THE TASTE OF
SPAIN

XAVIER   DOMINGO

p h o t o g r a p h y   b y

PIERRE   HUSSENOT

translated by Maev de Laguardia

recipes adapted by Stephanie Curtis

food stylist Marianne Paquin

Flammarion

Design:
Marc Walter
and Sophie Zagradsky

Editorial direction:
Ghislaine Bavoillot
Copyediting:
Julie Gaskill
Composition:
PFC Dole
Photoengraving:
Colourscan France
Map by Léonie Schlosser
The photographs on the following pages
are by Leopoldo Pomès:
p. 26; p. 39; p. 86 (above); p. 87; p. 94; p. 108; p. 142;
pp. 198-199; p. 209
Recipes by Angel de Miguel
and Rosa Grau (for the mushrooms)

PREFACE

There are few human beings capable of expressing truly original views on literature, politics, art or food. Most of the opinions aired in conversation, books and in the media are borrowed or secondhand. And yet those who advance them are convinced that their response is perfectly genuine and personal. When their views change, it is often as a reaction to the tides of fashion, but they are of course unaware of this. These people are thought-mirrors, barometers of the reigning mood, the convention of the moment — and the avant-garde is as conventional as the rest, often the most insidious of all. So what an intellectual relief, what a gust of fresh air to meet one of those rare people who express what they have thought and felt *themselves*, their own, direct response to unmediated reality. Xavier Domingo is one of them. He is a threatened species in these days of media-packaged ideas; whether he is right or wrong (and of course he is usually right), it is he and he alone who is doing the talking or the writing. In the domain of intellectual activity, whose noblest and most arduous manifestation is gastronomy, Xavier Domingo is an inexhaustible and completely original source.

This was something that struck me the instant I met him, shortly after the death of Franco and the beginning of Spanish democratization. I had been invited to Madrid by the Spanish weekly *Cambio 16*, and he was kind enough to meet me at the airport as the magazine's representative. Between picking up my case from the luggage conveyor and getting into the car, we had already managed to criticize fifty restaurants, ninety-seven politicians and seventy-six food critics from countries all over the world. On the drive into Madrid, we praised a number of others, which proves, at least, our serene open-mindedness. We have been friends now for over twenty years, and during all this time we have never lost that serenity, despite the fact that when it comes to food, it can be difficult, even for two amiable and easy-going gentlemen, to avoid an almost permanent state of discord and exasperation.

Xavier Domingo, "cuisinologist."

Domingo is a Catalan who spent a good deal of his youth in the Basque country, where his father was placed under house arrest by Franco's police. Much of his adult life was spent in Paris, from where he returned to Madrid only at the end of the dictatorship. He is a cosmopolitan who can berate a chef not only in Catalan, Spanish and French, but also in Portuguese, Italian and English. His ability to write with such talent on "the taste of Spain" is not surprising — his knowledge and experience of world cuisines are absolutely encyclopedic. At the University of Santander I heard him give a lecture on Chinese cuisine that was impressive in its subtlety and scholarship. Then, straight afterward, he took two other friends and me to Santillana del Mar for a lunch of fresh sardines, the rare, very lean kind that are caught only off the Cantabrian coast. The combination of that conference and that lunch throws a light on the nature of a true international gastronomic *culture*: it is totally and mightily opposed to the dreadful phenomenon of "international *cuisine*." It is based on recognizing and safeguarding *authenticity*, the originality of local products and preparations. True, every generation produces one or two great chefs who create new dishes or develop traditional ones along new lines, but the so-called "nouvelle" fad, which would have every cook serve only dishes of his or her own invention, has proved to be a catastrophe. The idea of entirely re-inventing cuisine from top to bottom every generation is a spurious, utopian notion and pure commercial and media fraud. What suicidal mania is behind the desire to deal a deathblow to centuries of delicate adjustment and patient research in perfecting the selection of food products and methods of preparing them? Can an orchestra conductor who conducts nothing but his own compositions be considered great? Should all the museums in the world burn every work produced before 1970? We must reject the cliché of the mutual exclusivity of ancient and modern, convention and invention, popular cooking and "sophisticated" cuisine. Most so-called popular dishes are much more ingenious than the insipid concoctions that turn up nowadays on the depressingly uniform menus of certain large restaurants in Tokyo, Munich, Milan and Paris. Xavier Domingo is not one to deny the genius of a creative chef when it really exists. In fact it was he whose articles revealed and launched the truly innovative talents who have emerged in Spain over the last twenty years. But it was also he who, at the risk of his own life, extracted from a tottering pile of old books in a ruined house in Extremadura, a collection of recipes carefully handwritten by two elderly ladies who had been the watchful heirs and trustees of the wonderful peasant cooking of that austere province. For Domingo knows that a good dish is like a good novel: its unique details, which make it unlike anything else in the world, give it its greatness.

As a matter of fact, Xavier Domingo is also a novelist. He is also a historian, an accomplished political journalist and an excellent reporter. He is a tremendous connoisseur of soccer: during the 1982 World Cup held in Spain, his articles denouncing dirty refereeing won him such bitter enemies among FIFA (Federation of International Football Associations) officials that they tried to discredit him by spreading the rumor that he was on a diet and had given up drinking wine! That calumny was too preposterous to be believed — and readers will see that this book's chapter on Spanish wines displays an erudition that could have been acquired only through much experience. Too many books on wine and cooking lack dimension because their authors fail to see their subject within a larger context. Domingo can expound rigorously and at length on Spanish wines because he is familiar with those from other parts of the world. This is a man who himself has so many facets that nobody can count them anymore, and who is well aware that apart from the authenticity I spoke of earlier, the taste of Spain is born of a thousand years of diversity.

Jean-François Revel

INTRODUCTION

It seems to me that a knowledge of food and wines, especially if one is lucky enough to have been born in a country with a great culinary and wine-making tradition, should be part and parcel of the general and humanistic culture of every citizen.

The culinary phenomenon can be approached from many angles. It is a cultural and social manifestation of the similarities and the differences among cultures, and has become the subject of sociological and anthropological study, as well as an integral part of the history of food and its transformations through the ages. As we know, the discovery of America was not what Christopher Columbus had in mind when he set sail from Palos de Moguer. He had hoped to find a shortcut to the spice route that would avoid the long and dangerous voyage around the Cape for the ships plying their way to and from the Indies. True, he did find spices in America, but his discovery also led to the introduction of potatoes, tomatoes, and green peppers into European cooking, along with many other products without which our cuisines would never have become what they are today. Hence, cooking is also an important element in the history of trade, economics and geographical discovery.

Finally, we can understand cooking and its place in culture simply by looking at cook-books. These are not as innocent as they might seem, and should really be called "books of precepts," canons or dogma prescribing the orthodoxy of each cuisine and laying down the immutable perfect ritual of each dish. In his writing, Jean-François Revel has defined them as ideological treatises. And so they are, whether from a platonic, social or nationalistic point of view.

There cannot be said to be "a" Spanish cuisine, for there are many, each very different from the others. But they do have certain elements in common: olive oil, garlic, bread, legumes, pork and pork products. Philo-sophically, they have in common straight-forwardness, simplicity, unpretentiousness, generosity, an abundance of flavor and a closeness to nature, and freedom from an over-reliance on sauces.

Spanish cuisines can be divided into three major areas: Mediterranean, central, and Atlantic. Catalonia, Valencia, Murcia and coastal Andalusia belong to the first area. The two Castiles, Extremadura and inland Andalusia comprise the second, and the third includes the Basque Country, Cantabria, Asturias and Galicia.

Historically, the roots of these cuisines are Roman, with Gothic and Germanic off-shoots during the High Middle Ages and Arabic input at a later stage. An Italian admixture occurred throughout the fourteenth, fifteenth and sixteenth centuries, especially in the Mediterranean area, and finally, the whole of the last three centuries has been influenced by France.

I myself am Catalan, which implies a lengthy epicurean tradition. A compatriot, the bishop Eiximenis, wrote in the fourteenth century that the Catalans ate and drank better than anyone else in the world, and with more merriment and sensuality to boot. Of course, this is just one more example of culinary chauvinism, but it does give a good idea of Catalan attitudes toward food. Eating is for enjoyment, even if the only thing on the table is modest tomato bread, olive oil and ham.

I would enjoy telling you about my childhood breakfasts under the sun-dappled climbing vines, the fried eggs with *cansalada virada,* the great slices of *pá de pagës* rubbed with garlic and spread with tomato, the green virgin oil from the olives in the fields in Tortosa, the honey-sweet red-fleshed figs.... And reminisce about my uncle, a fisherman who would arrive at the house with baskets overflowing with live red mullet, and the fried fish and sautéed shrimps prepared by my grandmother and godmother. I have an everlasting memory of Sunday rice casse-

Rocío is a biennial pilgrimage in which the Virgin of Almonte is carried to the Rocío chapel by the sea. Crowds from neighboring villages and even as far away as Seville come on horseback and carts to participate in this colorful festival (above).

In all of Mediterranean Spain and particularly in Catalonia, bread and tomatoes are appreciated at all hours of the day — at breakfast, as an afternoon snack, as an appetizer and, as in the photo, in a delicious mushroom dish flavored with garlic and parsley (facing).

A small fishing harbor in Andalusia, between Seville and Cádiz (above).
The internal provinces retain their mystery for tourists, who prefer Spain's gentle beaches. The small villages in these regions hide culinary treasures of surprising sophistication (facing).

Even though that menace known as "creative cuisine" is also on the rampage in Spain, one can still find many skillfully prepared popular dishes.

Paradoxically, the cuisine of the most visited country in Europe is the proverbial light under a bushel in the Old World. Responsibility for this situation lies with the state policy of attracting cheap, large-scale tourism with "fixed-price tourist menus." The application of this policy was compulsory for years (the Franco years, to be precise), and it translated into a monopoly of paellas, as offhand and arbitrary as they were dangerous to health. As far as foreigners were concerned, the colossal richness and variety of Spanish cuisine were reduced to a single, badly made dish.

This heavy-handed state intervention narrowly missed destroying the cuisines of Spain. The state is, among other things, a lousy cook. Fortunately, the arrival of democracy in Spain has saved them.

The establishment of the new autonomous states in Spain is largely responsible for the renewal of each Spanish region's interest in its cuisine, now considered a mark of identity and distinctive character. Throughout the country the autonomous authorities have given their official sponsorship to activities aimed at saving their cuisines. These gestures have validated Brillat-Savarin's phrase, "Tell me what you eat, and I'll tell you who you are."

The future of Spanish cuisines, then, can be contemplated with some optimism. For the moment the main handicap is the lack of qualified professionals — the quality product, on the other hand, is present in abundance. An interesting upshot of the autonomy program has been the widespread creation of cooking and hotel management schools, which have already produced a number of young chefs bubbling with talent and love of their profession.

With the decline of mass tourism, which was a prime source of revenue in Spain, gastronomy is becoming a major attraction for a new kind of tourist. The game will be won when people come here not only for our sunshine, but for the talent of our chefs and the variety and delight of our cuisines.

roles with rabbit from the farm, sliced artichokes, green peas, spring garlic and zucchini: green rice, my grandmother called it, a recipe from the Ebro delta where she was born. After that, life took me first to the Basque Country, which is a culinary paradise on earth, and then to France, where I discovered the extraordinary richness of the regional cuisines and the concept of cuisine as culture.

In fact, everyday popular cooking is what interests me most. Not only for what goes onto the plate, but also for the intellectual and even poetic pleasure that it provides. This kind of cooking may be totally anonymous; it is definitely not "signature" cuisine. When I go to France I never look for the three-star restaurants — not even two — or the designer establishments. I have no desire to waste my time and money on dubious dishes of metaphysical proportions: I want the carrots and beef *gros sel* to have big, real carrots with real carrot flavor, not miserable little insipid vegetables. I go directly to wherever I've heard that filleted herring is well prepared, or salt pork and lentils done just right, or where I will find a good fatty *boeuf en daube* (there's no such thing as good boiled beef that's not fatty) or a nutmeg-perfumed stew of *blanquette de veau*. Alas, finding these dishes is becoming more and more difficult.

BREAD

OIL

AND

GARLIC

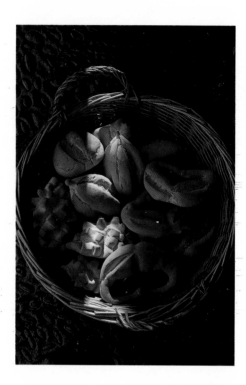

The delicious aroma of bread fills the early-morning streets of villages and cities — wheat, rye, barley or oat bread, according to the region (above).
In this ancient Argentona bakery near Barcelona, Josep More Rabassa makes a variety of breads for different purposes: one is served at breakfast, another accompanies soup or grilled meats (facing).

G o to any village in the Iberian peninsula, take a morning walk through the streets of any city, wander the length and breadth of the high plateau of Castile, the mountains of Galicia, or the Andalusian plain — wherever you go, you will be bathed in the warm, penetrating and familiar smell of fresh bread just out of the oven. There are huge loaves of bread as white as snow, round black rye breads, dense cornmeal breads, crusty *llonguets*, and decorative, sculptural Chinchón loaves.

For centuries bread has been the main food staple throughout Europe, and politics and society have gravitated around cereals and bread on this continent from Roman times to today. The major conflicts that arose in medieval society were often linked to a shortage of bread — war, rebellion, torture and bloodshed, all were suffered to gain a mouthful of it. The bread of the poor at times became a luxury found only on the tables of the high and mighty.

However, Spain may be the only European country in which bread has long been the source of a wide-ranging culinary art. This art includes dishes that vary from elementary to complicated, richly flavored to subtle, coarse to refined, hearty to frugal. They symbolize the essential difference between the cuisines of Spain and those of the rest of the world: the ability to use humble ingredients to create flavors of extraordinary succulence and sensual quality.

After a breakfast that might include fried eggs and bread dipped in milk, leave the village and take a look around. We might be in Tarragona, once a Roman stronghold, Moorish Córdoba or Jaén, perhaps in Mozarabic Aragon or Lleida, which was both Roman and Christian, but wherever we are, our village is certainly surrounded by masses of olive trees.

Bread and oil: these are the two basic elements of what might be called, to paraphrase the art term, "minimal cooking." Something was missing, though; some addition, some condiment was needed. Salt was not enough,

and pepper was a luxury from the Indies and the Americas, far beyond the means of those who invented this poor man's food. What they could afford, however, was garlic.

There are many different varieties of cooking in Spain, but garlic is one ingredient they all share. These Liliaceae are deeply rooted in the Iberian peninsula's culture, and every imaginable virtue is ascribed to them. Whenever someone reaches a hundred years of age, it is invariably discovered that the centenarian has been a fervent garlic-eater all of his or her life. After the San Fermín Fiestas in Pamplona, those extravagant displays of virility, the young men take home enormous strings of garlic for consuming throughout the next year. Not only are these a souvenir of the cuisine of Navarre, with its omnipresent taste of garlic, but they also serve as a guarantee that the young men's courage will not fail them in the following year's bull-runs.

In the words of Julio Camba, an excellent Spanish writer, and one of the many with an interest in cooking, "Spanish cooking is thick with garlic and religion." Whatever the accuracy concerning the second ingredient, the basic cuisine of the Iberian region certainly consists of of bread, olive oil and garlic.

The preeminent recipe involving garlic is to mix it with oil for an *all i oli* in its purest, most orthodox form — garlic pounded into a thick emulsion with oil and a little salt, and strictly nothing else. Above all: no egg. From Catalonia to Murcia, the whole of the Spanish Mediterranean is a sea of *all i oli* from horizon to horizon. The art lies in getting the thick sauce to such a consistency that the pestle stands in it unaided, and perfection is attained when the pestle is held tight and the mortar can be turned without either the sauce or the pestle coming away from each other. Few people can manage this. But anyone who wants to taste a truly great *all i oli* should try the one served at the Can Peixerot, in the port of the same name. It is outstanding, and there is nothing better to accompany the two main dishes of the local

Bread, olive oil, garlic and tomatoes are the basic ingredients in many dishes, including the delicious Andalusian gazpacho, the crusty cocas and the famous tomato bread described by the celebrated Catalan writer-photographer, Leopoldo Pomès (above and facing).
The vast olive groves in Spain supply rich and fragrant oil. Its beautiful deep color glows within unusual and original bottles (following double page).

cuisine: *el rossejat* and the *all cremat*, a casse-role of crisp-fried garlic, potatoes and anglerfish.

Bread, garlic and oil are the basic ingredients of a large family of traditional Andalusian dishes, including gazpacho soups, *salmorejo* sauces, and the *ajo blanco* (white garlic) sauces made with raw garlic and breadcrumbs. And although other products gradually crept into these recipes and eventually became an accepted part of them, they can in fact be considered purely "cosmetic" elements.

These include ingredients introduced from America, particularly Mexico and Peru, after the discovery and conquest of the New World: tomatoes, many varieties of peppers and spices, potatoes and other elements that, albeit slowly, became such an integral part of Iberian agriculture and cooking that it is impossible to imagine either without them today. The facts are simple: Spanish popular cuisines are the off-spring of Roman and pre-Hispanic Indo-American cuisines, with an Oriental lover lurking somewhere about (in the fragrances and spices that were, in fact, well known to Roman cooks).

An example of this blend of cuisines is the Cordoban *salmorejo*, which you will find prepared to perfection at the Caballo Rojo restaurant in the city of the caliphs, and at Las Camachas in Montilla, another town in the province of Córdoba. It was familiar to country folk in the environs of ancient Rome and to the Roman legionnaires.

The *salmorejo* also constitutes the basic elements of the gazpacho, which can really be defined as a *salmorejo* to which water has been added, with garden products such as cucumber, green peppers, onion and so on.

Today gazpacho, along with paella, is the most universally known dish in all of Span-ish cooking, although usually in adulterated, oversophisticated versions that are far re-moved from the authentic recipe.

The dish originated among the common Andalusian people — peasants and day laborers — who used up the dry bread from

previous days by dampening it with water and squeezing it in their hands, then mixing this paste with tomatoes crushed in the same way, together with garlic ground in a mor-tar, salt, oil, vinegar and, if there were any available, a few chopped vegetables, espe-cially cucumbers and green peppers.

Salmorejo and the varied range of the gazpacho family bring together the simple everyday food of the people of ancient Rome and the Aztecs. They have even recently come to include gazpachos made with avo-cado pears, a fruit to which the Aztecs and other Indian cultures attributed highly aphrodisiac qualities, by virtue of its testicle-like shape. This is one case where the modern world has not betrayed its origins.

But perhaps the most obvious of the many instances of the mingling of Roman and pre-Hispanic elements is, paradoxically, found in Catalonia, where the popular dish par excellence is bread and tomato. The paradox arises from the fact that the Cata-lans took no part in either the discovery or the conquest of the New World, and toma-toes and the possibilities they offered were recognized at a very late stage.

From then on, however, the Catalans have done miracles with these two ingre-dients plus olive oil, and have even invented shapes and types of bread especially for this kind of food, which can be served as an entrée, a salad, breakfast or lunch. It comes in forms such as the *coca* from Maresme, north of Barcelona. In Arenys de Mar is a restaurant called the Hispania, considered one of the best in Spain, where the *coca* with tomato and oil is quite sumptuous. It is interesting to observe how this "minimal" cuisine of bread, oil and garlic has developed in two recipes under the heading of *ajos blancos*: the *ajo blanco de Peloche* — Peloche is a sheep-rearing village in the autonomous community of Extremadura — and the *ajo blanco de Málaga*. The latter is a nineteenth-century urban variation that was in fact orig-inally a country dish, refined by the good ladies of the local bourgeoisie.

These are cold, refreshing dishes that orig-

inated in the South, with its long, dry and extremely hot summers, and hundreds of variations exist, both rural and urban. In other regions the longest part of the year is winter, a drawn-out time of piercing winds, snow and rain and, most of all, prodigious freezes. The succulent Castilian bread and soup mentioned earlier is a delicious way to keep out the cold.

Now we come to a more substantial product of the minimal world of bread, oil and garlic: *migas de pastor* — "shepherd's crumbs." I suspect that these originated a very long time ago. Some of the dish's variants offer evidence that some Maghrebian specialties, such as couscous, were part of everyday cooking in Visigothic Spain. The same might also be true of the famous Moroccan *pastela*, which harks back to ancestral times and is still being made in bakeries in the town of Murcia. The nomadic Arab army had no specific cuisine of its own, and created an amalgamation of what it encountered of other people's along the way. They did add their own touch, though, with the adaptations imposed by religious taboos.

The *migas* are usually made from bread. Their simplest form is the *migas canas* — "white-hair breadcrumbs" — prepared in the Andalusian countryside for farmers' breakfasts. A two-pound loaf is cut into thin slices which are placed in salted water to soak, while in another pan three peeled heads of garlic are fried in deep oil. When these are browned the bread is added and stirred until it breaks and separates into golden crumbs. Hot milk is then sprinkled over, giving the crumbs the pale color indicated by their name. The most important directive in all the variants of this dish is to use old, dry bread. This is generally put to soak the previous day, left to crumble and then wrapped in a white cloth, to be fried the next morning.

In Euskera, the harshly beautiful ancient language of the Basques, *zurrup* is an onomatopoeic word meaning "to sip," and *kutuna* connotes warm contentment. *Zurru-*

kutuna is the name of one of the most splendid soups ever to spring from the simple alchemy of bread, garlic and oil in the Iberian peninsula. The agglutinated name is as expressively warming as the soup itself, which is a dish truly meant to be savored slowly, in the intimacy of a dimly lit country kitchen, beside the fire or at the table of one of the many Basque gastronomical societies (about which, more later), shared among lifelong childhood or village friends. One of its great exponents is Don Lorenzo Zapiaín, a cooking enthusiast who belongs to the Ondar Gaiñ Society in Lazkano. *Zurrukutuna* is still served in some Basque restaurants, such as the Patxi Kintana in San Sebastián, where it is a much-loved specialty of the house.

Galicia, which lies in northwestern Spain, with the prow of its Cape Finisterre jutting into the Atlantic, is a land of superb bread. Much of it is baked in huge loaves meant to last for several days. I remember a time — fortunately, long past — when bread constituted the basic, if not the only, food for a great many families in mountain and coastal areas.

These monumental, rough loaves with their thick crusts and simple, elemental shapes call to mind ancient times, Roman

This modern Barcelona bakery makes special breads in the shape of hearts, crowns and animals. They can be ordered for weddings or simply offered as gifts (above). The coca de Recapte, made with bread, olive oil and tomatoes, is a specialty of the Hispania restaurant north of Barcelona, and illustrates one of the many ways in which bread can be used in a dish (facing).

Bread and olive oil are the foundation of Mediterranean cooking (above).
In Andalusia, this 500-year-old olive tree still bears fruit, helping to make Spain the foremost olive oil producer in the world (right).

Empanadas may be made with wheat, rye or barley flour, while some versions, such as those made with cockles or mussels, require corn flour. Some culinary theoreticians hold that *empanadas* are of humble popular origin, while others declare that they originated in monasteries. Professor Botero's discovery invalidates any theory claiming a purely Galician source for them, but this is of little importance. What matters is that this delicious pastry or bread stuffed with a filling that bakes along with the dough is so much a part of Galicia's cuisine that it is impossible to imagine a Galician meal without *empanadas* being served at some point along the way.

Empanadas, to my way of thinking, represent the initial qualitative leap from the "minimal" cooking of bread, oil and garlic into the realm of more sophisticated, complex cuisine. Structurally speaking, *empanadas* are the first step across the threshold between pure breadmaking and the rest of the culinary universe. It is by no means the only instance, however. There is another that is even more elemental though no less succulent, and this is the *gazpacho manchego* or *alicantino*, which should not be

abbeys and cloisters, the bygone universe of ovens and horse-driven flour mills, wood fires, and ox-drawn carts making their way through forests haunted by witches and fairies. The cultural shock of the discovery of the Americas had a great impact here too, and corn and potatoes are essential elements of Galician cooking and breadmaking.

Galician cooking is full of mysteries made all the more impenetrable by the region's ancient roots. Several years ago, Professor Jean Botero deciphered some Babylonian tablets and found what is undoubtedly the oldest recipe known to man. It was for a quail pie, the *mutatis mutandis* that is still made in Galicia as *empanada de codornices*. This Babylonian pastry dish followed a long road throughout the Mediterranean, with many halts along the way before finding its way to Galicia and finally settling in the easternmost parts of Europe. After that it leapt across the ocean to Chile and other Latin American countries.

In the final analysis, an *empanada* is essentially a pastry with a filling, and in Galicia that filling can consist of almost anything: eel, lamprey, salt cod with raisins, cockles, scallops, sardines or *xouba*, conger eel, mussels, onion, garlic, tomato, chili peppers, veal, pork, thrush, quail or rabbit.

confused with the Andalusian gazpacho.

Like any kind of bread, the crusty *empanadas* and their juicy fillings require an oven, whereas gazpacho provides a delicious, appetizing meal even in the desolate rural wilds.

Theories on gazpacho are as emphatic and abundant in La Mancha and the mountains of Alicante as they are on *empanadas* in Galicia and El Bierzo.

Basically, the dish consists of a *torta*, a kind of large flat pie crust cooked over an open fire and covered with a stew that may be simple or elaborate, and may include game, mutton or goat's meat, garlic, onions, dried peppers and aromatic or spicy condiments.

The stew itself is made in a special frying pan called a *gazpachera*, and the ingredients include crumbled bread, which could justify its being considered also a particularly rich form of *migas*. All the different meats must be well cooked and the other ingredients thoroughly mixed in; once this is done the stew is put onto one of the *tortas* and eaten using other pieces of crust that serve as a kind of spoon. In this very practical dish, the bread itself becomes the plate, and every last morsel is eaten.

In other words, it is really an *empanada* without the covering and, instead of baked in an oven, it is cooked lovingly over the embers of a rustic fire in the open air.

If you happen to be going to America via the port of Vigo, then before you make the journey, cross the estuary toward Cangas del Morrazo, take the road to Balea — until recently the site of a whale factory — go to Pepe Simón's place and have Doña Pilar prepare her *empanadas* with cockles, *xoubas*, or salt cod with raisins. Golden-brown, steaming hot from the oven, filling the air with the fragrant smell of fresh bread, crispy and moist, just waiting for you to sink your teeth into them, accompanied by a glass of Albariño or Rosal, a subtle, intelligent, cold wine with a slight mistiness. . . . None of this would have been possible if somebody had not, long ago, brought back pepper and tomatoes from America.

OLIVES TO WHET THE APPETITE

Spain is the world's foremost producer of olives and olive oil.

Whether virgin or pure, olive oil is the most frequently used in Spanish cooking, for frying and stewing as well as cold in salads or as seasoning.

Many different varieties of olives are grown in Spain, of which the greater part is used for making oil. Some olive oil-producing areas have been granted vintage status, and operate under the aegis of a regulating council.

Furthermore, much of the annual harvest, particularly from exceptionally high-quality varieties, goes into what is known as *verdeo* — preserved or semi-preserved olives. These *verdeo* olives are packed in special brines or used in marinades with the addition of aromatic herbs, the zests of oranges or lemons, mild or hot spices, garlic, onion, or other elements. They are a favorite Spanish appetizer, as well as an ingredient in many recipes.

The most highly appreciated preserved olives are:

– The pale green apple- or pear-shaped *manzanilla*. This is the best-known and most popular variety. It is a wonderful accompaniment to all kinds of aperitifs, especially the fine, dry Oloroso Jerez wines.

– The large, olive-green or dark green *gordal* or *sevillana*, which is a fleshy, very tasty variety.

– The horn-shaped *cornezuelo*, green with a white tip, which has a strong flavor with a hint of bitterness.

– The round, smallish black or blue-black *cuquillo* olive goes particularly well with beer. It is usually prepared with chopped onion and one of the hot spices.

– The *negral* or *negrilla* is served spiced or dried and pickled. Native to Aragon, it is perfectly suited to red wines.

– The tiny green or purplish-green *arbequina* is a delicious, pleasantly bitter aromatic olive whose name comes from the village of La Arbeca in Lleida (Catalonia). This is the customary appetizer in many Catalan restaurants.

As suggested above, the best wines to accompany olives are the Fino and dry Oloroso Jerez wines or the Manzanilla from Sanlúcar de Barrameda.

*The delicious Jerez wine adds
incomparable flavor to salmorejo
(cold Andalusian soup) served
with hard-boiled eggs at the
Salinas tavern in Córdoba
(above).
Nourishing and tasty, this
Castilian soup of garlic, bread
and eggs is an example of Spanish
"minimal" cooking (facing).*

WARM GARLIC SOUP
SOPA DE AJO
Castile-La Mancha

Preparation time: 5 minutes
Cooking time: 10 minutes
For 6 servings:
6 thin slices (5 oz/150 g) day-old white bread
6 tablespoons (3 fl oz/9 cl) olive oil
6 cloves garlic, peeled
1 tablespoon paprika
Salt
6 cups (48 fl oz/1 1/2 l) water

Method:
　　Remove crusts from the bread.
　　Heat the olive oil in a large
earthenware casserole or saucepan. Add
the garlic cloves and cook until they begin
to color. Reduce the heat, add the bread
and cook until browned on both sides.
Add the paprika and salt, stirring
constantly to prevent the bread from
burning.
　　Bring the water to a boil in a separate
saucepan. Stir it into the bread mixture
and let cook for 5 minutes longer.
　　Serve immediately.

COLD GARLIC SOUP
SALMOREJO
Andalusia

Advance preparation time: 1 hour
Preparation time: 10 minutes
For 6 servings:
**30 thin slices (1 1/2 lb/750 g) day-old,
　　firm white bread**
3/4 cup (6 fl oz/18 cl) olive oil
3 cloves garlic, peeled
3 tablespoons sherry vinegar
Salt
Ice water (about 4 cups/32 fl oz/1 l)
2 hard-cooked eggs, quartered

Method:
　　Remove crusts and place the bread
slices in a shallow bowl with enough
water to barely cover. Let soak for 1 hour.
Squeeze bread firmly between the palms
of the hands to remove excess water.

　　In a food processor, combine the
bread, oil, garlic, sherry, and salt, and
process for 5 minutes or until smooth.
　　Transfer the mixture to a soup tureen
and stir in ice water to the desired
consistency. (The texture should be that
of a thick gazpacho.) Decorate with the
egg quarters and serve cold.

EXTREMADURA-STYLE
SAUTÉED BREAD
AND BACON
MIGAS EXTREMEÑAS
Extremadura

Advance preparation time: 8 hours
Cooking time: 50 minutes
For 6 servings:
**40 thin slices (2 1/4 lb/1 kg) day-old,
　　firm white bread**
1 cup (8 fl oz/25 cl) water
Salt
3/4 cup (6 fl oz/18 cl) olive oil
5 oz (150 g) fillet of pork, diced
5 oz (150 g) slab bacon, diced
6 cloves garlic, peeled
1 tablespoon paprika

Method:
　　Remove crusts from the bread, tear
into small pieces and spread in a large
shallow dish. Combine the water and salt
and drizzle evenly over the bread. Cover
with a damp towel and set aside for 6 to
8 hours until the bread is well soaked.
　　Heat the oil in a large skillet. Add the
pork and bacon and sauté until lightly
browned. Remove from the skillet and set
aside. Gently squeeze the soaked bread
between the palms of the hands to
extract a little of the water.
　　Add the garlic to the hot oil remaining
in the skillet and cook until garlic begins to
color. Add the paprika, stirring rapidly. Add
the bread and meats, and cook over
medium heat, turning gently with a
spatula until the bread pulls away from the
sides of the pan and turns golden brown.
　　Serve hot, accompanied by fried eggs,
if desired.

WHITE GARLIC GAZPACHO
AJO BLANCO
Andalusia

Advance preparation time: 1 hour
Preparation time: 5 minutes
Refrigeration: 2 hours
For 6 servings:
6 thin slices (5 oz/150 g) firm white bread
1 cup (5 oz/150 g) almonds, peeled
2 cloves garlic
6 tablespoons (3 fl oz/9 cl) olive oil
2 tablespoons sherry vinegar
Salt
Ice water (about 4 cups—32 fl oz/1 l)
30 white grapes

Method:

Remove crusts and place the bread in a shallow bowl with enough cold water to barely cover. Let soak for 1 hour. Squeeze bread between the palms of the hands to remove excess water.

Combine the bread, almonds, garlic, oil, vinegar, and salt in a food processor, and process until well blended. (Or, grind the bread and almonds together in a large mortar and stir in remaining ingredients.) Add about 1/2 cup (4 fl oz/12 cl) of the ice water, and process. Scrape the mixture into a bowl and refrigerate for 2 hours.

When well chilled, stir in enough additional ice water to obtain the desired consistency, which should be that of a thick gazpacho.

Just before serving, garnish with the grapes, and serve very cold.

Mortars are often used for making sauces like the picada, which includes grilled almonds, pine nuts and garlic. Picada is served with many meat and fish dishes in Mediterranean Spain.

SCALLOP EMPANADA
EMPANADA DE VIEIRAS
Galicia

Preparation time: 25 minutes
Cooking time: 40 minutes
For 6 to 8 servings:
Pastry dough:
3/4 cup (6 fl oz/18 cl) milk, at room
    temperature
3/4 cup (6 fl oz/18 cl) water, at room
    temperature
3 1/2 teaspoons active dry yeast or
    1 oz (30 g) compressed yeast
3/4 cup (6 fl oz/18 cl) olive oil
8 cups (2 1/4 lb/1 kg) all-purpose flour
3 eggs, Salt

Filling:
24 sea scallops
1 1/4 cups (10 fl oz/30 cl) olive oil
2 cloves garlic, peeled and chopped
4 large onions, peeled and chopped
2 red bell peppers, seeded and diced
2 bay leaves
3 medium, ripe tomatoes, peeled
    and chopped
Pinch saffron threads (see glossary)
Salt
1 tablespoon lard
1 egg, beaten

Method:

In a large mixing bowl, combine the milk, water, yeast, and oil.

Add the flour, eggs, and salt, and mix until well combined.

Knead the dough. Cover with a damp kitchen towel and set aside to rest in a warm place (about 75° F /25° C) for 20 minutes.

Meanwhile, prepare the filling: rinse the scallops, pat them dry, and set aside. Heat the oil in a large skillet. Add the garlic and cook until it begins to color. Add the onions, peppers, and bay leaves, and cook for about 20 minutes. Add the tomatoes, saffron and salt, cook for 5 minutes longer and remove from the heat.

Divide the pastry dough into two parts. Roll the pastry out into two large, very thin rounds, one slightly larger than the other.

Grease the bottom and sides of a large round quiche pan with the lard. Line the bottom of the pan with the larger dough round. Spread the vegetables and scallops evenly over the dough. Lay the second dough round over the top, pinching and rolling the edges firmly together.

Brush the top of the pastry with the beaten egg. Bake in a preheated 400° F (200° C) oven for 15 minutes.

BASQUE-STYLE DRIED SALT COD SOUP
ZURRUKUTUNA
Basque Country

Advance preparation time: 12 hours
Preparation time: 25 minutes
Cooking time: 45 minutes
For 6 servings:
1 lb (500 g) dried salt cod
6 tablespoons (3 fl oz/9 cl) olive oil
1 large onion, finely chopped
3 cloves garlic, peeled
1 1/2 teaspoons paprika
Salt
7 or 8 thin slices (7 oz/200 g) firm
    white bread, toasted

Method:

A day in advance: Place the cod in a large basin of cold water and soak for 24 hours, changing the water 3 or 4 times.

The same day: Drain the cod and pat dry. Place it on a grill over hot coals (or in the broiler of an oven) and cook, turning once, for about 12 minutes, depending on the distance from the heat. Remove from the grill and flake the fish into pieces with a fork, removing any skin or bone.

Heat the oil in a large earthenware casserole or skillet. Add the onion and cook until lightly browned. Add the garlic cloves and cod, and cook, stirring, until lightly browned. Add the paprika, stirring quickly.

Add water to cover and let cook over low heat for 30 minutes. Taste and season with salt, if needed.

Remove the toast crusts, arrange toast in the pan with the cod and cook for 5 minutes longer. Place under a very hot broiler and cook for another 5 minutes.

Serve immediately.

ANDALUSIAN GAZPACHO
GAZPACHO ANDALUZ
Andalusia

Advance preparation time: 1 hour
Preparation time: 10 minutes
Refrigeration: 3 hours
For 6 servings:
2 thin slices (2 oz/50 g) bread
2 1/4 lb (1 kg) ripe tomatoes, peeled
    and seeded
2 cloves garlic, peeled
6 tablespoons (3 oz/9 cl) olive oil
3 tablespoons sherry vinegar
1 tablespoon coarse salt
2 cups (16 fl oz/50 cl) water

Garnishes (optional):
1 small onion, peeled and diced
1/2 cucumber, peeled and diced
1 medium green bell pepper,
    seeded and diced
1 1/2 cups toasted croutons

Method:
    Remove crusts and place the bread
slices in a shallow bowl with enough
water to barely cover. Let soak for 1 hour.
Squeeze bread firmly between the palms
of the hands.
    Combine the bread, tomatoes, garlic,
oil, vinegar and salt in a food processor
and blend for 5 minutes.
    Strain the mixture through a fine sieve
into an earthenware bowl. Correct
seasoning if necessary.
    Stir in the water and refrigerate until
well chilled, about 3 hours.
    Serve very cold, garnished, if you
wish, with the onion, cucumber, pepper,
and croutons.
    Note: The garnish is a fairly recent
addition. In Andalusia, gazpacho is
traditionally served at the end of a meal
or as a cool, refreshing drink.

LA MANCHA-STYLE GAZPACHO
GAZPACHO MANCHEGO
Castile-La Mancha

Preparation time: 20 minutes
Cooking time: 3 hours 25 minutes
For 6 servings:
1 partridge, cleaned
10 oz (300 g) hare
9 oz (250 g) wild rabbit
10 oz (300 g) chicken, cut in pieces
8 cups (64 fl oz/2 l) cold water
Salt
1/2 cup (4 fl oz/12 cl) olive oil
1 tablespoon paprika
2 galettes de Cercena, cut in small
    pieces (see note)
Freshly ground black pepper

Method:
    Combine the partridge, hare, rabbit,
chicken, salt, and cold water in a large
stock pot or soup kettle and bring to a
simmer. Simmer over low heat for
3 hours.
    Remove the meats from the stock.
Bone and skin the meats and chop finely.
    Combine the olive oil and paprika in a
large shallow earthenware casserole. Add
the stock in which the meats cooked, and
season with salt and pepper as needed.
Bring to a boil, add the galettes, and boil
for 20 minutes, stirring occasionally.
    Add the meats and continue to cook
for 5 minutes. Serve hot.
    Note: Galettes de Cercena are crepe-
like rounds of unleavened bread. They can
be replaced with flour tortillas, or other
thin unleavened breads.

MINORCAN BREAD SOUP
OLIAIGUA BROIX
Minorca-Balearic Islands

Preparation time: 10 minutes
Cooking time: 15 minutes
For 4 servings:
4 cups (32 fl oz/1 l) water
2 tablespoons olive oil
4 cloves garlic, peeled
2 sprigs parsley
1 sprig thyme
2 tablespoons salt
1 very ripe tomato, peeled and
    chopped (optional)
1 green bell pepper, seeded and
    chopped (optional)
24 very thin slices (1 1/4 lb/600 g) day-old,
    firm white bread
4 egg yolks

Method:
    In a large saucepan, combine the
water, oil, garlic, parsley, thyme, salt, and
tomato and pepper, if using, and bring to
a boil. Let boil for several minutes.
    Remove crusts from bread and divide
the slices among four shallow soup
plates. Place an egg yolk in each plate.
    Bring the hot broth to the table and let
each guest ladle it over the bread and egg
in his bowl.

*Olive oil is the main product of
Baena, in the province of Jaën
(Andalusia). After pressing, the
oil ages in huge earthenware jars,
acquiring richness, a beautiful
amber color and superb flavor
(above).*
*The ingredients for a top-notch
gazpacho are assembled at the
headquarters of the Friends of
Cordobès at the San Basilio in
Córdoba. Admirers of the famed
matador can taste this traditional
chilled soup that unites all the
flavors of Andalusia (facing).*

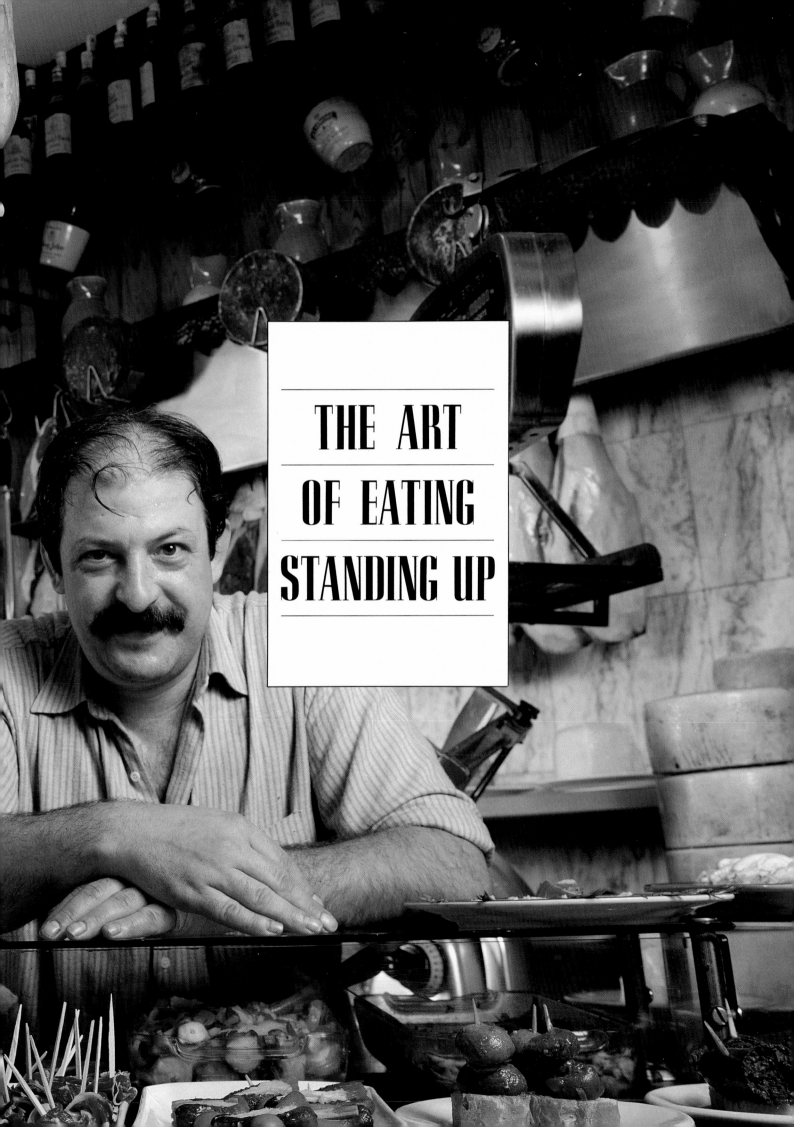

THE ART
OF EATING
STANDING UP

At nightfall — a sacrosanct time of day — Spaniards meet in tascas (bistrots) to drink wine and nibble on their favorite tapas (above and right). Córdoba's picturesque taverns offer mouthwatering specialties such as oxtail, grilled eggplant and homemade omelettes — excellent with a Fino Amontillado wine from Sanlúcar de Barrameda (facing).

T apas, the snack-like assortments of appetizers, came into vogue worldwide in the early 1980s, at about the same time as *sevillanas* and other edibles of purely Spanish origin.

What was less exportable, however, was the art of eating on one's feet, the traditional manner of consuming *tapas*. This is done at a succession of bars in which one nibbles *tapas* accompanied by *chatos* — small glasses of white, red or rosé wine. There are even dedicated specialists in the *tapeo* or the *chateo* circuits who have mapped out routes through town that are calculated to include particularly good *tapas* or wines. In almost every city there are streets or even entire neighborhoods full of bars and taverns with well-stocked *tapa* counters. Such is the case in all the towns and cities in northern Spain, Old and New Castile, Extremadura, Andalusia and Murcia, whereas there are far fewer in Catalonia and Valencia.

What was the origin of the *tapas*, and how did they get their name? *Tapa* literally means "lid," and initially *tapas* were round slices of ham, bacon or sausage such as loin, chorizo, and blood sausage, which were used to cover the tall narrow glasses of wine served in Andalusian taverns.

The term was later extended to include any kind of hot or cold aperitif, and the *tapa* evolved from a single tiny meatball, a few snails or a skewered pickle or two, generally offered as an accompaniment to a glass of wine or beer, to a small selection of sausages, cheese and prepared dishes.

The philosophy of the *tapa* lies in its original, Andalusian sense of the *tapadera*. Andalusians are a refined, contemplative people with a great fondness for eating exquisite morsels of pork chitterlings, yet who make a point of appearing to attribute little importance to material things, least of all anything to do with food. Everyday eating to them is a pleasurable activity that requires none of the pomp and circumstance of tablecloths or cutlery. These are reserved for great occasions. The enjoyable thing is the slow, quiet walk, in a group, from one tavern to the next, sipping Fino and Manzanilla with a *sevillana* olive here, a small slice of good ham there, a piece of potato omelette farther on, all of which are eaten with epicurean sobriety, with the time for a leisurely chat with friends and acquaintances met along the way.

The slices of sausage and other meats covering the Jerez glasses were not simply for eating, but also preserved the bouquet of the

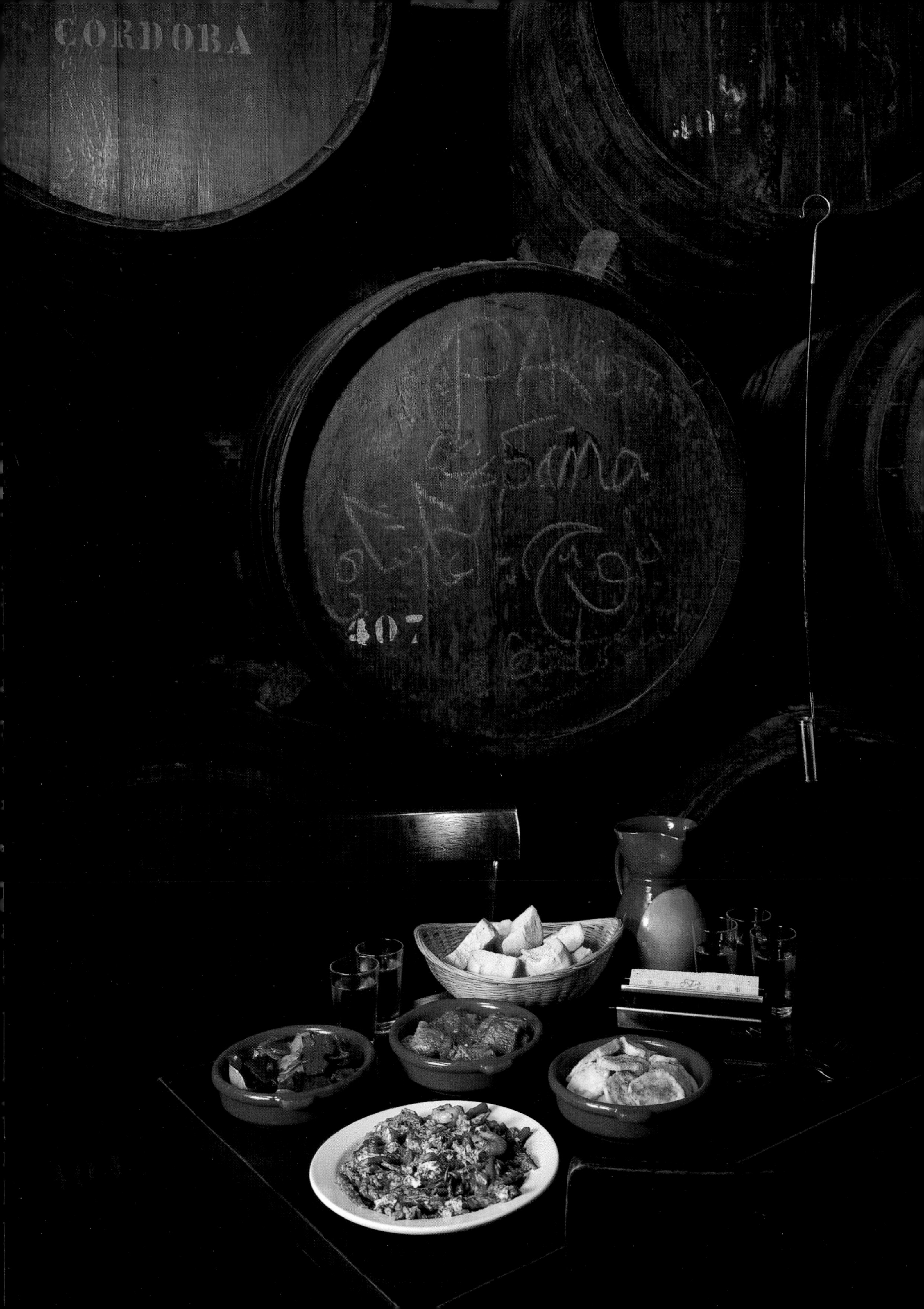
CORDOBA
407

A delectable zucchini omelette makes an ideal mid-morning tapa with a glass of chilled white wine (above).

The infinite range of tapas amazes visitors to Spain. Here they will find classic tapas such as seafood, meatballs and snails, as well as many regional specialties (right and facing).

wine. What wisdom on the part of the Andalusians, whose eating customs are in such harmony with their civilization and their climate, as well as so in tune with aesthetics!

Is it possible, for example, to have a truly serious, deep discussion about art without going through the motions of art oneself? What I really mean, of course, is a discussion about bulls and bullfighters. . . . No one can talk about bulls sitting down — you must be standing up. The conversation requires bullfighting gestures and a vertical stance such as is expected of any man worthy of the name, in the face of life and death. Body erect, or perhaps slightly leaning at an elegant angle against the bar. Subtle refinement in the movement of the hand as the glass is grasped and carried to the lips. Sublime indifference to the delicacies being consumed, however choice they may be. Never must one lose face, especially when it comes to eating.

The original, Andalusian *tapa* is for people with breeding and pride — mystics and adepts of the bullfight. None of this implies disdain for people from the North, like myself. It is simply a matter of making distinctions. The dividing line between Andalusia and La Mancha and Castile marks the beginning of another Spain as far as *tapas* are concerned: a more material, down-to-earth country entirely. More in the Sancho Panza style. Northerners also do the *tapa* rounds, but for much more serious eating.

The *tapa* repertoire overlaps that of ordinary home cooking. Any dish can be turned into a *tapa* simply by reducing the portion to a half or a quarter of the amount that would normally be served at table, so that by the

time one has visited several bars and tried a number of *tapas* of this size, there is no longer any need for lunch or dinner. Not that this necessarily stops anyone from finishing off a proper meal at mid-day or at night, of course.

Some cold or casserole *tapas* are more common than others. The little fricassees of snails, tripe, shrimps in garlic, fried chorizo and black pudding, meat- or fish-balls and potatoes in a spicy sauce are among the favorite hot dishes, while, in addition to olives and pickles, the cold ones include fresh anchovies in vinegar, sardines or anchovies marinated in *escabeche*, and the famous though underestimated potato omelette, as well as ham and a wide variety of sausages.

Doing the *tapa* rounds is above all an occasion to mix socially. It is called *alternar*, an expressive verb that connotes meeting with different people in different places to have drinks together and talk. There is even a term — *chicas de alterne* — which designates the young ladies found in particular bars along the circuit. The specific time for this event is the hour or two between leaving the office and arriving home, the pause between work and the cares of home life. For many Spanish people it is both a daily form of socializing and a kind of fourth meal, along with breakfast (which itself often consists of *tapas* halfway through the morning), lunch and dinner.

Another significant aspect of *tapas* and the *tapa*-rounds is the Spanish attitude toward wine. For centuries, writers from other countries who visited Spain and wrote about their experiences there were unanimous in remarking upon the Spaniards' sobriety. All noted that drunkards were rarely seen in the streets and that inebriation in public was an unpardonable breach of good taste. The French were especially surprised at what they saw as an absurd custom of never drinking wine without water added to it. Alcoholism was virtually unknown in Spain, despite the vast quantities of wine produced there.

All this has changed, of course, but even today the Spanish palate is ill at ease when

One of the finest restaurants in Spain is the Jockey in Madrid (they cater the official banquets at the royal palace), particularly famed for its casserole of "Madrid-style" tripe. This succulent dish — which is usually even better when prepared the day before — is another favorite among the typical hot *tapas*. So much so, in fact, that in many bars a single piece of tripe is served on a cocktail stick to accompany a glass of wine, free of charge. But besides beef tripe, the dish contains black pudding, chorizo, pieces of muzzle, calves' feet or pigs' trotters all cooked together until the sauce, deliciously gelatinous, has been reduced to almost nothing. A dish like this is one of those culinary monuments that have arisen from humble but inspired origins.

Some bars in Madrid (in and around the Plaza de Cascorro, for example) serve a curious kind of tripe consisting of the large intestine of lamb rolled into a small bundle and fixed with a cocktail stick top and bottom. These go by the name of *zarajos*, or sometimes *gallinejas*. They originated in the northern part of La Mancha and the Guadalajara region but are also characteristic of northern Aragon, especially the town of Barbastro (Huesca). In fact they bear a resemblance to the typical *pieds-paquets* of Marseille, though only the Barbastro variety of *zarajos* or *gallinejas* contains lambs' feet. They are all prepared with tomato sauce and onions and must be cooked until very tender.

There is another special *tapa* that is a great favorite in springtime in Extremadura: sheep's tails, which the female sheep frequently lose when they give birth; once stripped of wool and skinned they are an incomparable delicacy. Then there are the lambs'-foot *tapas* that are served in abundance throughout Castile. . . .

The most orthodox *tapeo* devotees adhere to a basic rule: the morning aperitif must be white wine, while in the evening and at night it is red. To go with the white wine, two *tapas* are served across Spain, one hot and one cold. The hot *tapa* is gambas with

The most devoted tapas-lovers exchange the addresses of tascas offering the best specialties. Friends get together before a meal to "practice the art of eating standing up."

alcohol is not accompanied by something to eat. Furthermore, the Spaniards tend to drink outside the home, and rarely on their own. Which explains the necessity, or at least the custom, of the *alterne* and the *chateo* — or *copeo*, as it is also known.

Let us take a look at some of the classic cooked *tapas*. Snails, for instance. The preferred variety is the *caracol de viña*, known in France as the *petit gris*. This snail actually has an annual fair in its honor in Lérida, attended by thousands of enthusiasts from all over the world, who cook and consume millions of gastropods in every street and square in town in a single day.

As a rule snail *tapas* are served in small earthenware pots, cooked with a rather spicy sauce that usually includes tomato, garlic, onion, hot red peppers and chopped ham, laced with an herb such as bay leaf, thyme or rosemary and, almost invariably, mild or strong paprika. That is one of the variants of the *caracoles a la madrileña*, or "Madrid-style snails" consumed in huge quantities in the bars of the state capital. The snails are served in their shells, with cocktail sticks to winkle them out. Before being put into the sauce they are sometimes cooked in water mixed with vinegar or white wine, or in a stock made from ham bones.

garlic, and the cold, anchovies in vinegar.

The former is prepared in a small earthenware pot with oil, peeled gambas, garlic, parsley and chopped red peppers with a little lemon juice to bind it all together. The latter can be fresh or pickled anchovies, it makes no difference: the fish is put on a plate and a very hot mixture of water and vinegar is quickly poured over it, then it is left to marinate all night with garlic-steeped oil and finely chopped garlic and parsley. In fact, this turns it into a kind of anchovy *cebiche*.

And then hot or cold, the potato omelette cut into thick, solid cubes is marvelously filling when one starts the *tapeo* on an empty stomach.

The potato omelette is one of the great symbols of the "direct and simple" school of Spanish culinary art. The best I have ever eaten was in the Edreira restaurant in the Galician town of Betanzos, although in this case it was served as a meal, not as a *tapa*. It was juicy, tender and delicious, partly because of the quality of the Galician potatoes, but also because of a secret technique whereby two omelettes are prepared simultaneously, each in its own pan, and one is slipped on top of the other at the last moment, before the eggs (home-produced, of course) are completely done.

According to persistent legend, the potato omelette was invented in the nineteenth century, during an episode of the Carlist or dynastic wars between traditionalists and liberals. The Carlist general, Zumalacárregui, half dead with hunger, came to a hamlet demanding food. A peasant woman is supposed to have had some eggs and a few cooked potatoes, which she chopped and made into an omelette with the beaten eggs.

However, the most Spanish of all the popular dishes is in fact of Belgian origin. The first potato omelette documented in an actual recipe appeared in a book called *Ouverture de Cuisine*, published in Liège in 1557. Its author was Lancelot de Casteau, cook to Monsignor Robert de Berghes, Count of Walhain and bishop of that town. This same cook later pursued a splendid career among the ovens of Monsignor Gerard de Groesbeck, cardinal-archbishop of Liège, and those of Prince Ernest, duke of Bavaria and archbishop of Cologne. This high-born ecclesiastic nobility was enjoying potato omelettes centuries before the humble folk of Spain adopted it and brought it into the lowliest, most unassuming taverns.

There is another detail that is worth observing in the eminently Spanish art of eating standing up: the *tapeo* transcends class barriers.

As for restaurants, there are establishments for the very wealthy, for the middle classes, for the workers, and even for people with hardly any money at all. But the bars and taverns with their *tapa* counters are there for all and sundry, and everyone mixes there regardless of social or economic status. Today there is even a further attraction that would have been unthinkable some years back: a considerable feminine clientele. The evening *tapeo* is a very mixed affair, including unmarried couples, singles, husbands and wives, usually in groups and of all ages, everybody talking all at once and at the top of their voices.

Sheep tails, prepared in the spring with tomato sauce, crushed almonds and fresh hot green peppers, makes an original tapa in Extremadura (above).
Juanito is one of the most popular men in Barcelona. After a late night, party-goers flock to his tiny bar in the middle of the Boquería market (left).

SPANISH OMELETTE
TORTILLA ESPAÑOLA

Preparation time: 20 minutes
Cooking time: 55 minutes
For 6 servings:
3/4 cup (6 fl oz/18 cl) olive oil
1 large onion, chopped
1 3/4 lb (750 g) potatoes, peeled
    and sliced very thinly
Salt
8 eggs

Method:
Heat the oil in a large (12-inch/30 cm) non-stick skillet. Add the onions and cook over medium-high heat for 5 minutes, or until tender.

Add the potatoes, season with salt, and cook over low heat for 40 minutes or until the potatoes are tender, shaking the pan from time to time to prevent the potatoes from sticking. Drain the potatoes in a sieve, reserving 1 tablespoon of the oil in which they cooked.

In a large bowl, beat the eggs and season with salt. Add the potatoes, mixing well.

Heat the reserved tablespoon oil in the same skillet until it is very hot. Add the egg mixture, lower the heat, and cook for 5 minutes. Use a plate to carefully turn the omelette, and continue to cook for 5 minutes.

Spanish omelettes can be served hot or at room temperature.

SACROMONTE OMELETTE
TORTILLA SACROMONTE
Andalusia

Preparation time: 10 minutes
Cooking time: 17 minutes
For 6 servings:
1/2 cup (1 3/4 oz/50 g) fresh shelled peas
6 tablespoons (3 fl oz/9 cl) olive oil
3 1/2 oz (100 g) lamb kidneys
3 1/2 oz (100 g) lamb brains
8 eggs
Salt
3 1/2 oz (100 g) Serrano ham, chopped
    (see glossary)
1 large red bell pepper, seeded and chopped
1 3/4 oz (50 g) chorizo sausage, chopped
    (see glossary)

Method:
Place the peas in a saucepan filled with lightly salted boiling water, bring back to a boil and boil for 2 to 4 minutes, until peas are tender but still firm. Drain.

Heat 2 tablespoons of the oil in a skillet. Add the kidneys and brains and cook over high heat, turning, for 5 minutes. Remove, drain, and chop.

Beat the eggs in a large bowl. Season with salt. Add the kidneys, brains, ham, bell pepper, peas and chorizo.

In a large non-stick skillet, heat the remaining 4 tablespoons oil. Turn the omelette mixture into the skillet and cook for about 6 minutes on each side, using a plate to carefully turn the omelette.

Note: The traditional version of this omelette also includes lamb testicles, omitted from this recipe.

POTATOES WITH RED PEPPER SAUCE
PAPAS ARRUGADAS CON MOJO PICON
Canary Islands

Preparation time: 15 minutes
Cooking time: 50 minutes
For 4 servings:
8 medium red potatoes
1 1/3 cups (12 oz/350 g) coarse salt
Red pepper sauce:
1/2 slice firm white bread
1 small clove garlic, peeled
1 dried hot red pepper
1 tablespoon paprika
Pinch ground cumin
Salt
1/3 cup (2 1/2 fl oz/8 cl) olive oil
2 tablespoons wine vinegar
3/4 cup (6 fl oz/18 cl) water

Method:
Place the potatoes and salt in a saucepan. Add enough water to cover generously, and cook for 40 minutes. Drain off the water and return the potatoes to the heat until the skins are dry, shaking the pan from time to time to prevent sticking.

To prepare the sauce: Remove crusts from the bread, dampen with a little water and set aside. Place the garlic, pepper, paprika, cumin, and salt in a mortar and grind together with a pestle. Squeeze excess water out of the bread and add it to the spices, along with the oil and vinegar. Mix well. Add the water and mix again.

Pour the sauce over the hot potatoes and serve.

Note: In the Canary Islands, garlic is not included in this dish. Instead, a type of paprika called azafran del pais, or local saffron, is used.

Spanish omelette
(facing page).

MARINATED FISH ROE
HUEVAS ALIÑADAS
Andalusia

Preparation time: 15 minutes
Cooking time: 5 minutes
Marinating time: 2 hours
For 6 servings:
1 3/4 lb (750 g) fish roe (from cod, hake, etc.)
Fish broth (optional — see glossary)
1 bay leaf
2 tomatoes, ripe but firm, peeled and
   chopped
1 green bell pepper, seeded and thinly sliced
1 small onion, peeled and chopped
Salt
1/2 cup (4 fl oz/12 cl) olive oil
1 1/2 tablespoons wine vinegar

Method:
   Rinse the roe thoroughly, removing the outer membrane. Place them in a saucepan filled with the fish broth or salted water. Add the bay leaf and simmer for 5 minutes. Remove from the heat and let the roe cool in the broth.

   Remove the roe, drain, and place it on a plate. Sprinkle with the chopped tomatoes, green pepper, and onion. Season lightly with salt. Drizzle with the oil and vinegar and mix gently.

   Place in the refrigerator to marinate and chill for at least 2 hours. Serve accompanied by toasted slices of country bread.

FRESH ANCHOVIES IN VINEGAR
BOQUERONES EN VINAGRE
Madrid

Preparation time: 20 minutes
Marinating time: 8 hours
For 4 servings:
1/2 lb (250 g) fresh anchovies
3/4 cup (6 fl oz/18 cl) wine vinegar
2 1/2 tablespoons water
Salt
3 cloves garlic, peeled and chopped
Chopped parsley
6 tablespoons (3 fl oz/9 cl) olive oil

Method:
   Remove the heads from the anchovies and bone them, lifting off the fillets. Rinse the fillets and pat dry with paper towels.

   Place the fillets in an earthenware terrine or shallow glass baking dish. Add the vinegar and water, and set aside to marinate for 8 hours.

   Carefully drain the anchovy fillets and arrange them on a serving plate. Season lightly with salt. Sprinkle with the garlic and parsley. Drizzle the olive oil evenly over all and serve.

Anchovies are used in many dishes, and make delicious tapas, like these grilled toasts with anchovies and peppers in oil (above).

The best bulls for the corrida are from Andalusia, where bullfighting is closely linked to the world of tapas and Jerez wine. Enthusiasts expound on the exploits of their favorite matador while sampling tasty specialties, often served under the menacing gaze of a stuffed bull (facing).

PORK
AND
BACALAO

The severe Lenten periods of abstinence have made cod the typical dish in many areas of Spain, even in regions far removed from the sea. More than one hundred recipes exist for this cornerstone of Spanish cooking.

The conflict — and the symbiotic relationship — of the three cultures embodied in three religions, Jewish, Islamic and Christian, that clashed and eventually merged in Spain, left its indelible traces on Spanish cuisine.

There was a time when making a public show of an immoderate liking for pork was a demonstration that one's veins held not a drop of Jewish blood, and not surprisingly this gave rise to a huge variety of pork delicacies. Similarly, from an epoch when Lenten fasting and abstinence were strictly observed, we have inherited an anthology of delicious recipes for dried salt cod, or *bacalao.*

During the Inquisition people were burned at the stake for showing a distaste for pork products, which was taken as incontrovertible evidence that they were either Muhammadans or Jews. Conversely, the annual prohibition against eating meat during Lent spawned costly recipes for fish and seafood accessible only to the nobility and high-ranking clergy. Today Spain is second only to Japan as the world's biggest consumer of fish, of which some varieties can be wildly expensive.

For centuries *bacalao,* salt cod, was a poor man's dish, not only the Lenten repast par excellence, but a year-round staple. Today, however, it has become a luxury food that is presented as the specialty of the house on the menus of the best-known and most expensive restaurants. Traditional popular recipes, which are often surprisingly refined, have been used by some of the most famous chefs as a starting point for new recipes. These are always an assured success because their basic ingredient, dried salt cod, is held in the greatest esteem by Spaniards everywhere.

Bacalao and pork, then, have taken on almost sacramental connotations for Spanish palates. They could be considered culinary baptismal waters, Catholic authority represented in the kitchens of a people. Salt cod and pork and their derivatives also have in common a significant economic feature: both are products that keep well. They are well adapted for long-term storage and for use in times when fresh foods are not available. This was of vital importance during Spain's protracted history of poverty and famine.

Bacalao was long a metaphor for fasting, abstinence and the wrath of God, but pork, ham, fat strings of chorizo, blood sausages and black puddings, *bisbes* and pork sausages, on the contrary, were and still are symbols of wealth and prosperity blessed by God.

However, while there is nothing strange about finding pork on the table in Spain, the presence of cod merits some thought. The fact is that not a single codfish has ever been caught off the coast of the Iberian peninsula. And yet in Spain, and even more so in Portugal, it is the most highly consumed fish in the country. Furthermore, in both countries it is the main ingredient of many recipes that belong to areas far removed from the sea, which explains why it is often called *pescado de tierra adentro,* "inland fish."

Before the cod reaches the drying sheds (in Spain and Portugal *bacalao* refers strictly to the dried fish — it has only recently been introduced in non-dried form, and this has received a distinctly cool welcome), it is fished from the distant, cold seas of Scotland, Denmark, Norway, Iceland and, especially, Newfoundland.

Whalemeat and other whale products were widely consumed in the European Middle Ages; whales were therefore an important source of trade, and the most expert whalers were Spanish and French Basques. While following the great cetaceans, which were themselves in hot pursuit of krill, the diminutive shrimp that is its customary food, the Basque fishermen discovered immense shoals of what to them was an unknown species of fish swimming toward the estuary of the St. Lawrence River. They caught these fish and salted them on board ship, just as they did parts of the whale, and the result quickly became highly appreciated by buyers and sellers alike. Let it be mentioned in passing that, along with *bacalao*, the Basques discovered America five centuries before Christopher Columbus, whose sole true discovery was the Caribbean!

In any case, without the hard discipline of Lenten abstinence from meat, *bacalao* would never have achieved such prominence in the cuisines of the Iberian peninsula. Thanks are also due here to an odd ethnic group and to a profession: the *maragatos*, inhabitants of a district in the province of León, and the *arrieros*, or muleteers, who were responsible for transporting sea products — including *bacalao* — from the misty North as far south as the plains of Andalusia.

The *maragatos* have handed down to us a recipe called *bacalao al ajo del arriero* (muleteer's garlic *bacalao*), although the present-day preparation has little of the healthy simplicity prescribed in the original version:

Once the cod was desalted it was soaked in plain water, then put into an earthenware pot that was set on red-hot coals. In a separate pan a great quantity of garlic was fried in oil or lard until it was well browned. When the temperature rose to the point where the fish began to exude water, the boiling oil was thrown onto it with the garlic. Finally, it was seasoned with a splash of good wine vinegar. The mule drivers would then gather around the pot, spread the delightful mixture on hunks of bread and devour some of the *bacalao* they were taking south. Gustave Doré even executed some illustrations featuring the courageous *maragato* muleteers and their long strings of mules and wagons. Cervantes himself enjoyed their unsophisticated, healthful *bacalao*, and mentions it in his writing. *Bacalao al ajo arriero* today has degenerated into an emasculated stew cooked in a little casserole with a tomato sauce and the odd peeled shrimp.

Fortunately, there are still reasonably faithful variants of the authentic *bacalao al ajo del arriero* found under the name of *tiznao* at inns in La Mancha. In this region, during the autumn of 1986, I had the honor of pre-

siding over the jury of a competition for home-made *tiznaos*. There were many finalists — thirty or so — and their culinary art could hardly be described as light. The splendid ladies of La Mancha were unequivocal enthusiasts of garlic and red-hot peppers, the greatest amount of oil possible, discernible quantities of vinegar and cumin, and non-desalted *bacalao*, as employed in the unadulterated orthodox version of the recipe. The *tiznao* tasting began at seven o'clock in the evening and was followed by a dinner at which the main dish was another *tiznao*.

It was the *margato* muleteers who transmitted the ancestral dish to the shepherds of La Mancha. That is how a country is made, no doubt — especially in winter, when the icy north wind blows.

Ecclesiastical might (which was mainly political) was harsh in its prohibition of meat during Lent, but laid a far gentler hand on *bacalao* than did the *maragatos* and the Manchegan shepherds. One of the oldest and best recipes for *bacalao* is of monastic origin: this is the *potaje de Cuaresma* — Lenten soup, also known as *potaje castellano*. The ingredients required for this dish, which is cooked in a pot or casserole, are salt cod (it must be cut thin), chickpeas and Swiss chard or spinach. And some water, of course, oil and a few herbs, cumin and a dash of saffron. It may also be cooked in the oven. It is generally better with chard than with spinach, and is delicious, subtle, light and dietetic — food for monks of refined taste. Even overly ascetic, perhaps.

Bilbao, the great Basque industrial center, with its ironworks, its oil-soaked estuary, its afternoons frequently blanketed by a smog worthy of a town in Britain, and its heavy fogs and thin, sharp drizzle; Bilbao, a mecca of football, a port city both working-class and bourgeois, torn today by political strife, its streets plastered with autonomist slogans and, at times, the site of pitched battles between young *"abertzales"* and the state police: Bilbao is the place of pilgrimage for all truly dedicated lovers of *bacalao*.

Basque whaleboats discovered cod around the year A.D. 1000. Spaniards are capable of detecting subtle differences in the many kinds of cod (even those fished far from their coast), and know how to choose between Scottish or Norwegian cod, depending on the recipe.

Traditional Spanish cuisine includes dried fish, salted sardines, conger or smoked tuna fillets, served with delicious bread that has been toasted and drizzled lightly with olive oil (above). Desalted cod is featured in this salad with olives and peppers served at Rosimar, one of the best Spanish restaurants in Paris (facing).

In this city there is a man by the name of Emilio Alberdi. This stone-faced, husky gentleman runs a bar in the Calle Enrique Eguren, near the San Mamés stadium. It is a tiny, totally unpretentious place, its kitchen a minute room with little more than a few gas rings in it. It is called the Bolaviga. The tables are formica, the tablecloths made of paper. There are no waiters. Of course, at the Bolaviga, no one expects fancy surroundings. The customers are there to eat *bacalao* — in earnest. There are plenty of places in Bilbao that serve excellent *bacalao* — the Guria, for example, which is a classic, or the Bermeo, and many others. But anyone who wants to eat *bacalao* with the worshipful reverence due a divinity must go to Emilio Alberdi's. Why? Because elsewhere there is *bacalao* and many other things as well, but Señor Alberdi serves *bacalao* and nothing else — and only two *bacalao* dishes, at that. The two best, of course: *bacalao al pil-pil* and *bacalao a la vizcaína*. A word of warning, though: when I say you must go to the Bolaviga, it would be more exact to say that you must go to the Bolaviga . . . if you can get in. Emilio Alberdi doesn't accept just anyone. He has his clients and his friends, and if he doesn't take a liking to you, you can eat *bacalao* anywhere you like, but not at his place!

Don Emilio has been working on his *bacalao al pil-pil* and *bacalao al la vizcaína* for years, and knows all the secrets of their respective sauces. He selects none but the finest dried cod as his raw material, and is an expert at rendering it so juicy, soft and tender that it melts in the mouth, the flesh flaking apart piece by piece with slender threads of luscious tasty gelatin in between. I once called the Bolaviga the Sistine Chapel of *bacalao*, and Don Emilio Alberdi its Michelangelo. I hope that my words do not tempt him to abandon his rigorous selection of customers or his austere, unwaveringly orthodox approach.

Watching a *bacalao al pil-pil* being cooked is quite a show. The preparation of this dish, like paella in Valencia, is a male

prerogative: in theory only men cook it. This is logical, in fact, because making *pil-pil* for a number of people requires a good strong pair of arms.

The authentic version of *bacalao a la vizcaína* is a splendid dish whose secret lies in its somewhat elaborate sauce. Every so often in the Basque region tremendous arguments erupt over the genuine recipe for this sauce, arguments that are even carried on in the newspapers. Purists feel that there should be no tomato in it, while heterodox thinkers claim that there should. Personally, I side with the purists. The blasphemous introduction of tomatoes is due solely to considerations of a vulgar economic nature, when chorizo-pepper becomes scarce.

As I mentioned earlier, the two great Catalan *bacalao* dishes are known as *bacalao a la llauna* and the typical *bacalao a la catalana*, dishes that admit few variations and that can be perfected only with much skill on the part of the cook.

Ferrán Agulló was a great journalist, writer, poet and politician at the beginning of this century. He was for many years the director of *La Veu de Catalunya*, the foremost Catalan newspaper of his day, as well as an important figure in the center-right nationalist party, the Lliga Catalanista. But what is of particular interest to us here is the fact that Agulló was a gourmet who collected and published a series of recipes in a book that has today become a classic: the *Llibre de la cuina catalana*. He wrote a preface that included some very sensible assertions, such as the following:

"Catalonia, just as it has a language, a body of law, customs, its own history and a political ideal, also has a cuisine. There are regions, nationalities, and groups of people who have some particular characteristic dish or other, without having a true cuisine of their own, but Catalonia does. It has more than that, for it possesses a great faculty for assimilating dishes from other culinary traditions, such as French or Italian: it incorporates these dishes into its own cuisine and modifies them to suit its taste and style."

*In this tiny shop in an
Andalusian market, cod, olive oil
and ham are sold side by side,
symbols of Christian traditions
in Spanish cooking (above).
The variety of Spanish preserved
meats is endless, and each region
has its specialties. Castilian blood
sausage with rice and nutmeg can
be tasted at the Mesón de la Villa
at Aranda de Duero (facing).*

In our search for the "soul" of Spanish cooking, we have already run into religion several times. One of the key texts of early Spanish literature was the *Libro del Buen Amor* (Book of Good Love), written by Juan Ruiz, archpriest of Hita. This masterpiece is a collection of medieval light verse containing, among other things, a brilliant account of the annual combat between Don Cuaresma and Don Carnal (Sir Lent and Sir Non-Lent). The sensual archpriest of Hita, with his rebellious cast of mind, could well be considered a forebear of Rabelais.

Its hundreds of different recipes has won *bacalao* its full Spanish credentials and entry into what might be called "ideological cooking" by virtue of its connection with Lent; the same applies to pork, though in this case it was because of its association with transgression.

There is a medieval monastery in Salamanca that has a huge kitchen with an appropriately channeled small river flowing through it. The story has it that when it became time for the harsh disciplines of Lententide the monks there used to throw pigs into the river and "fish" them out when the current carried them into the kitchen. Since anything that came out of water counted as being "fished" (*"pescado"* is the past parti-

ciple of the verb *pescar*, to fish), they gaily consumed the pork with a clear conscience. Allegorically speaking, they had the wit to transform *pecado* (sin) into *pescado* (fish) simply by adding an "s"!

Nevertheless, fresh pork is rarely eaten in Spain. Almost all of it goes into jars, preserves and sausages, and these products, like chorizo, different varieties of blood puddings, *botillos*, dry bacon, and other specialties, are used enormously in Spanish cuisine, especially in the vast universe of casserole dishes, stews, and *escudellas.*

One of the best examples of Spanish "winter" dishes is the Galician *lacón con grelos.* This is one of those specialties that are strictly identified with their own region, because it can be made only with local products.

Lacón is partly salted shoulder of pork, and *grelos* are the leaves of new turnips. It also needs a few Galician chorizos and some potatoes, or *cachelos,* the Galician potatoes that grow in salty soil close to the sea — a large, white potato of exceptionally fine quality.

Galicia is the westernmost part of Spain, and is often compared to Brittany in France. Like Brittany, Galicia juts into the raging storms of the Atlantic, its dagger-like Cape Finisterre projecting from the Costa de la Muerte: the Death Coast. This is named for the countless shipwrecks that have occurred there — tragedies that still strike almost every year, shrouding the lovely fishing villages in mourning. This coast, battered by the icy waters of the Atlantic, produces what is probably the finest seafood in the world. Behind the coastline, however, Galicia is also a large inland territory, a hard, poverty-stricken land with the highest percentage of emigrants in all of Spain. Nonetheless, it is the area with the greatest number of celebrations, all of which are accompanied by Pantagruelian feasting on popular dishes that can be exquisitely refined, such as those made with lamprey when in season, or richly flavored, like *lacón con grelos* and the famous *pulpo da feira.*

Jabugo is a small Andalusian town famed for its hams and chorizos, which are considered among the best in Spain. They are prepared with Iberian pork from the pata negra, a rare species of pig that is fed almost exclusively on acorns (above and right).

Serrano ham was considered the most desirable delicacy of Spanish culinary mythology long before the dreadful postwar famines struck. The finest of all the hams is from Jabugo, a tiny village in the Sierra de Aracena in Huelva (Andalusia). Two factors concur in the making of this superb product: first, the animal itself, which is the *cerdo ibérico,* a black-haired breed of pig native to Galicia and raised in woodland areas where in theory it feeds primarily on acorns. The special characteristic of this breed is that its meat has a high fat content. In addition, after being salted it is hung to cure in high-ceilinged rooms where a particular degree of humidity and other microclimatic factors facilitate the production of a blue penicillium mold, and this microscopic fungus on the outer skin gives it its unique flavor. Jabugo ham, and *pata negra* products from the black-haired pig in general, fetch high prices on the market, because the breed is extremely limited in number.

The meat is cut with special ham knives that have attenuated, broad blades, and the slices must be so fine as to be almost transparent, with the same amount of fat in each one. This is the only way to ensure that the *pata negra* ham releases the full fragrance of the oak woods and sun-ripened acorns that give the ham fat its ivory color and its characteristic hazelnut or almond-like flavor.

Spain has marvelous regions for producing great ham — dry mountainous country redolent of wild herbs, where temperatures drop sharply at night. Among the best are Trevélez hams in the Sierra Nevada, which are cured in snow-covered caves, and those from Sierra de Teruel in Aragon.

Each of the autonomous regions in Spain has its own typical sausages, and the selection of pork products is enormous: chorizos from Cantimpalos, Salamanca and Pamplona; blood sausages with rice from Aranda de Duero, and with onion, from Castile and Aragon; *fuets, longanizas, bisbes,* and black and white *butifarra* sausages from Catalonia; Andalusian loin sausages; Extremadura's black puddings; *botillos* from El Bierzo. And, lording it over all, the fine-textured *sobrasada* from Majorca, a kind of highly seasoned pâté sausage made from the best Majorcan hams and seasoned with a sweet pepper found only on the island itself.

The king of Spanish pork dishes, of course, is roast suckling pig. Its greatest exponent was undoubtedly Cándido, the Castilian innkeeper in Segovia, but it is also prepared extremely well in other establishments, such as the Casa Botin in Madrid.

Roast suckling pig requires a special technique, and it has to be cooked in an old-fashioned baker's oven — in other words, a brick or clay, but never a refractory oven. Ash wood, pinecones or broom are best for the fire. Once the pig is roasted it is spread with lard mixed with chopped garlic, and in some restaurants it is flambéed with rum and branches of thyme before serving.

*The climate of the dry
mountainous south
produces the exceptional
Jabugo ham, the most prized
in all of Spain (above).*

LENTEN SOUP
POTAJE DE VIGILIA
Castile-León

Advance preparation: 24 hours
Cooking time: 1 hour 50 minutes
For 4 servings:
1/2 lb (250 g) dried salt cod
2 cups (14 oz/400 g) chickpeas
1 onion, peeled
1 bay leaf
Salt
12 cups (1 lb/500 g) fresh spinach leaves, finely chopped
1 large potato, peeled and diced
1/3 cup (2 1/2 fl oz/8 cl) olive oil
2 cloves garlic, peeled and chopped
1 tablespoon paprika

Method:

A day in advance: Place the cod in a large basin filled with cold water and soak for 24 hours, changing the water 3 to 4 times. Place the chickpeas in a bowl of cold water and soak for 8 hours.

The same day: Drain the chickpeas, place them in a large soup kettle or Dutch oven and cover with water. Cut the onion in half and add one half to the pan along with the bay leaf and salt. Place over medium heat and cook for 1 hour.

Drain the cod, removing any remaining bones or skin, and flake with a fork.

When the chickpeas have cooked for 1 hour, add the cod, spinach and potato to the pan and continue to cook over low heat for 40 minutes.

Meanwhile, chop the remaining onion half. Heat the oil in a skillet. Add the chopped onion and garlic and cook until tender. Add the paprika, stirring rapidly. Stir this mixture into the soup, season if necessary, and cook 5 minutes longer.

Serve hot.

Cod esqueixada is a salad made with raw, desalted cod, olive oil, chopped tomatoes, white beans and onions. This Catalan specialty, which is served cold, is both refreshing and nourishing (facing page).

BACALAO — WHICH TO CHOOSE?

"Vigil-day beef" was what *bacalao* was called by good Spanish Christians, when there were any of them around. Today it has become a luxury food, as is apparent from the surprising appearance in major Spanish cities, especially Madrid, Barcelona and Bilbao, of "*bacalao* boutiques," which sell an amazing selection of varieties and cuts.

There are thick loin cuts for *bacalaos a la llauna*, square-cut, medium-thick pieces for the *vizcaína* and *pil-pil* recipes, thinner strips for stew or for cooking with potatoes . . . all nicely presented and labeled with the place of origin of the dried and salted cod.

Although there are a number of Spanish drying and salting plants for handling large fish, usually from Newfoundland, Spain also imports processed *bacalao* from other countries.

As to the best source, experts are divided between Norway — preferred by most — and Scotland. Norwegian cod, which is fatter and more fleshy as well as whiter, is ideal for cooking in the oven, especially the more compact, thicker cuts. The Scottish variety is smaller and tends to have a yellowish cast; it has a much stronger taste, and is particularly good for dishes in which the *bacalao* is accompanied by other ingredients such as potatoes, rice, or a large quantity of vegetables. Many people prefer the small Scottish *bacalao* to the Norwegian for this reason.

Icelandic cod also has its enthusiasts: it is tender, very white, and excellent eaten raw or macerated as in Catalan *esqueixada*.

BAY OF BISCAY SALT COD
BACALAO A LA VIZCAÍNA
Basque Country

Advance preparation: 24 hours
Preparation time: 5 minutes
Cooking time: 30 minutes
For 6 servings:
1 3/4 pound (750 g) dried salt cod, with skin
6 hot red peppers
3/4 cup (6 fl oz/18 cl) olive oil
8 cloves garlic, peeled
2 large onions, peeled and chopped
2 ripe tomatoes, peeled and chopped (optional)
Flour
Salt

Method:

A day in advance: Cut the cod into 12 pieces. Place them in a large basin of cold water and soak for 24 hours, changing the water 2 or 3 times. Soak the peppers in a bowl of warm water for about 12 hours.

The same day: Drain and pat dry the cod, removing any bones. Drain the peppers.

Heat 4 tablespoons of the oil in a skillet. Add the onions and garlic and cook briefly. Add the tomatoes, if using, and peppers, and cook for 8 to 10 minutes. Press this mixture through a fine sieve, and keep warm.

Dust the cod pieces lightly with flour. Heat the remaining oil in a large shallow earthenware casserole or skillet. Add the cod and cook until lightly browned on both sides. Spread the sauce over the cod, season with salt if necessary, and simmer over very low heat for 15 minutes, shaking the pan from time to time.

Serve hot.

SALT COD WITH GARLIC AND PEPPERS
BACALAO AL PIL-PIL
Basque Country

Advance preparation: 24 hours
Preparation time: 3 minutes
Cooking time: 20 minutes
For 6 servings:
2 1/4 lb (1 kg) dried salt cod, with the skin
1/2 cup (4 fl oz/12 cl) olive oil
6 cloves garlic, peeled
2 hot red peppers, seeded and thinly sliced
Salt

Method:

A day in advance: Cut the cod into 18 pieces. Place them in a large basin filled with cold water and soak for 24 hours, changing the water 3 or 4 times.

The same day: Heat the oil in a large shallow earthenware casserole or a skillet. Add the garlic and cook over medium heat until it begins to color. Stir in the peppers and cook for 1 minute. Remove the garlic and peppers and set aside. Pour off most of the olive oil and reserve.

Drain and pat dry the cod pieces. Arrange them, skin side down, in the pan in which the garlic and peppers cooked, and let cook over low heat for 15 minutes, continually moving the pan in a circular motion. This is important to the success of the dish; hold the casserole and swirl gently and continually, sliding the pan on and off the heat. Add the reserved garlic, pepper and oil in a slow stream, continuing to swirl the pan to obtain a sauce that will thicken and bind with the gelatin from the cod. Season lightly with salt, if necessary.

Arrange the cod on a serving platter, pour the sauce, garlic and peppers over the top and serve hot.

Salt cod with garlic and peppers (facing page).
Spain has many simple cod recipes, like this Catalan preparation with potatoes —a specialty of the Hispania restaurant at Arenys de Mar (above).

SEVILLIAN SALT COD WITH POTATOES AND OLIVES
BACALAO A LA SEVILLANA
Andalusia

Advance preparation time: 24 hours
Preparation time: 10 minutes
Cooking time: 40 minutes
For 4 servings:
1 lb (500 g) dried salt cod
6 tablespoons (3 fl oz/9 cl) olive oil
1 lb (500 g) potatoes, peeled and sliced thinly into thin rounds
2 medium onions, peeled and sliced
4 cloves garlic, peeled
1 lb (500 g) tomatoes, peeled and chopped
2 green bell peppers, seeded and diced
2 red bell peppers, seeded and diced
1 cup (1/3 lb/150 g) pitted black olives
2 bay leaves
3/4 cup (6 fl oz/18 cl) water

Method:

A day in advance: Place the cod in a large basin of cold water and let soak for 24 hours, changing the water 3 or 4 times.

The same day: Drain the cod and pat dry. Remove any bones or skin and cut the cod into thin slices.

Place 1 tablespoon of the oil in a Dutch oven. Line the bottom of the pan with a layer of potato slices. Arrange the cod, onion, garlic, tomatoes, green and red peppers, olives, and bay leaves over the top. Drizzle the water and the remaining olive oil evenly over the ingredients. Season lightly if necessary.

Cover and bake in a preheated 375° F (190° C) oven for 40 minutes. Serve hot.

SALT COD WITH CATALAN MIXED VEGETABLES
BACALAO CON SANFAINA
Catalonia

Advance preparation time: 24 hours
Preparation time: 10 minutes
Cooking time: 30 minutes
For 6 servings:
1 1/3 lb (600 g) dried salt cod, with the skin
1/2 cup (4 fl oz/12 cl) olive oil
3 eggplants, diced into 1/4-inch cubes
1 red bell pepper, seeded and diced
1 green bell pepper, seeded and diced
2 medium onions, peeled and chopped
11 oz (300 g) tomatoes, peeled and chopped
Salt

Method:

A day in advance: Place the cod in a large basin of cold water and soak for 24 hours, changing the water 3 or 4 times.

The same day: Drain the cod, pat dry, and cut it into pieces. Heat the oil in a large skillet, add the cod and cook for 5 minutes, turning. Remove the cod with a slotted spatula and drain.

Add the eggplant to the hot oil remaining in the skillet and cook over low heat for 15 minutes. Remove from the pan and set aside. Cook the peppers, onions, and tomatoes in the same skillet until tender, adding a little more oil if necessary and seasoning with salt.

Return the cod and eggplant to the skillet with the peppers, onions and tomatoes, and cook for about 2 minutes. Serve immediately.

BORRETA OF SALT COD
BORRETA DE BACALAO
Valencia

Advance preparation time: 24 hours
Preparation time: 10 minutes
Cooking time: 20 minutes
For 4 servings:
14 oz (400 g) dried salt cod
1 lb (500 g) potatoes, unpeeled and cut
into pieces
1 lb (500 g) cauliflower, cut into flowerettes
6 cloves garlic, peeled and coarsely chopped
6 dried sweet peppers
Pinch saffron threads (see glossary)
1 cup (8 fl oz/25 cl) olive oil

Method:
A day in advance: Place the cod in a
large basin of cold water and soak for
24 hours, changing the water 3 or 4 times.
The same day: Drain the cod, pat dry,
and cut into large pieces.
Fill a large saucepan with water. Add
the cod, potatoes, cauliflower, garlic, and
peppers and cook over low heat for about
20 minutes.
Just before serving, season with the
saffron and stir in as much olive oil as
desired.
Serve immediately.

*Salt cod fritters may be served
alongside a delicious dish of cod
with white beans (facing).*

SALT COD FRITTERS
SOLDADITOS DE PAVIA
Andalusia

Advance preparation time: 12 hours
Preparation time: 1 hour
Cooking time: 5 minutes
For 6 servings:
1 lb (500 g) dried salt cod, cut from
the thickest part of the fillet
2 cups (16 fl oz/50 cl) olive oil
1 tablespoon dry white wine
Juice of 1 lemon
1 teaspoon paprika
Freshly ground black pepper
13 tablespoons (100 g) all-purpose flour
1 1/2 teaspoons baking powder
3 tablespoons eau-de-vie or brandy
Salt

Method:
A day in advance: Cut the cod into
2 by 3/4-inch (5 by 2 cm) strips. Place
them in a pan of cold water and soak for
12 hours, changing the water 2 or 3 times.
The same day: Drain the cod and pat
dry. Cut the strips in half lengthwise and
set aside.
Prepare the marinade: In a bowl,
combine 1/3 cup of the oil with the wine,
lemon juice, paprika, and pepper, and mix
thoroughly. Add the cod and let marinate
for 45 minutes.
Meanwhile, sift the flour into a mixing
bowl. Form a well in the center and add
the baking powder and eau-de-vie, along
with a tablespoon of the oil. Gently
combine the ingredients, adding enough
water to form a rather wet dough, and
season with salt. Set aside and let rest
at room temperature for 15 minutes.
Heat the remaining oil in a heavy
skillet until very hot. Dip the cod fillets in
the batter to coat and fry in the hot oil, a
few pieces at a time, for about 5 minutes.
Serve immediately.

CATALAN SALT COD WITH AÏOLI SAUCE
BACALAO CON ALIOLI
Catalonia

Advance preparation time: 24 hours
Preparation time: 5 minutes
Cooking time: 45 minutes
For 4 servings:
3/4 lb (300 g) dried salt cod
1 lb (500 g) potatoes
2 cloves garlic, peeled
Salt
1 cup (8 fl oz/25 cl) olive oil
Freshly ground pepper
2 hard-cooked eggs, sliced into rounds

Method:
A day in advance: Place the cod in a
large basin of cold water and soak for
24 hours, changing the water 3 or 4 times.
The same day: Cook the potatoes,
unpeeled, in a large pan of salted water
for 40 minutes.
Drain the cod. Place it in a saucepan of
simmering water and cook for 3 minutes.
Drain. Remove any bones or skin. Using a
fork, flake the cod into pieces.
Meanwhile, prepare the aïoli sauce: In
a large mortar, grind the garlic and a little
salt to a paste with a pestle. Add the oil in
a slow steady steam, whisking constantly
to form an emulsion.
Drain and peel the potatoes, and cut
them into 1/4-inch (1/2 cm) rounds.
Arrange them on a large serving platter
and season to taste with salt and pepper.
Arrange the cod on top.
Spoon the aïoli sauce evenly over
the potatoes and cod.
Serve immediately, decorated with
the hard-cooked egg rounds.

EGGS "SOLLER"
HUEVOS AL MODO DE SOLLER
Balearic Islands

Preparation time: 5 minutes
Cooking time: 30 minutes
For 4 servings:
2 cups (16 fl oz/50 cl) oil
1 cup (3 1/2 oz/100 g) fresh shelled peas
1 large leek, cut into rounds
1 medium carrot, cut into rounds
1 cup (8 fl oz/25 cl) milk
1/4 cup (2 fl oz/6 cl) fish broth (see glossary)
1 sugar cube
Salt
8 eggs
8 thin slices sobresada (see glossary)

Method:

Heat 6 tablespoons of the oil in a large skillet. Add the peas, leek, and carrot and cook until tender. Add the milk, fish broth and sugar cube, season lightly with salt and cook over low heat for 20 minutes.

Strain the mixture through a fine sieve and correct the seasoning if necessary. Set aside and keep warm.

In the remaining oil, fry the eggs, one by one, in a skillet. In a separate skillet, sauté the sobresada slices without oil.

Divide the sausage slices among 4 serving plates. Place a fried egg on each plate. Spoon the sauce over each serving and serve immediately.

Serrano ham, particularly appreciated with aperitifs, is enjoyed throughout Spain (above).
The Hispania restaurant near Barcelona serves excellent local pork products. These include butifarra and Bisbe (bishop) black or white sausage — a huge, truly episcopal slice (facing).

GALICIAN-STYLE PORK RIBS WITH CHESTNUTS
COSTILLAR DE CERDO CON CASTAÑAS
Galicia

Preparation time: 20 minutes
Cooking time: 1 hour 20 minutes
For 4 servings:
6 tablespoons (3 fl oz/9 cl) olive oil
2 bay leaves, crumbled
1 sprig thyme, crumbled
2 teaspoons salt
Freshly ground pepper
2 1/4 lb (1 kg) pork spare ribs
1/2 cup (4 fl oz/12 cl) chicken broth
3/4 lb (350 g) fresh chestnuts (see note)
3 tablespoons lard

Method:

Combine the olive oil, bay leaves, thyme, salt, and pepper in a bowl. Brush the mixture over the spare ribs.

Place the ribs on a rack over a shallow pan filled with the broth, and bake in a preheated 425° F (220° C) oven for 45 minutes. The fat given off by the ribs during cooking will mix with the broth and may be used to baste the ribs during the cooking and before serving.

Meanwhile, peel the outer shells from the chestnuts and place them in a large saucepan filled with salted water. Cook for 30 minutes over medium heat, being careful not to let them burst. Drain thoroughly and peel off the inner skin.

Melt the lard in a skillet. Add the chestnuts and sauté until lightly browned.

Arrange the ribs on a serving platter surrounded by the chestnuts.

Note: Canned unsweetened chestnuts, available in many specialty food shops, may be substituted. Drain them, rinse and sauté in the lard to brown and heat through.

EXTREMADURA-STYLE EGGS AND HAM
HUEVOS CON TORREZNOS A LA EXTREMEÑA
Extremadura

Preparation time: 5 minutes
Cooking time: 11 minutes
For 4 servings:
3 1/2 oz (100 g) slab bacon, cut into
    1/4-inch (3/4 cm) matchsticks
4 slices Serrano ham (see glossary)
1 cup (8 fl oz/25 cl) olive oil
8 very fresh eggs
Salt

Method:

Sauté the bacon and ham over medium-high heat for about 3 minutes. Remove from the skillet and keep warm.

Heat the oil in the skillet. Fry the eggs one at a time, keeping the oil at the same high temperature throughout the cooking. Remove the eggs with a slotted spatula, gently shaking off excess oil, and keep them warm while frying the remaining eggs. Salt, if necessary.

Serve the eggs immediately, accompanied by the ham and bacon and slices of toasted or fried country bread.

ROAST PORK
WITH CARAMEL SAUCE
CINTA DE LOMO AL CARAMELO
Murcia

Preparation time: 5 minutes
Cooking time: 1 hour 25 minutes
For 6 servings:
2 1/4 lb (1 kg) pork loin end or fillet roast
3 tablespoons oil
Zest of 1 orange
Zest of 1 lemon
4 cups (32 fl oz/1 l) milk
1 cup (7 oz/200 g) sugar
1/2 cinnamon stick
2 cups (16 fl oz/50 cl) water
3/4 cup (6 fl oz/18 cl) liquid
  caramel (see glossary)
Salt

Method:
   Brush the pork generously with the oil. Place it in a Dutch oven over high heat and cook until browned on all sides. Add the orange and lemon zest, along with the milk, sugar and cinnamon stick. Stir in the water and cook over low heat for 1 hour.
   Remove the meat from the pan, set aside and keep warm. Stir the liquid caramel into the pan juices and continue to cook and reduce over low heat for 20 minutes.
   Just before serving, slice the roast and serve hot, napped with the reduced sauce.

Fresh pork is rarely eaten in Spain, but dried and preserved pork, particularly dry blood sausage, is used in many dishes, notably the wide range of cocidos (stews).

In Aragon, the marinade for pigs' feet with truffles is prepared with leeks, bay leaves, onions and tomatoes, and is one of the many recipes featuring pork (facing).

SLOW-SIMMERED PORK LOIN
LOMO EN MANTECA
Andalusia

Preparation time: 5 minutes
Cooking time: 15 minutes
For 4 servings:
1 lb (500 g) lard
1 lb (500 g) pork loin, cut into 1/2-inch
  (1 cm) slices
10 cloves garlic, peeled
2 bay leaves
1 1/2 teaspoons oregano
2 sprigs thyme
Salt

Method:
   Melt the lard in a large, deep-sided skillet or Dutch oven.
   Add the pork slices, garlic, bay leaves, oregano, and thyme, and season with salt. Let simmer over low heat until the pork is nicely browned on all sides, about 15 minutes. Remove from the heat and let cool slightly.
   Transfer the contents of the skillet to a large earthenware crock for storage. The pork will keep well in a cool place for several months.
   To serve, remove the pork slices from the fat and serve cold, or melt a little of the fat in a skillet and sauté over high heat until heated through.

PORK TENDERLOIN WITH
SERRANO HAM
SOLOMILLOS DE CERDO MECHADOS
Andalusia

Preparation time: 5 minutes
Marinating time: 2 hours
Cooking time: 10 minutes
For 4 servings:
2 pork tenderloins
4 1/2 oz (125 g) Serrano ham (see glossary)
4 sprigs parsley
4 cups (32 fl oz/1 l) dry white wine
Salt
Freshly ground pepper

Method:
   Make several lengthwise slits in the tenderloins. Cut the ham into lengthwise strips, and insert them into the tenderloins. Place a parsley sprig in each slit.
   Place the tenderloins in a shallow dish, add the wine and let marinate for 2 hours.
   Remove the tenderloins from the wine, reserving the wine, and pat the meat dry. Season with salt and pepper, and place on an oiled and heated wire grill set over a hot wood fire or barbecue. Cook for about 10 minutes, turning to cook evenly and basting 4 or 5 times with the wine in which the meat marinated.
   Serve hot, cut into slices and accompanied by French-fried potatoes.

THE
AROMA
OF THE
STEWPOT

Chicken is an essential ingredient in Spanish stews, always in combination with other meats (above).

The savory aroma of fish stock permeates the kitchens of Andalusian restaurants, where dishes are always prepared simply — like the swordfish stew with onions, cuttlefish with potatoes, and marinated rock salmon served at Sanlúcar de Barrameda, north of Cádiz (facing).

One of the few dishes of traditional Spanish cuisine adopted by the celebrated French chef Antonin Carême was the *olla podrida* stew. This is of course the stew to end all stews, and cooking it means embarking on an adventure, a long journey through Nature for whoever is preparing it, and through Nature's rich and nourishing gifts for those who eat it.

One of the characteristics of Spanish cuisine mentioned earlier is "minimal cooking," the result of a century of using whatever was available — sometimes barely survival fare — in a poverty-stricken country wracked by five civil wars and several revolutions. In his brilliant book, *Guide du Gastronome en Espagne*, Raymond Dumay wrote at length on Spanish cooking as "soldiers' food." From bread and tomato to potato omelettes (the latter albeit a Belgian invention) and chickpeas with bacon, much of Spanish food seems to hark back to the ancient Roman legions, with their backpacks full of flour and fat for the soldiers' meal of polenta.

Olla podrida is just the opposite. *Olla podrida* is "The Compleat Cuisine." Claude Lévi-Strauss saw in it the symbol of maternity and fecundity, and in the adjective *podri-da* (literally, "rotten"), an allusion to placental fluids or the mud and slime from which life emerged. I was told by someone from the Castilian province of Burgos that the word was not really *podrida*, but a corruption of *poderida*, from *poder*, or power, deriving from the fact that it was possible for *olla podrida* to be made in its entirety only in the homes of the rich and powerful.

Whatever the case, one thing is certain, and that is that *olla podrida* never was and never could have been a poor man's dish.

The two oldest known Spanish cookery books, both of which are Catalan, are the early fourteenth-century *El Llibre de Sent Sovi* and, from the end of the same century, *El Llibre de Coch*. Each of them mentions *ollas*, but without calling them *podridas*; furthermore, the dishes they refer to are simple stews containing only chicken, bacon and a few greens and other vegetables.

The earliest *olla podrida* recipes ever published appeared in books dating from the sixteenth century. The first mentions an *olla podrida en pastel* (in pastry), in the *Arte de Cocina, Pastelería, Vizcochería y Conservería* (The art of cooking, pastry-making, baking and preserving), written by Francisco Martínez Montiño, who was cook to Philip III, while the other is in the *Libro de Arte de Cocina* (The art of cooking) by Diego Granado (1599). The latter is a remarkable recipe that deserves to be recounted in its entirety:

"Take two pounds of salted gullet of pork and four pounds of desalted hock, two snouts, two ears and four split one-day-old pig's-feet, four pounds of wild boar with its fresh tripe, two pounds of good sausages, all clean. Cook in unsalted water; in another copper or earthenware pot also cook, in salted water, six pounds of lamb and six pounds of calves' kidneys, and six pounds of good fat beef and two capons or two chickens, and four plump domestic pigeons; and of all these things, those that were set to cook first must be removed from the pot before they fall to pieces, and be kept in a receptacle, and in another pot of earthenware or copper, with the stock from the said meat.

For most Spanish and French gourmets and food critics, Juan Mari Arzak in San Sebastián is the best chef on the Iberian peninsula. His brilliant, poetic cuisine is inspired by products from the Basque region.

Then cook two hindquarters of hare cut in pieces, three partridges, two pheasants, two plump, fresh mallards, twenty thrushes, three black partridges and, when all this is done, mix the two stocks together and strain them through a sieve, taking care that they are not too salty.

"Have ready prepared black and white chickpeas that have been left to soak, whole heads of garlic, onions cut in two, peeled chestnuts, boiled French beans or boiled red beans, and put all these to cook together with the broth, and when the vegetables are almost done, add Savoy cabbages, white cabbages, turnips, forced meats of giblets and sausages, and when everything is cooked, firm rather than over-softened, mix everything well together. Taste frequently for salt and add a little pepper and cinnamon, and after that have large dishes ready and set upon them a portion of the combination, without the stock, and cut all the fowl into four parts and the large pieces of meat and the salted flesh trimmed into slices, and the small birds left whole, and set dishes upon the mixture and on them put the other mixture of forcemeats in slices, thus making three tiers of dishes, and cover with another dish, and serve hot with sweet spices. Some of the birds can be roasted after they have been boiled."

You can see why the word could well be *poderida* rather than *podrida*!

Olla podrida today belongs to the realm of culinary archaeology. It is prepared only on very rare occasions by members of some gastronomical society or other, and it is a momentous event. It has been replaced in everyday home cooking or in restaurants by stews such as *cocidos*, *pucheros*, and *escudellas*. Every region has its own recipes, of varying degrees of complexity and divergence from the original.

The specialty of the city of Madrid, for example, is the *cocido madrileño*. It is rare for a metropolis to have something as rustic as a *cocido* as its traditional dish, but then Madrid is a hybrid city whose growth has been alluvial, created by generations of farmers streaming in from rural areas, and for whom the "Monday stew" or the "Tuesday hotpot" is a way of maintaining contact with their roots.

Indeed, as soon as autumn comes round, both luxury and popular restaurants include the house *cocido* on their Monday and Tuesday menus. Even the restaurant of the Hotel Ritz in Madrid has a much-loved *cocido*, as does the old Lhardy and, in more sophisticated, modern versions, the Lúculo, which belongs to Ange García from Perpignan.

Who said there was no connection between food and politics? At the beginning of this century, the American Congressional Cooks' Club collected and published a huge book of recipes, selecting those that were considered the "national" dishes of each country.

Spain's contribution was the *cocido madrileño*, and to dispel any possible doubt as to the "national" character of this recipe, it was signed by the head of state himself, H. R. H. King Alfonso XIII, the grandfather of the present King Juan Carlos.

In fact, the recipe for the *cocido* was created by Cándido Collar, who ran the kitchens of Her Royal Highness *la Infanta Isabel*.

"A good *cocido* for five people takes a half pound of Castilian chickpeas; one pound of gelatinous meat, preferably elbow or back; half a chicken, not too old — for although the popular saying has it that it produces a better broth, the fact is that it gives it an unpleasant taste of the chicken-run; three and one-half ounces bacon; the same amount of Serrano ham; one salted pig-foot and a 'ball' made by kneading together ground meat, breadcrumbs, an egg and seasoning. The pot for cooking the *cocido* in must be wide-based and is set on the fire with sufficient cold water to cover the meat, bacon, chicken and ham, which are put in first. When scum begins to form it is removed with a slotted spoon, and when the water starts to boil, the chickpeas and the pig's foot, which have been soaked for at least ten hours beforehand, are added to the pot. When the water comes back to the boil, the pot is put to the side of the flame and left there to cook as slowly as possible, without interruption, for the space of three hours, or more if the quality of the water or the kind of ingredients require it. As soon as it begins to boil, the appropriate amount of salt is added, together with half a small onion spiked with a clove. The vegetables to accompany the *cocido* (cabbage, Swiss chard, Savoy cabbage, green beans, cardoons, et cetera) are cooked in a separate pan or stewpot, together with the chorizo and blood sausage, taking care that all the ingredients are properly cooked and salted at the right time. Fifteen minutes before serving, six small egg-shaped peeled potatoes are added or — for a more attractive appearance — are cooked separately in a little stock from the stew. When it is required, the soup is made by removing some stock from the stew and straining it through a muslin cloth or a very fine sieve. The ingredients selected for the soup (pasta, rice, bread, etc.) are cooked in the strained stock and served as the first course. The chickpeas are thoroughly drained and placed in a dish; the meat is cut into small, regular pieces and arranged in a band from one side of the dish to the other on top of the chickpeas. The ham, bacon, pig's foot, chicken and the 'ball,' all cut into pieces or slices, are placed as artistically as possible on either side of the meat. The well-drained vegetables are lightly fried in a little oil in which a clove of garlic has been well browned, and are then put into another dish with the sliced chorizo and blood sausage, together with the previously prepared potatoes. The two dishes are served at the same time, usually accompanied by a sauceboat containing tomatoes that have been chopped into small pieces and fried to obtain a kind of sauce."

This is perhaps the only recipe ever signed by a reigning monarch in the history of cooking. It was sent by cable and broadcast throughout the United States over the microphones of the station WRC. This happened while Calvin Coolidge was president, and the recipe for *cocido madrileño* was read on the radio by the wife of the secretary of labor.

In one of the seminars on culinary anthropology that I ran at the Menendez Pelayo de Santander Summer School, the writer Manolo Vásquez Montalbán, famous gourmet and cooking enthusiast, gave a brilliant lecture entitled "An interpretation of Franco-style autarchy in Spanish cuisine," in which he referred to a hit song from the 1950s entitled "Cocidito Madrileño":

No me hable usted
de los banquetes que hubo en Roma
ni del menu del Hotel Plaza en
Nueva York
ni del faisan
ni de los foiegrases de paloma
ni le hable usted de la langosta a un
servidor.
Porque es que a mí sin discusión me
quita el sueño
y es mi alimento y mi placer,
la gracia y sal que al cocidito madrileño
le echa el amor de una mujer.

Don't bother to tell me
about banquets in Rome
or the Hotel Plaza menu
in New York
or pheasants
or pigeon *foie gras*
and don't talk about lobster to me.
For what keeps me awake at night
what's my food and my delight
is all the charm and spice
that a woman's love puts right
into the *cocidito madrileño*.

But to go back to the great *olla podrida*: it was so elaborate and expensive that it soon disappeared from Spanish cookbooks entirely, yet it nevertheless lingered on in French cuisine and cookery books as the archetypal Spanish dish.

The *olla*, or *oille* in its French version, reached Antonin Carême — who never actually went to Spain — from a number of sources, which he divulged in the chapter on Spanish stews in his *L'Art de la cuisine*

The Mesón de la Villa restaurant in Aranda de Duero serves excellent food, and evokes centuries-old tradition with its ancient bakers' ovens and vaulted cellars full of the best Rioja wines. Eugenio and his wife Seri focus on Castilian cooking, the least known of the Spanish cuisines.

Paul Bocuse was enchanted by patatas a la riojana, a traditional dish of the Rioja wine harvesters, made with braised potatoes and chorizo (above).
This delectable stew is served on festive occasions in Catalan villages. Everything that can possibly be made from pork is included here.

francaise au XIX siècle (The art of French cooking in the nineteenth century). His primary source was "a number of our distinguished chefs who had worked in Madrid," who recounted that "in the mansion houses of the natives [*sic*] they prepare a stew consisting of a great quantity of meats, roots and vegetables." This kind of information was not enough for him, and he adds that the first *olla* he ever saw being prepared was made by the great Laguipierre, "but he was making this for a great piece of meat, not for a stew, which is quite different."

Carême discovered the definitive details in *Le Cuisinier Moderne qui apprend à donner toutes sortes de repas* (The modern chef, who learns how to prepare all manner of meals), by Vincent La Chapelle, who was chef to the Prince of Orange and Nassau, and whose book was published in 1735. This is a rare work, and difficult to come by, but it is of great interest to anyone researching eighteenth-century cooking, and Carême thought very highly of it.

The brilliant Frenchman saw the *olla podrida* as the basis for an entire family of "soups that could be useful to any of our colleagues who might have occasion to serve important Spanish personages, whether in Paris or abroad, taking the typical ingredients of the Spanish-style *ollas* as a guide."

Carême derived eight different kinds of soup from the *olla podrida*. Vincent La Chapelle executed a virtually literal translation of the above-mentioned Diego Granado recipe for *olla podrida*. In his commentary, Carême qualified it as "a badly-prepared hash," saying that "this stew must have looked vile, but at that time the art of cooking was still in its infancy."

However, Carême did also take note of two soups, which he refers to as *potage national espagnol* and *potage soufflé à l'espagnol* ("Spanish national soup" and "Spanish-style souffléed soup") for which the recipes were given to him by "M. A., maître d'Hôtel de la princesse . . ." who also "gave me new details on how to make the truly distinctive *olla española*": cooking meat and vegetables separately, mixing the stocks, seasoning with nutmeg and saffron, and so forth. This drew praise from Carême, who justified his own variations on the *olla* by saying that "my soups nevertheless have the flavor and taste of the Spanish *ollas*. Once again, I break with established routine, which is how the arts and crafts are perfected. I know that the traditionalists are repeatedly astounded by any imaginative soul who dares to challenge convention."

Carême first became interested in the *olla podrida* around 1830. In 1818, however, a book had been published, *La cuisinière de la Campagne et de la Ville* by Louis-Eustache Audot, which was one of the most popular French recipe books and a tremendous bestseller in the culinary field. By 1861 it was in its forty-first edition.

Audot included in his book two recipes for *olla podrida* (he used the Spanish name): the *olla podrida simple* and the *olla podrida para un Grande de España* (Simple *olla podrida* and *olla podrida* for a Spanish Grandee). He also gave a recipe for a *potage espagnol,* which anticipated by some years the same dish to which Carême gave the name *potage national espagnol* (could Carême have perhaps plagiarized it?).

Audot's *olla podrida para un Grande de España* is the best *olla* I have tasted. I have made it several times at home, and it is wonderful. According to the author of *La Cuisinière,* Audot got the recipe from a friend who was "once a cook in a rich convent in Spain, which from time to time had the honor of lodging the Emperor Charles V." Audot, who besides being extremely well informed about cooking also had a sense of humor, wrote: "As you see, the *olla podrida* is an encyclopedia of good food, and whoever invented it also solved the problem of how to create a banquet with a single recipe."

This stew provides an eight-course meal: 1, soup; 2, beef accompanied by chickpeas and garnished with carrots; 3, stewed chicken with white rice; 4, mutton served with chickpea purée; 5, veal with tomato sauce

Thyme, laurel and garlic enhance the flavor of a Catalan roast chicken surrounded by chopped smoked bacon (above).
Soup is often made with fresh vegetables to which fish — usually cod — or meat is added (facing).

Urbain Dubois and Emile Bernard, who were chefs to the emperor of Germany and his family, in their important book *La Cuisine classique,* published in 1856. Dubois and Bernard called it *potage oilla à l'espagnole,* and they essentially followed Audot's recipe.

Alexandre Dumas also gave two or three *olla podrida* recipes in his *Dictionnaire de Cuisine*; he took these from earlier works, convinced that it originated from the *"grande ouille"* made by the chefs of Louis XIII, and declared that it was "a dish so complicated that French cooks are not in the least interested in putting it on their menus, and furthermore, it is a dish so costly that it can be made neither indifferently nor frequently."

Escoffier's *Larousse Gastronomique* echoes Dumas's sentiments, in the same derogatory tone.

For my own part, I would like to point out that if the eight *olla podrida* courses are served in small portions, they look very much like one of those "long skinny menus" typical of *nouvelle cuisine.*

Spanish conquistadores and settlers brought to America the dish that most reminded them of home: the *olla.* In America new ingredients were added that no European stew could do without today. Potatoes, in particular, but a good many other "exotica" as well. The Canary Island stew, for example, contains not only pears, but also chayote and maize. The Canaries were the real starting point for Christopher Columbus's caravels, as well as a compulsory port of call for all ships coming and going between "The Indies" during the Conquest and the Spanish Colonial period, and the pear and chayote stew is typical of the transition between Spanish cooking and that of the New World.

Similarly, the extraordinary Colombian boiled *sancocho,* especially as it is made in Cartagena de Indias, is a true *olla podrida,* but whose basic ingredients are cassava, yams, pumpkin, sweet potatoes, sweet corn, green and ripe plantains — the latter used with the skin on — cabbage, oxtail, pork ribs, veal ribs, salted meats, chicken, pig's

and giblets; 6, lightly salted ham, stuffing, chorizos, blood puddings and sausages with cabbage and turnips; 7, chicken or capon brushed with egg yolk and browned in the oven; 8, partridge, quail and pheasant, served with a red-hot spicy sauce.

The *olla podrida* was also included by

head, celery, tomatoes, garlic and different varieties of chili peppers.

The *olla* was also adopted by Africans who had arrived in America as slaves, and the same specialty can be found in Jamaica and Haiti under different names. In Jamaica it is called "pepper pot," and in Haiti it has exactly this same name in French, *poivrière*, because of the enormous amount of hot spice they manage to put into it. In both cases the adjective *podrida* (rotten) would be appropriate: what you are eating today could actually have begun to cook dozens of years ago. As the meal is served from the pot, the amount removed is continually replenished by similar quantities of meats, roots and vegetables. It truly is the bottomless pot.

An *olla* had been presented to Don Quixote when the government of the Isle of Barataria was deceitfully promised to him. When he saw it, he commented, "It seems to me that this great dish steaming before me is *olla podrida*, and from the great diversity of things that are put into such *ollas podridas* I shall most certainly come across something to my taste and appetite."

CHICKPEAS: THE NATIONAL VEGETABLES

Chickpeas came from Central Asia, and Charlemagne is supposed to have loved them. They were introduced to Spain by the Phoenicians, to become ever after the culinary consolation of the poor and a delicacy rarely disdained by the rich.

Never are they — never must they be — absent from any self-respecting *cocido, puchero* or *olla*. And, their rich fiber content makes them a healthful, dietetic food.

In Spain they are eaten in many ways: in stews, of course, but also in soups, purées, salads, or boiled and then fried, or even raw or simply toasted. They can even be made into a dessert with quinces. In some regions the chickpeas are toasted thoroughly, ground and made into a "coffee" that not only tastes good but has the virtue of not keeping one awake at night.

There are several varieties of chickpeas, of which the best are from the current year's crop, while those from Fuentesauco and from Méntrida in Castile are considered especially good. The varieties include: large, round, denticulated and black, although the latter are becoming increasingly scarce.

Chickpeas are a rewarding crop that grow well on arid land. They were among the vegetables taken by the Spaniards to America, and Mexico is today the leading exporter of this highly nutritious product. Chickpeas are the common thread linking the popular cuisines of North Africa, Spain and Latin America.

Chickpeas should be of good quality; they should be large rather than small, and have a fine skin. They need to be soaked for at least twenty-four hours before being put into the pot. An old trick for making them more tender is to add a teaspoon of bicarbonate of soda to the soaking water, and some believe that cooking them in the same water produces the best results. When the chickpeas have finished cooking it is preferable not to take them out of the water immediately, otherwise the sudden change of temperature will make the skin peel.

In cities like Barcelona and Valencia, chickpeas are ready-cooked and sold the same day at the market stalls. They are also good for preserving, especially in glass jars.

There is an old Spanish recipe for "sweet and sour chickpeas" that has curious Chinese overtones. Here it is:

"Cook the chickpeas in water with salt, good oil and a few whole onions; then chop the onions very small, smother them in new oil, and throw them into the pot with the chickpeas.

"Have toasted bread ready, soaked in good vinegar. Take some of the chickpeas out of the pot and put them in the mortar. Mash them with a small amount of chopped greens. Take the soaked bread, squeeze out the vinegar, put it in the mortar and pound all the ingredients together.

"Liquefy the mash with a little of the vinegar from the bread and with some of the stock from the chickpeas and pour it into the pot. Add sweet-and-sour seasonings, cinnamon, saffron and honey, and serve on slices of bread."

EXTREMADURIAN LENTILS AND HAM
LENTEJAS A LA EXTREMEÑA
Extremadura

Advance preparation time: 8 hours
Preparation time: 10 minutes
Cooking time: 1 hour 40 minutes
For 6 servings:
4 cups (1 3/4 lb/750 g) lentils
1 head garlic, whole, unpeeled
Salt
6 tablespoons (3 fl oz/9 cl) olive oil
9 oz (250 g) Serrano ham, diced (see glossary)
1 medium onion, peeled and chopped
2 medium tomatoes, peeled and chopped
6 tablespoons (3 fl oz/9 cl) dry white wine
1/2 teaspoon paprika
8 black peppercorns

Method:

The night before: Pick through the lentils, removing any grit or stones, rinse them and place in a bowl filled with cold water to soak for 8 hours.

The same day: Drain the lentils. Place them in a large Dutch oven, add enough cold water to cover and cook over low heat for 30 minutes. Add the garlic head, season with salt, and continue to cook over low heat for 1 hour.

Heat the oil in a skillet. Add the ham and onion and sauté for 5 minutes. Add the tomatoes and cook over low heat for 10 minutes.

Stir in the wine and paprika and let the mixture cook and reduce over medium heat for several minutes. Add the peppercorns and turn this mixture into the lentils. Let cook over low heat for 10 minutes longer. (If the mixture becomes too thick, add a little more water or chicken broth.)

Correct the seasoning and serve immediately.

CATALAN MIXED MEATS AND CHICKPEAS
ESCUDELLA
Catalonia

Advance preparation time: 8 hours
Preparation time: 15 minutes
Cooking time: 2 hours 20 minutes
For 6 servings:
1 1/4 cups (9 oz/250 g) chickpeas
1 cup (7 oz/200 g) dried white beans
12 cups (96 fl oz/3 l) water
1 pound (500 g) top round of beef or short ribs
1 1/2 pounds chicken pieces or 1/2 broiler or fryer
1 pig's foot
1/2 pound (250 g) pig's ear
5 oz (150 g) side pork or fresh, unsmoked bacon
1 ham bone
1 beef marrow bone
1 medium carrot, peeled
1 large turnip, peeled
Salt
1 egg
3 1/2 oz (100 g) lean pork, diced
5 oz (150 g) butifarra blanca, diced (see glossary)
2 tablespoons fresh white breadcrumbs
1 clove garlic, peeled and chopped
1 tablespoon chopped parsley
1/2 teaspoon ground cinnamon
Freshly ground pepper
1 tablespoon flour
1/2 pound (250 g) butifarra negra (see glossary)
1/2 pound (250 g) potatoes, quartered
1 medium Savoy cabbage
3/4 cup (3 1/2 oz/100 g) elbow macaroni

Method:

In advance: Place the chickpeas and white beans in a large bowl filled with lukewarm water and soak for 8 hours.

The same day: Fill a large soup kettle or stock pot with the water. Add the beef, chicken, pig's foot and ear, side pork, ham bone, marrow bones, carrot and turnip. Bring to a boil, skimming off and discarding the foam that rises to the surface.

Drain and rinse the chickpeas and white beans, and tie them in a fine mesh bag or a square of cheesecloth to prevent the beans from mixing with the meats. When the water in the stock pot begins to boil, add the beans and season with salt. Reduce the heat to low and simmer for 1 1/2 hours.

Meanwhile, combine the egg, diced pork and butifarra blanca, breadcrumbs, garlic, parsley, cinnamon and pepper in a bowl and mix until well blended. Form the mixture into a long cylinder and dust with the flour.

When the meats and beans have simmered for 1 1/2 hours, add the floured sausage roll, along with the butifarra negra, potatoes, and cabbage. Let simmer for 30 minutes longer. Then ladle about half of the cooking broth into a saucepan. Add the macaroni and simmer for about 20 minutes.

This dish is served in three consecutive courses: 1. Soup; 2. The meats, sliced and arranged on a serving platter with a little of the broth; 3. The vegetables and beans arranged on a separate serving dish.

Dried beans, lentils and chickpeas are popular everyday fare. Ready-to-eat chickpeas can be found in most markets and feature in many recipes (above).
Catalan mixed meats and chickpeas (facing page).

PARTRIDGE AND WHITE BEANS
JUDIONES CON PERDIZ
Castile-La Mancha

Advance preparation time: 12 hours
Preparation time: 10 minutes
Cooking time: 1 hour 35 minutes
For 6 servings:
4 cups (1 3/4 lb/750 g) giant white beans
    ("La Granja," if possible)
1 medium Savoy cabbage
6 small partridges
2 bay leaves
6 cloves garlic, peeled
3 hot peppers
1 ham bone
1 carrot, sliced into rounds
Salt
Freshly ground black pepper
1 lb (500 g) potatoes, peeled
5 oz (150 g) side pork or slab bacon
3/4 cup (6 oz/18 cl) olive oil
2 medium onions, peeled and chopped
3 tomatoes, peeled and chopped
5 oz (150 g) chorizo (see glossary)

Method:

A day in advance: Place the beans in a large bowl with enough lukewarm water to cover, and let soak for 12 hours.

The same day: Drain the beans. Remove and discard the outer leaves of the cabbage. Blanch the white inner leaves in a saucepan filled with boiling salted water, and drain.

In a large stock pot, combine the beans, cabbage leaves, partridges, bay leaves, garlic, hot peppers, ham bone, and carrot. Season with salt and freshly ground pepper. Add enough water to cover generously, bring to a boil and cook for 30 minutes.

After 30 minutes, add a cup of cold water to stop the boiling. Add the potatoes and side pork and cook 30 minutes longer.

Remove the partridges and bone them. Return them to the stock pot.

Heat the oil in a skillet. Add the onion and cook over low heat for 5 minutes until lightly browned. Add the tomatoes and cook with the onions for 6 minutes.

Slice the chorizo into rounds, and add to the skillet with the tomatoes and onions. Moisten this mixture with 3 tablespoons of the cooking liquid from the stock pot. Then stir this mixture into the stock pot, holding back any excess oil. Correct the seasoning, if necessary. Let cook over low heat for 15 minutes.

Let rest, without letting it cool off too much, before serving.

BOILED BEEF AND CHICKPEAS MADRILENO
COCIDO MADRILEÑO
Madrid

Advance preparation time: 12 hours
Preparation time: 10 minutes
Cooking time: 3 hours 30 minutes
For 6 servings:
2 1/2 cups (1 lb/500 g) chickpeas
1 lb (500 g) top round of beef or short ribs
3/4 lb (350 g) chicken pieces
7 oz (200 g) side pork or fresh, unsmoked
    bacon
3 1/2 oz (100 g) ham end trimmings
1 ham bone
4 beef marrow bones
5 oz (150 g) chorizo (see glossary)
5 oz (150 g) morcilla (see glossary)
4 medium carrots, peeled
4 medium potatoes, peeled
2 1/4 lb (1 kg) cabbage
3 tablespoons olive oil
2 cloves garlic, peeled
2 1/4 cups (9 oz/250 g) elbow macaroni
Salt

Method:

A day in advance: Place the chickpeas in a bowl of lukewarm salted water and let soak for 12 hours.

The same day: Place the beef, chicken, side pork, ham, ham bone and marrow bones in a large soup kettle or stock pot and add cold water to cover.

Bring to a boil over medium heat, skimming off and discarding the foam that rises to the surface.

Drain and rinse the chickpeas and tie them in a small mesh bag or a square of cheesecloth (to keep them from mixing with the meats) and add to the meats. Cook over low heat for 1 hour.

Add the chorizo and morcilla and continue to cook for 1 hour.

Add the carrots and cook for 30 minutes. Add the potatoes, and cook until tender, about 30 minutes longer.

Meanwhile, cook the cabbage separately in a large saucepan filled with salted water for 40 minutes. Drain and cut into pieces.

Heat the oil in a large skillet, add the garlic and cabbage pieces and sauté until tender.

Drain the broth from the meats into a large saucepan. Add the macaroni, season lightly with salt, and cook over medium heat for 15 minutes.

Meanwhile, slice the meats, arrange them on a large platter and keep them warm. Arrange the chickpeas, potatoes, carrots and cabbage on a large platter and keep warm.

The cocido is traditionally served in three courses, presented in the following order: 1. the macaroni soup; 2. the vegetables; 3. the meats and sausages.

Note: If you prefer a less spicy soup, sauté the chorizo and morcilla separately with a little oil in a skillet just before serving. These sausages can be served with a tomato sauce. The chickpeas are often drizzled with a little olive oil before serving.

Boiled beef and chickpeas Madrileno (facing page).

ASTURIAN BEAN AND SAUSAGE STEW
FABADA ASTURIANA
Asturias

Advance preparation time: 12 hours
Preparation time: 5 minutes
Cooking time: 2 hours
For 6 servings:
5 cups (2 1/4 lb/1 kg) dried white beans
1 salted pig's ear
1 1/2 to 1 3/4 lb (750 g) salted pork hocks
3/4 lb (300 g) Asturian morcilla (see glossary)
3/4 lb (300 g) Asturian chorizo (see glossary)
Salt

Method:
A day in advance: Place the beans in a large bowl filled with cold water and soak for 12 hours. Place the pig's ear and hocks in a large bowl filled with lukewarm water and let soak for 12 hours.

The same day: Drain the beans and the pig's ear and hocks. Place them in a large stock pot along with the morcilla and chorizo. Add enough cold water to cover.

Bring to a boil, skimming off and discarding the foam as it rises to the surface. Cover and simmer over very low heat for 2 hours.

Add a glass of cold water 2 or 3 times during the cooking to stop the boiling—this will make the flavor of the beans more delicate. Taste the broth during the cooking and season lightly with salt if necessary.

If the cooking liquid is too thin, remove a few beans and crush them in a mortar. Stir them back into the stew to thicken the broth slightly.

Remove from the heat and let rest, without letting it cool off too much, and serve.

Asturian bean and sausage stew (right).

POTATOES AND SAUSAGE A LA RIOJANA
PATATAS A LA RIOJANA
La Rioja

Preparation time: 5 minutes
Cooking time: 35 minutes
For 4 servings:
3 tablespoons olive oil
7 oz (200 g) chorizo (see glossary), chopped
1 small onion, peeled and chopped
2 cloves garlic, peeled
1 1/2 lb (750 g) potatoes, peeled
   and cut into large cubes
Salt

Method:
Heat the oil in a saucepan. Add the chorizo, onion and garlic cloves, and cook over medium heat until lightly browned. Add the potatoes and mix together well.

Add enough water to cover. Season with salt and let cook over medium heat for 30 minutes.

Serve immediately.

ANDALUSIAN GYPSY FEAST
BERZA GITANA
Andalusia

Advance preparation time: 8 hours
Preparation time: 10 minutes
Cooking time: 2 hours 30 minutes
For 6 servings:
1 1/4 cups (9 oz/250 g) chickpeas
1 1/4 cups (9 oz/250 g) dried white beans
1 dried hot red pepper
12 cups (96 fl oz/ 3 l) water
2 salted or pickled spare ribs (see note)
1 1/2 lb (680 g) chicken pieces or 1/2 fryer
14 oz (400 g) veal leg or shoulder
7 oz (200 g) slab bacon
1 beef marrow bone
1 ham bone
2 cloves garlic, peeled
1 teaspoon ground cumin
2 teaspoons olive oil
Salt
5 oz (150 g) green beans
5 oz (150 g) Swiss chard
1 rib celery
2 medium carrots
5 oz (150 g) chorizo (see glossary)
1 1/2 cups (7 oz/200 g) chopped pumpkin
2 small potatoes, peeled

Method:
In advance: Place the chickpeas and beans in cold water and soak for 8 hours.

The same day: Soak the dried pepper in lukewarm water. Fill a soup kettle with water. Add the pork ribs, chicken, veal, bacon, marrow bone and ham bone and bring to a boil, skimming off and discarding the foam as it rises to the surface. Drain the hot pepper. Grind it and the garlic, cumin, and oil to a paste with a pestle. Add to the stock pot and season lightly.

Drain the chickpeas and beans, add to the pot, and cook slowly for 1 1/2 hours.

Add the green beans, Swiss chard, celery, carrots, and chorizo. Let cook for 20 minutes longer. Add the pumpkin and potatoes, and let cook 30 minutes longer.

Serve meats and vegetables separately, accompanied by the hot broth.

Note: If unavailable, blanch fresh spare ribs in boiling salted water and drain. Then simmer them in water with a bay leaf for about 1 hour before proceeding.

CANARY ISLAND PUCERA
PUCHERA CANARIO
Tenerife

Advance preparation time: 12 hours
Preparation time: 10 minutes
Cooking time: 2 hours 15 minutes
For 4 servings:
1/2 cup (3 1/2 oz/100 g) chickpeas
1/2 lb (225 g) pork loin
1/2 lb (225 g) lamb neck
1/2 lb (225 g) breast of veal
5 oz (150 g) bacon
1 beef marrow bone
1 pig's ear
1 small chicken, or 4 chicken thighs
4 potatoes, peeled
2 sweet potatoes, peeled
1 small slice pumpkin, peeled
1 chayote squash
1 ear sweet corn
2 firm pears, peeled
1/2 Savoy cabbage
4 tomatoes
4 cloves garlic, peeled
1/2 teaspoon saffron (see glossary)
2 teaspoons salt
1 teaspoon black pepper

Method:
A day in advance: Place the chickpeas in a bowl filled with cold water and let soak for 12 hours.

The same day: Drain the chickpeas and place them in a soup kettle or stock pot with the pork loin, lamb, veal, bacon, marrow bone, pig's ear and chicken. Add water to cover. Bring to a boil and cook for 2 hours.

Add the potatoes, sweet potatoes, pumpkin, chayote, corn, pears, cabbage and tomatoes and let cook for 15 minutes longer.

In a mortar, grind the garlic, saffron, salt and pepper to a paste with a pestle. Stir this paste into the other ingredients, cook briefly and serve hot.

GALICIAN STEW
POTE GALLEGO
Galicia

Advance preparation: 12 hours
Preparation time: 10 minutes
Cooking time: 2 hours 20 minutes
For 6 servings:
1 1/2 cups (11 oz/300 g) dried white beans
1 lb (500 g) top round of beef
5 oz (150 g) chorizo (see glossary)
1/2 lb (250 g) Serrano ham (see glossary)
5 oz (150 g) morcilla (see glossary)
5 oz (150 g) side pork or slab bacon
1 lb (500 g) Savoy cabbage
5 oz (150 g) potatoes, peeled and cut into pieces
Salt

Method:
A day in advance: Place the beans in a large bowl filled with cold water and soak for 12 hours.

The same day: Place the beef, chorizo, ham, morcilla, and bacon in a large Dutch oven or soup pot. Add enough cold water to cover generously and cook over low heat for 2 hours, skimming off and discarding the foam that rises to the surface.

Drain the beans. Place them in a large saucepan with salted water to cover and cook for 1 1/2 hours.

In a separate large saucepan of salted water, cook the cabbage for 40 minutes.

Drain the beans and the cabbage and add them to the pan with the meats. Add the potatoes, season with salt, and let cook 20 minutes longer.

Slice the meats and serve surrounded by the other ingredients in a large shallow earthenware bowl or on a serving dish.

Galician stew (above).

RICE:
MORE THAN
JUST
PAELLA

Many recipes exist for paella, but purists do not believe in mixing meat with fish or seafood. Depending on the region, there is fisherman's paella and farmer's paella, the latter using only rabbit and chicken.

Now that the imperial *olla podrida* that bore the banner of Spanish cooking throughout the civilized world has fallen somewhat out of favor, the most representative Spanish dish is paella. Unfortunately, however, few really good paellas can be found in public restaurants in Spain, and none anywhere else. Mass tourism and the policy that gave rise to it have ruined the dish by imposing single prices for tourist menus featuring paella.

First, it should be pointed out that paella is actually the name of the utensil used to prepare the dish: a kind of low-sided frying pan with two handles instead of a long single one. They come in many different sizes to suit the amount being prepared, from individual serving sizes up to gigantic pans for 1,000 people or more, specially made for aspirants to the Guinness Book of Records. Second, many different kinds of rice are made in this paella; and finally, it should be realized that none of these is the kind of rice usually served to tourists under the name of paella.

So let us ignore once and for all that indigestible, scurrilous tourist version of paella and enter the vast and varied world of Spanish rice.

Almost all the varieties of rice originated and still thrive on the Mediterranean coast, from Murcia in the south, through the three Valencian provinces of Alicante, Valencia and Castellón de la Plana, up to Catalonia in the north. There are innumerable recipes for cooking them other than in paellas.

There are also varieties of rice that grow inland, like the delicious *arroz a la zamorana* from the province of Zamora in the north, along the Portuguese border. This rice is cooked with pig's lips and ears, a dish that is probably another invention of the *maragato* muleteers who brought the product from the Valencian rice fields up to Galicia.

The rice trail from east to west was extremely long. The grains came to Spain in the bags of Arab farmers, five thousand years after it had become a staple of Oriental cooking far and wide. The earliest "Spanish" recipes using rice appeared in Arab cookery books such as the thirteenth-century *Fadalat al-jiwan*: its recipe for *manjar blanco* — rice with almonds — was so widely adopted by Christians that Saint Louis, King of France, supposedly ate rice prepared according to this recipe in Sens on his way to Aigues-Mortes, where he set sail for the Crusades.

The earliest known Spanish cookbooks are *Sent Sovi* and *Llibre de Coch*, both from the fourteenth century. Each gives a number of recipes for rice, which by then was being widely consumed. Both reflect a preference for sweet dishes such as *manjar blanco,* and meat and rice stew to which sugar or honey is added at the end of cooking. Some of these recipes, such as the delightful rice pudding *arroz con leche,* have come down to us almost unchanged.

Rice belongs to the Mediterranean world of conviviality, sunshine, the sea, and warm, fragrant fruit-growing plains; to the pine forests, rocky hills and the sea breezes scented with rosemary and thyme: rice truly belongs to the same Mediterranean universe as vines and olives.

Whether it is made in a paella or a *cazuela* (a casserole — the usual method in Catalonia), rice is the ideal dish for large groups and for sharing among friends. In fact the size of the paella is calculated for the exact number of participants at the meal, who traditionally sit in a circle around it, eating out of the recipient it was cooked in.

Imaginary lines from the edge of the paella to the center mark the area into which each guest may stick his or her fork without trespassing on his neighbors' territory — a tacit, genial accord that establishes harmony within the group. Aromas waft in the steam from the dish toward the blue sky like a mythical column of incense in homage to some hedonistic Mediterranean god.

Everyone takes part in some way in the preparation and cooking of the rice. The fire is critical: experts say that the best kindling is vine shoots, and the fire is perfect when the wood is glowing red-hot but still flaming,

In Valencia, making paella is considered a man's job. Experts believe the best paellas are cooked in the open air. Friends make paella on the beach or, as here, on the banks of Lake Albufera near Valencia. The success of a good paella depends above all on the fire and the right proportions of rice to water (above and facing).

with a fine layer of blue ash. The fire should be a circle of the same size as the pan, and it is quite an achievement to maintain an even heat throughout. Mastering the fire is a consummate skill of the great rice cooks. Paellas can of course be made on a gas fire, and it is possible to obtain special spiral tubes that distribute the gas evenly, but the result is not the same at all. It lacks the magic of the open fire and, more importantly, the slight smoky flavor that comes only from a wood fire, and especially one made with vine shoots.

Experts in making fires for cooking rice know which vine stems to select and how to arrange them so that the wood will burn evenly, and they know exactly how to feed the fire when the heat slows in one spot or another.

Another important aspect of this technique is laying the right kind of fire for the right kind of rice. The cooking time, which is of paramount importance, depends on the fire as well as on the variety or quality of the rice used and the consistency desired. The precise amount of water is yet another factor.

Ordinary rice takes thirty minutes to cook, but for the new processed and washed types this can be reduced to twenty. Experts advise one measure of oil to two of rice (although less oil may be used), and two and a half measures of water to one of rice. Whatever method is used, well-prepared paella can be removed from the fire a few minutes before the end of cooking to allow the rice to rest and finish cooking in its own heat. That it goes on cooking means that once it is ready it must be eaten immediately, otherwise it will be overdone. There is no worse insult to a Valencian that to arrive late for a paella, as this means ruining a dish that requires perfect timing and exceptionally sensitive handling.

Some purists claim that an authentic paella consists merely of lightly fried garlic and parsley, both rice and eels from the local rice fields, green beans or *garrofó,* which are dried white beans, mountain snails, or *ba-queta,* and rice seasoned with saffron. Nothing else. Rice prepared this way is exquisite, but it is very hard to find. The gelatinous smoothness of the eel gives the rice and its stock particularly delicate flavors. This combination of ingredients is natural and logical, and could almost come under the heading of "country cooking," given the usual abundance of eels in the rice fields and their irrigation canals. Today, however, eels are exported by the ton to Germany and northern countries, where they are smoked and eaten as appetizers, so that there are less and less available on the market in Spain. Spanish consumers have gradually stopped buying them, much less taking the trouble to skin, clean and cook them.

Another splendid and typical dish from the rice fields is also disappearing: *all i pebre* (garlic and pepper). In fact *all i pebre* contains no rice — it is a sauce served with eel, though it also goes well with other fish and even with meat. A good quantity of oil is heated in a casserole with two or three cloves of chopped garlic, green pepper and several chopped hot red peppers, then the eel is cut into slices and added with water and salt. In some parts of Valencia two or three almonds are crushed with the garlic, and ground pepper and cloves are mixed in with the red peppers.

But to go back to the rice: as we have seen, paella is really a dish to be eaten by a group of people out of doors. The natural surroundings are part of its ritual: it can be on the seashore, in the mountains or in an orchard, and in each instance the ingredients culled from the environment are as much part of the paella as the rice. This has

In fact, paella is not the name of
the world-famous dish, but the
pan it is cooked in. It comes in all
sizes, from individual serving sizes
to pans serving a thousand (the
latter usually for aspirants to the
Guinness Book of World Records).
Here the utensil is used to cook
rice with snails (facing).

inspired hundreds of rice recipes whose sole common denominator is the paella pan.

Valencians will tell you that the one place never to ask for a paella is in a restaurant. That is going a bit far, but it is true that there are few places open to the public in which a really good paella is served.

An exception is Don Rafael Vidal's restaurant in the Valencian village of Benissano, not far from the capital of the province. Señor Vidal has a popular roadside restaurant called the Levante, and there he produces nothing but paella, for the simple reason that it is the only thing he knows how to cook. Otherwise, he is incapable of even frying an egg. This gentleman used to run a garage, to which at some point he added a bar. One day — a long time ago, for Don Rafael is now a grandfather — a traveler who stopped at the garage asked if he could get a meal. Señor Vidal killed one of his own chickens and cooked some rice. It turned out very well. So well, in fact, that the driver told his friends, who in turn went to the garage and asked Vidal to make them his chicken and rice. In the end, Don Rafael had no alternative but to shut down the garage and open an eating-house — for paella, of course. He has not stopped since, and has even cooked paella for the king of Spain. His spe-

cialty is chicken and rabbit paella, with white beans when they are in season.

In the city of Valencia, the Galbis restaurant is highly recommended for its rice dishes, especially its delicious rice with duck.

Other rice recipes may require specific utensils, such as the *perol,* a cauldron-like metal or earthenware pot for rice dishes that contain meat and large quantities of vegetables (the fabulous *arrós amb fésols i naps* and the *arrós a banda,* for example); round-bottomed casseroles for soupy rice eaten with a spoon, such as the Catalan *arrós a la cassola;* and flat-based pots for rice cooked in the oven, like the *arrós amb crosta* and *rosetjat.* Some rice dishes are made in an ordinary long-handled frying pan, although the non-stick variety should be avoided, because many people love the browned crust of rice that sticks to the bottom of the paella or the cooking pot.

Arrós amb fésols i naps is a rich, succulent winter dish that could as well have been included in the chapter on stews. It is made throughout the province of Valencia, and many enthusiasts claim that it is the greatest rice dish of all.

Valencia — all of eastern Spain, in fact — consists of two separate worlds: the inland area and the coast. Within the inland world a further distinction exists between the cultivated plains and the mountains. This is a broad simplification, of course, but it nevertheless reflects a geo-culinary reality.

The farmlands of the Spanish Mediterranean areas (Valencia and Murcia) are among the most fertile in Europe. The landscape is exuberant and rich, bathed in the perfume of orange and lemon groves. The fruit and vegetables grown there are of exceptional quality, and the Valencians themselves are as complicated and eloquent as their cooking.

What is really impressive about the Levantines, however, is their incredibly imaginative use of raw materials like rice.

Oriental peoples were growing and eating rice thousands of years before the Valencians, but even today the range of

Chinese, Japanese and Vietnamese recipes for rice is surprisingly limited. On the other hand, there are hundreds of Spanish Mediterranean rice recipes.

There are delicate, subtle dishes such as *arrós vert,* which is made in a paella dish with whatever vegetables are in season: beans, artichokes, peas, Swiss chard; tasty rice soup with cuttlefish and cabbage; rice with frogs' legs; rice for fast days and for feast days. Devotees can even try rice with water rat, a purely vegetarian rodent with white meat, and another famous, though strictly illegal dish: rice with squirrel. There is rice for every day and rice for holidays, but there is no such thing as a week without rice at all.

THE SPANISH ROSE

"Spain overflows with harvest; she is delightful with milk and all that is made from it; she is covered with cattle; rich in horses; prosperous in mules; joyous with good wines; she enjoys an abundance of bread; is sweet with honey and sugar; alight with beeswax; sated with oil; radiant with saffron."

This is how Mediterranean Spain was described in the thirteenth century by Alfonso the Wise, king of Castile, in his *Primera Crónica General.*

This royal description of life in Spain was idyllic, but not totally unrealistic. Interestingly, it mentions *azafrán* — saffron — as one of the country's treasures, and indicates how far back the use of this spice and colorant goes in Spanish cooking. It is employed in numerous dishes, from soups and *migas* to meat and fish stews, and above all, as the essential condiment for most rice recipes. Essential, and increasingly expensive — today thousands of paellas served in Spain are dyed with yellow vegetable or even chemical food coloring.

Saffron is an herbaceous plant native to the Mediterranean; it originally grew wild, but was quickly removed from its native habitat and cultivated for commercial purposes.

It is a bulbous perennial that flourishes in dry soil, and whose first leaves sprout with the spring rains. Hot temperatures do not suit it, and it stays practically underground until the rain begins to fall again in the autumn. Toward November the "mantle" of saffron appears, usually around the first of November. The saffron flowers appear to have suddenly bloomed in a single day, covering the fields with a velvet purple dotted with golden, red and orange stamens.

The Spanish call the saffron flower a "rose" and the pickers (usually women) *roseras* — rose-gatherers. Saffron is derived from the stalks of the flowers, the tubular and funnel-shaped stigmas, filaments and styles, which are dried before being sent to market.

There are two main saffron-producing regions, La Mancha and Lower Aragon, in addition to some isolated spots on the Mediterranean coast from southern Catalonia to the south of Andalusia.

Before putting the saffron into the dish being prepared — rice, for example — it should be ground in a mortar with a little stock until it colors the liquid, then added to the paella or the pot before all the cooking liquid has evaporated.

Saffron should be used judiciously — not too much or too little. Just a pinch of the stigmas is enough for a paella or rice dish serving four to six people.

It adds color and flavor to a dish, but it also imparts a special, very characteristic taste, which should be perceptible but not overwhelming.

VALENCIAN-STYLE FISH AND SEAFOOD RICE
ARROZ A BANDA
Valencia

Preparation time: 25 minutes
Cooking time: 1 hour 20 minutes
For 6 servings:
3/4 cup (6 fl oz/18 cl) olive oil
6 potatoes, cut into large cubes
4 onions, peeled and cut into large pieces
2 teaspoons paprika
8 cups (64 fl oz/ 2 l) water
Salt
1/2 lb (250 g) monkfish or angler fish
1/2 lb (250 g) grouper
1/2 lb (250 g) conger eel
7 oz (200 g) small squid,
cleaned (see glossary)
5 oz (150 g) medium shrimp
1/2 lb (250 g) Dublin Bay prawns
1 small (5 oz/150 g) tomato, peeled
and chopped
3 garlic cloves, peeled and chopped
Pinch saffron threads (see glossary)
3 cups (1 1/3 lb/600 g) short-grain rice

Method:

In a Dutch oven, heat 6 tablespoons of the oil. Add the potatoes and onions and sauté until lightly browned. Add 1 teaspoon of the paprika, stirring rapidly. Stir in the water, season with salt, and cook over medium heat for 30 minutes.

Meanwhile, clean the fish. Rinse and pat dry the shrimp and prawns.

Add the monkfish, grouper, and conger eel to the potatoes and broth. Cover and simmer over very low heat for 10 minutes. Add the shrimp and prawns and cook 5 minutes longer.

Heat the remaining oil in a paella pan or wide, shallow earthenware casserole. Add the squid, tomato, and garlic and cook briefly until the squid turns opaque. Remove and set aside.

Stir the remaining teaspoon paprika into the paella pan along with 6 cups of the broth from the Dutch oven. Bring to a boil and add the saffron. Correct the seasoning if necessary.

Sprinkle the rice evenly over the boiling broth in the paella pan and let cook over high heat for 10 minutes. Reduce the heat and continue to cook for 10 minutes.

Remove the paella pan from the heat, cover with a kitchen towel and let rest for 5 minutes.

Arrange the fish, shellfish, and squid on one platter and the potatoes and onions on another.

Serve with the rice in the paella pan, accompanied by an aïoli (see glossary).

GRATIN OF RICE WITH PORK AND CHICKEN
ARROZ CON COSTRA
Murcia

Preparation time: 15 minutes
Cooking time: 30 minutes
For 6 servings:
6 tablespoons (3 fl oz/9 cl) oil
7 oz (200 g) pork chop, cut into pieces
7 oz (200 g) pork spare ribs, cut into pieces
3 breakfast sausages
7 oz (200 g) lightly cured chorizo
6 chicken thighs
4 cups (32 fl oz/1 l) beef broth
1 small tomato, peeled and chopped
1 teaspoon paprika
Salt
3 cups (1 1/3 lb/600 g) short-grain rice
6 eggs

Method:

Heat the oil in a large shallow earthenware casserole or paella pan. Add the pork chop, spare ribs, sausages, chorizo, and chicken, and cook over medium heat until lightly browned.

Meanwhile, place the broth in a saucepan and bring to a boil.

Add the tomato and paprika to the browned meats, stirring rapidly. Season with salt. Sprinkle the rice evenly over the meats. Add the boiling broth, stirring to distribute the rice evenly in the pan.

Bring the broth back to a boil, then transfer the pan to a preheated 425° F (220° C) oven for 12 minutes.

Beat the eggs in a small bowl. Pour them evenly over the meats and rice, making sure that the eggs completely cover the surface. Return the pan to the oven to cook for 4 minutes longer.

Serve immediately.

RICE WITH SQUID INK
ARROZ NEGRO
Valencia

Preparation time: 15 minutes
Cooking time: 30 minutes
For 6 servings:
1 lb (500 g) small squid, cleaned
6 tablespoons (3 fl oz/9 cl) olive oil
1 small tomato, peeled and chopped
1 small onion, chopped
3 cloves garlic
6 cups (48 fl oz/1 1/2 l) fish broth
(see glossary)
1 teaspoon paprika
3 cups (1 1/3 lb/600 g) short-grain rice
Salt
5 small sacs squid ink (see note)

Method:

If the squid are large, cut them into pieces.

Heat the oil in a large paella pan. Add the squid and cook until lightly browned. Add the tomato, onion, and garlic, and cook briefly.

Remove and set aside 6 tablespoons (3 fl oz/9 cl) of the fish broth. Pour the remaining broth into a saucepan and bring to a boil.

Add the paprika and rice to the squid and vegetables, stirring rapidly. Pour the boiling broth into the paella pan. Season with salt and let cook over high heat for 10 minutes.

Meanwhile, break the squid ink sacs into a small bowl. Stir in the reserved fish broth and mix thoroughly. Stir this mixture into the paella pan and lower the heat. Correct the seasoning if necessary. Let cook for 10 minutes longer.

Remove from heat, cover with a kitchen towel and let rest for 5 minutes before serving.

Note: Ask your fishmonger to clean the squid, reserving the ink sacs. Or you may clean them yourself: pull out the tentacles and peel off the silvery ink sac located underneath the tentacles, being careful not to break it. Reserve the tentacles, discarding the slimy white portion below the eyes. Remove the quill and rinse the squid body thoroughly inside and out.

RICE AND CLAMS IN BROTH
ARROZ CALDOSO CON ALMEJAS
Andalusia

Preparation time: 10 minutes
Cooking time: 45 minutes
For 6 servings:
1/2 cup (4 fl oz/ 12 cl) olive oil
1 large onion, peeled and chopped
11 oz (300 g) tomatoes, peeled and chopped
3 cloves garlic, peeled
1 red bell pepper, seeded and diced
1 green bell pepper, seeded and diced
Pinch saffron threads (see glossary)
1 lb (500 g) cherrystone clams in their shells
1/2 teaspoon paprika
5 1/2 cups (44 fl oz/140 cl) water
2 1/4 cups (1 lb/500 g) short-grain rice
Salt

Method:
Heat the oil in a large Dutch oven or heavy saucepan. Add the onion, tomatoes, garlic and bell peppers, and cook over medium heat for 10 minutes.

Mix the saffron with 2 tablespoons water in a mortar, crushing the saffron threads with a pestle, and add to the vegetables. Stir in the paprika, the clams, and about 1/2 cup (4 fl oz/12 cl) of the water. Cook over medium heat for 5 minutes. Add the rice and the remaining water. Season with salt and let simmer for 20 minutes.

Serve immediately. This dish should be rather liquid.

Rice with seafood and red peppers (facing page).

ROSA GRAU'S RICE WITH SEAFOOD
ARROZ A BANDA ROSA GRAU

Preparation time: 20 minutes
Cooking time: 50 minutes
For 4 servings:
1 lb (500 g) potatoes, peeled and cut into large pieces
1 onion , 1 bay leaf
6 cups (48 fl oz/1 1/2 l) water
1 3/4 lb (750 g) grouper (or monkfish, lemon sole, etc.)
3 sardines
Freshly ground black pepper
1/2 cup (4 fl oz/12 cl) olive oil
1 head garlic, separated and peeled
2 cups (14 oz/400 g) short-grain rice , Salt
Pinch saffron threads (see glossary)

Sauce:
2 cloves garlic, peeled
2 sprigs parsley, chopped
1 tablespoon wine vinegar
3 tablespoons olive oil, Salt
1/4 cup (2 fl oz/6 cl) fish broth (see glossary)

Method:
Place the potatoes, onion, bay leaf and water in a large Dutch oven or heavy saucepan and cook for about 10 minutes. Season with pepper, add the grouper and sardines, and continue to cook for 10 minutes, or until the potatoes are tender. Drain the fish and potatoes, straining and reserving the broth in which they cooked. Meanwhile, heat 1/2 cup oil in a separate saucepan. Add the garlic and rice, and cook, stirring, until lightly browned. Add all but 3 tablespoons of the reserved broth to the saucepan. Add the saffron, season with salt and pepper, and let cook for about 20 minutes.

To make the sauce, grind 2 garlic cloves and the chopped parsley to a paste in a mortar and pestle. Stir in the vinegar and oil and season with salt. Stir in the reserved 3 tablespoons warm broth a few drops at a time to bind the sauce.

Arrange the rice on a large serving platter. Arrange the fish on a separate platter, surrounded by the potatoes and accompanied by the sauce.

Serve the rice first, followed by the fish and potatoes.

RICE WITH SEAFOOD AND RED PEPPERS
ARROZ AL CALDERO
Murcia

Preparation time: 15 minutes
Cooking time: 55 minutes
For 6 servings:
11 oz (300 g) sea bream
11 oz (300 g) mullet
11 oz (300 g) grouper
1 1/3 lb (600 g) monkfish
3/4 cup (6 fl oz/18 cl) olive oil
3 hot red peppers
1 head garlic, whole and unpeeled
6 cups (48 fl oz/1 1/2 l) fish broth (see glossary)
Pinch saffron threads (see glossary)
2 small tomatoes, peeled and chopped
1 1/2 teaspoons paprika
3 cups (1 1/3 lb/600 g) short-grain rice
Salt

Method:
Cut the fish into large pieces.

Heat the oil in a large Dutch oven. Add the peppers and garlic head and cook over high heat until the garlic begins to color. Remove the peppers and garlic, and set aside. Add the fish to the Dutch oven (the oil should still be hot) and cook over medium heat for 3 to 5 minutes.

Bring the fish broth to a boil in a large saucepan.

Peel the fried garlic cloves, place in a mortar with the peppers, and grind to a paste with a pestle, adding fish broth to moisten. Spoon this mixture over the fish.

Add the tomatoes and paprika to the fish, stirring gently. Pour the boiling broth over the fish and let cook for 12 minutes.

Remove the fish from the pan, set aside and keep warm. Cook the broth 5 minutes longer, then strain it through a fine sieve. Correct the seasoning.

Wipe out the pan in which the fish cooked, add 6 cups of the strained broth and bring to a boil. Add the saffron. Sprinkle the rice into the pan and cook over high heat for 5 minutes. Reduce the heat and cook over low heat for 15 minutes.

Accompany the fish with aïoli (see glossary) and a tomato sauce. Serve the rice on a separate platter.

OVEN-BAKED RICE WITH CHICKPEAS AND GARLIC
ARROZ AL HORNO
Balearic Islands

Advance preparation time: 12 hours
Preparation time: 5 minutes
Cooking time: 1 hour 30 minutes
For 6 servings:
1 cup (7 oz/200 g) chickpeas
8 cups (64 fl oz/ 2 l) beef broth
1 head garlic, whole and unpeeled
6 tablespoons (3 fl oz/9 cl) olive oil
3 small potatoes, peeled and cut into rounds
3 medium tomatoes, halved
2 large tomatoes, peeled and chopped
Salt
7 oz (200 g) sobresada (see glossary), cut
    into pieces
3 cups (1 1/3 lb/600 g) short-grain rice

Method:
A day in advance: Place the chickpeas in a bowl of salted water and soak for 12 hours.

The same day: Drain the chickpeas. Place them in a saucepan with 2 cups (16 fl oz/50 cl) of the broth and cook over medium heat for 1 hour until tender. Drain.

Rinse the garlic and pat dry thoroughly. Place the remaining broth in a saucepan and bring to a boil.

Meanwhile, heat the oil in a large shallow earthenware casserole. Add the garlic head and cook for 3 minutes. Add the potatoes, tomato halves, and chopped tomatoes. Season lightly with salt and stir in the chickpeas and sobresada. Sprinkle the rice evenly over the vegetables. Pour the boiling broth over the rice and let cook for 2 minutes. Correct the seasoning if necessary.

Place the pan in a 350° F (175° C) preheated oven and cook for 18 minutes.

Remove the garlic head, separate it into cloves and arrange them over the top of the rice.

Serve immediately.

RICE WITH WHITE BEANS
ARROZ EMPEDRADO
Valencia

Advance preparation time: 12 hours
Preparation time: 15 minutes
Cooking time: 2 hours 30 minutes
For 6 servings:
1 1/4 cups (8 oz/250 g) dried white beans
1 head garlic, whole and unpeeled
8 cups (64 fl oz/2 l) chicken broth
Salt
Pinch saffron threads (see glossary)
6 tablespoons (3 fl oz/9 cl) olive oil
3 cloves garlic, peeled and chopped
1 medium tomato, peeled and chopped
1 teaspoon paprika
3 cups (1 1/3 lb/600 g) short-grain rice

Method:
A day in advance: Place the beans in cold water to soak for 12 hours.

The same day: Drain the beans. Add them to the head of garlic and 2 cups (50 cl) chicken broth. Season lightly with salt and add the saffron. Cook for 2 hours.

When the beans are cooked, drain them, reserving the garlic head.

Heat the oil. Add the chopped garlic and tomato and cook until tender. Add the paprika, stirring rapidly. Pour the remaining 6 cups chicken broth into the pan and bring to a boil over high heat. Sprinkle the rice over the broth and cook for 12 minutes over high heat. Spread the beans on top of the rice and cook over low heat for 8 minutes longer.

Let rest for 5 minutes before serving.

Separate the garlic cloves and use them to decorate the top of the rice.

RICE WITH WHITE BEANS AND TURNIPS
ARROZ CON ALUBIAS Y NABOS
Valencia

Advance preparation time: 12 hours
Preparation time: 15 minutes
Cooking time: 2 hours 35 minutes
For 6 servings:
1 1/2 cups (11 oz/300 g) dried white beans
1/4 cup (2 fl oz/6 cl) olive oil
6 cloves garlic, peeled
1 medium onion, peeled and chopped
11 oz (300 g) turnips, peeled and cubed
1 teaspoon paprika
11 oz (300 g) lean pork
1/4 lb (100 g) side pork or fresh,
    unsmoked bacon
10 cups (80 fl oz/2 1/2 l) water
Salt
6 morcilla de cebolla sausages (see glossary)
Pinch saffron threads (see glossary)
1 1/2 cups (11 oz/300 g) short-grain rice

Method:
A day in advance: Place the beans in a bowl with enough cold water to cover generously and soak for 12 hours.

The same day: Drain the beans thoroughly. Heat the oil in a Dutch oven. Add the garlic, onion, and turnips, and cook until barely tender. Add the paprika, stirring rapidly. Remove the vegetables from the pan and set aside.

Place the beans, lean pork and bacon in the Dutch oven, add the water, and season with salt. Cook over medium heat for 2 hours.

Add the reserved vegetables, the morcilla and saffron to the pan. Let cook for 5 minutes longer. Add the rice and continue to cook for 20 minutes.

Remove from the heat and let rest 5 minutes before serving.

LENTEN RICE WITH SALT COD AND ARTICHOKES
ARROZ DE AYUNO
Castile-La Mancha

Advance preparation: 24 hours
Preparation time: 10 minutes
Cooking time: 35 minutes
For 6 servings:
11 oz (300 g) dried salt cod
3 tablespoons (5 cl) olive oil
2 cloves garlic
1 lb (500 g) tomatoes, peeled and chopped
6 baby artichokes, trimmed and quartered
1 cup (3 1/2 oz/100 g) fresh peas
1 red bell pepper, seeded and sliced
6 cups (48 fl oz/1 1/2 l) water
3 cups (1 1/3 lb/600 g) short-grain rice
Salt

Method:

A day in advance: Place the cod in a large basin of cold water and soak for 24 hours, changing the water 3 to 4 times.

The same day: Drain the cod, removing any skin and bones. Flake the flesh into pieces with a fork.

Heat the oil over medium heat in a paella pan. Add the garlic and tomatoes and cook until tender. Stir in the artichokes, peas, bell pepper, and cod, and cook over low heat for 10 minutes.

Meanwhile, bring the water to a boil in a saucepan.

Sprinkle the rice evenly over the vegetables and cod, and stir in the boiling water. Season lightly with salt and let cook over medium heat for 20 minutes.

Remove the paella pan from the heat and cover with a kitchen towel. Let rest for 5 minutes before serving.

Canning and preserving are popular activities in Spanish homes, and housewives often sell their own produce at the market. Tomatoes, peppers and eggplants are the most commonly preserved vegetables (facing).

SHELLFISH PAELLA
PAELLA DE MARISCO
Valencia

Preparation time: 30 minutes
Cooking time: 1 hour 20 minutes
For 6 servings:
6 tablespoons (3 fl oz/9 cl) olive oil
6 Dublin Bay prawns
6 medium prawns
12 medium shrimp
1 large onion, peeled and chopped
2 medium tomatoes, peeled and chopped
8 cups (68 fl oz/2 l) water
1/2 pound (250 g) mussels
1/2 pound (250 g) clams
5 small squid, cleaned and cut into
    rounds (see glossary)
2 cloves garlic, peeled and sliced
3 cups (1 1/3 lb/600 g) short-grain rice
Pinch saffron threads (see glossary)
1 teaspoon paprika
Salt

Method:

Heat 3 tablespoons of the oil in a paella pan. Add the prawns and shrimp and cook, turning, until golden. Remove the shellfish and set aside.

Add the onion and tomatoes to the pan and cook in the same oil until tender. Add the water.

Peel the prawns and shrimp, leaving their tails intact and reserving their heads and shells. Process the heads and shells in a food processor until reduced to a powder. Stir this powder into the paella pan and cook over medium heat for 40 minutes.

Steam the mussels and clams in a separate pan until they have all opened. Pour any liquid remaining in the mussel and clam shells into the sauce in the paella pan. Remove the sauce from the heat, strain it through a fine sieve, and set aside.

Wipe the paella pan clean. Add the remaining oil to the pan and heat. Add the squid and garlic, and cook over medium heat until lightly browned.

Sprinkle the rice over the squid, stirring rapidly. Pour the reserved sauce over the rice. Add the saffron and paprika, seasoning with salt if necessary. Cook over high heat for 10 minutes.

Return the prawns, shrimp, mussels and clams to the paella pan and continue to cook for 10 minutes over low heat.

Remove from the heat and cover with a kitchen towel. Let rest for 5 minutes before serving.

VALENCIAN PAELLA
PAELLA VALENCIANA
Valencia

Advance preparation time: 12 hours
Preparation time: 30 minutes
Cooking time: 1 hour 15 minutes
For 6 servings:
1 1/3 cup (9 oz/250 g) dried white beans
1/3 lb (150 g) fresh fava beans
3/4 lb (300 g) green beans
3/4 cup (6 fl oz/18 cl) olive oil
1 chicken (2 1/4 lb/1 kg), cut into pieces
1 lb (500 g) rabbit, cut into pieces
2 medium tomatoes, peeled and chopped
12 cups (96 fl oz/3 l) water
Salt
18 snails, cleaned
1/2 teaspoon paprika
Pinch of saffron (see glossary)
3 cups (1 1/3 lb/600 g) short-grain rice

Method:

A day in advance: Soak the white beans in cold water for 12 hours.

The same day: Drain the white beans. Shell the fava beans. Rinse and trim the green beans.

Heat the oil in a very large paella pan or Dutch oven. Add the chicken and rabbit pieces and cook, turning, until lightly browned on all sides. Add the tomatoes and cook, stirring, for 5 minutes.

Add the white beans, favas, and green beans, and cover with the water. Season with salt and let cook over medium heat for 45 minutes.

Add the snails, paprika, and saffron. Sprinkle the rice into the pan and cook for 10 minutes over high heat. Reduce the heat and cook for 10 minutes.

Remove from the heat and cover with a kitchen towel. Let rest for 5 minutes before serving.

THE TASTE
OF THE
SEA

After Japan, Spain is the world's biggest consumer of fish. The genius of Spanish cooks can transform the most ordinary varieties (hake, whiting) into extremely flavorful, superb, dishes (above and facing).

Spain is a peninsula surrounded by the Cantabrian, Atlantic and Mediterranean seas and attached to Europe by the Pyrenees, which have for centuries been more of a barricade than a crossroads.

Euskadi, Cantabria, Galicia, Andalusia, Murcia, Valencia, Catalonia, the Balearic Islands and the Canary Islands: of the seventeen autonomous communities (*Comunidades Autónomas*) that comprise Spain, these nine face the sea, and a considerable percentage of their populations make their living from it. Their cooking is based on food from the ocean, and they produce and consume a bewildering variety of seafood dishes.

Madrid, the state capital, which is situated inland far from any coastline, has been defined as "the best port in Spain," and it is true that there are few cities in Europe that have fish as fresh as in Madrid. Madrid's citizenry is among the world's greatest consumers of fish, which an extremely efficient road transport system delivers on the same day that it is caught from the major ports in the north and south.

Madrilenians are prepared to make considerable economic sacrifices for fresh gambas, prawns and a good hake in green sauce. It is quite an experience to be in a Ma-

drid seafood bar at aperitif hour, with the shells of gambas, prawns, crabs and shrimps piling up on the floor, and the counters filled with small casseroles of prawns with garlic or clams *a la marinera*, while the beer-taps are pulled constantly and the smell of the amber liquid wafts through the noisy, happy atmosphere.

The traditional Christmas dinner is inconceivable in Madrid without a second course of fish, and the typical choice is *besugo al horno* — oven-baked sea bream. As Christmas approaches enormous quantities of the fish are brought into the city, and prices soar atrociously.

Sea bream is one of the four aces of Spanish fish cookery, along with turbot, hake and perch. When in season bream is consumed heavily throughout the North, especially in Euskadi.

In the winter months the sea bream get their incomparable flavor from the cold, stormy waters of the Bay of Biscay. On damp, foggy evenings in the Basque region, Cantabria and Asturias, there is no greater gastronomic pleasure than to wander into a grill or cider bar where the specialties are huge barbecued cutlets, salt cod omelettes and, especially, *besugo a la espalda*. At that time of year the bream needs nothing complicated in its preparation. It is full of the taste of the sea; it is firm and flavorful, and is enough by itself to satisfy the most demanding palates.

The bream is slit open and placed on the oiled grill skin side down. When it turns white it is dressed with chopped fried garlic and hot red peppers, the frying oil and a few drops of vinegar. It is healthy, simple and delicious.

Eating this fish in the magical atmosphere of the cider bars, where the golden liquid flows from the enormous casks, provides all the conditions necessary for pure, unadulterated pleasure. There is a ritual to it: the huge cask is pierced and the cider pours out in a strong, thin stream from which it is caught frothing in the bottom of a glass jug. Then the good-humored group goes back to

Fish from the Mar Menor at Murcia is in great demand, as the heavy salt content of the water adds an exquisite briney flavor (above).
The big seasonal catches of sardines, herrings and anchovies means a proliferation of economic but delicious dishes, both at home and in restaurants (right).

the table where the fragrant *besugo a la espalda* awaits them. It is never long before a song starts up among the diners. But beware! There are cider bars that are as solemn as a cathedral, where such strict orthodoxy is applied that women are not allowed inside. According to hyperorthodox thinking, women are the source of mysterious "emanations" that can ruin the whole year's cider production. However, such beliefs are gradually disappearing.

Fish has been the most unfortunate victim of the recent wave of *nouvelle cuisine*. It has been mauled and mashed, rolled, had its spine — a source of flavor — removed, and been drowned in all manner of strange sauces, until in the "signature restaurants" it has been turned into an unrecognizable substance that tastes of anything and everything except the sea. In Spain fish is still appreciated for its taste of fish, and nothing else. The favorite recipes are the classic ones, simple preparations derived from popular sources.

Turbot, for example, goes into the oven as it is, and that's that. It only has to be eaten one time in the Elcano restaurant in Guetaria for the diner to understand that it needs nothing more than simple boiled potatoes as an accompaniment.

Hake can be prepared in many ways, but the method that best enhances its natural qualities, and which is the most popular, is in *salsa verde* (green sauce). People in the North are particularly fond of large hake. The greatest delicacy is considered the back of the neck, which is often roasted in the oven, cooked with asparagus, or served with a garlic sauce. But the most peculiar delicacy is *kokotxas,* the subtly flavored gelatinous lower jaw, which prepared in a *salsa verde* or in batter is an unparalleled delight, to the Basques in particular.

Once this luxury morsel has been removed, the head of the hake, prepared *a la donostiarra* ("Donosti" is San Sebastian in the Basque language), is a succulent example of what I earlier called Spanish "minimal cooking" — cooking that is unpretentious, inexpensive and simple. This will not be found in any restaurant, but it is nonetheless a favorite dish with many northern cooks. They make it in an original way: first they remove the gills and cook the head (the larger the better) in enough water to cover, adding salt, bay leaf, parsley, chopped leeks and carrots. When the water comes to the boil, they take the fish head out of the pot and drain it.

Garlic and hot red peppers are then fried until nicely browned, and the head added to the pan and put into a very hot oven for ten

minutes or so. The fish head is then placed in a dish and half a glass of wine vinegar poured into the frying pan, which is set on the flame to reduce the liquid. When this is done, the head is put back into the pan and the whole thing goes back into the oven for another five minutes. Then it is served and eaten.

The Spanish consider tuna fish and bonito the marine equivalent of pork. The arrival of the migrating tuna shoals in Spanish waters, especially in the southern fishing areas, is an extraordinary spectacle. Once caught in the nets the tuna are slaughtered with harpoons; the sea becomes stained with red foam, and the event takes on the aspect of a wild ballet, full of strength and brutal energy — a scene immortalized in a famous work by Salvador Dalí.

Tuna fish is the basic ingredient of the *marmitako,* one of the most popular Basque dishes. It is so popular, in fact, that in Euskadi *marmitako* championships are held every year which draw huge crowds and numerous entries from professional and amateur cooks. One of the most reputed specialists in the field is Currito de Santurce, a frequent *marmitako* national championship winner. He sports a Basque beret on his head and owns a large Basque restaurant named after himself in the Casa de Campo in Madrid. His son carries on the flame in their native town of Santurce, near Bilbao.

The *marmitako* was originally a fishermen's dish, invented for cooking on board ship. All over the coasts and ports of Spain can be found versions of *marmitako,* which is basically a ragout of fresh tuna and potatoes.

Thus, as long as the basic ingredients are respected, the recipe for *marmitako* is a matter of individual inspiration. Every fisherman and every cook has his or her own version, and there are some that reach sublime heights. It is extremely substantial and nutritious and, as its name suggests, it is a single-dish meal.

Currito won the Spanish *marmitako* championship with the following recipe. For

six people, take three pounds of tuna fish (or bonito), two pounds of potatoes, two-fifths of a pint of oil, an onion, a green bell pepper, six dried hot red peppers, and salt.

Heat the oil in a large pan and fry the chopped onion until it is nicely browned — about half an hour on low heat.

In a separate pan make a stock using the head and tail or any bones of the fish, a leek, two green bell peppers and a whole onion.

Mince another bell pepper and add it to the onion, along with the sliced potatoes. (Be careful not to cut through with the knife: cut part-way down and pull them apart afterward.) Stir thoroughly and pour in the fish stock, covering the potatoes.

Currito's secret is to add a few ladles of *salsa vizcaína,* a sauce similar to that used in the recipe for Bay of Biscay salt cod described earlier, and the skinned, boned tuna cut into small cubes.

He then brings this to the boil, lets cook for no more than four minutes, and leaves it to rest for two hours until the sauce thickens and absorbs the flavor of the fish. He heats it again just before serving.

The Basque *marmitako* is the equivalent of the Mediterranean *all cremat* from the coast of Tarragona. This is beautifully prepared at the El Peixerot restaurant in Vila-

Countless visitors throng the markets in the fishing port. The fish glistening in the sun, the overpowering smell of the sea, and the vendors shouting out their wares make the scene unforgettable (above). Pressed and salted, neatly arranged in barrels, the small sardinas de sorra are eaten grilled in the week that follows their salting (following double page).

The return of the fishermen is the occasion for tasting the excellent charcoal-grilled sardines or breaded, fried anchovies at the snack bars along Galician beaches (above). Catalonia is a paradise for seafood-lovers, who can relish baby octopus with garlic mayonnaise, tiny calamars on skewers, or, as in the photo opposite, calamar fritters.

nova i la Geltrú, south of Barcelona, which is one of the finest places on earth for fish dishes. The Mestre brothers, who have opened a similar establishment with the same name in Barcelona, come from an old fishing family, and have inherited all the culinary secrets of their grandfather Peixerot.

If it is ordered beforehand, the Mestre brothers themselves will make *bull de tonyina,* which is one of the most unusual dishes on the coast. This is a stew whose basic ingredient is the dried viscera of bonito or tuna fish, soaked and then boiled with the same vegetables as for a stew: potatoes, cabbage and chickpeas, accompanied by a sauce of tomatoes and red bell peppers.

Another of the Mestres' spendid yet simple dishes is baby octopus and potatoes with a layer of *aioli* on top. This can only be made during the season for fishing the newly spawned octopus, which is from winter to spring.

The best local cooking is produced when the really big catches of anchovies and winter sardines arrive in the fishing ports.

Fresh anchovies, dredged in flour and fried, or prepared in a casserole with garlic and parsley, make for Pantagruelian collations in the bars and open-air restaurants along the seashores. In Galicia tons of sardines are grilled in long rows over coals while new potatoes, *cachelos,* cook in huge pots. The surrounding cornfields are filled with the smell of the grilling sardines, their sea-tangy fat melting and spluttering in the flames. The crusts of huge loaves of rye crack as the bread is sliced, and the local, pleasantly acidic white wine flows freely.

Galician-style octopus is a favorite dish in Spain; it is served at every local celebration and festivity in Galicia, and is prepared in public in the *pulpeiras.* The octopus is cooked in large copper pots, then the tentacles are cut into slices and set on a board, where they are seasoned with a little oil, coarse salt and hot paprika. The contrast of the white octopus with the red splash of paprika makes an appetizingly attractive dish.

Scallops also abound. Doña Pilar pre-pares an unforgettable dish with scallops at the Casa Simón in Cangas del Morrazo; casserole-simmered with onion preserves. It is one of those dishes that leave a lasting impression.

Andalusia is the land of *pescaito frito* — fried fish — although it also boasts some excellent, elaborate dishes such as the *urta a la roteña,* the larded Roteña-style tuna fish baked with brandy, and cuttlefish with new broad beans and fresh mint sauce.

One of the outstanding fried fish dishes is the *chanquete* — whitebait — of Málaga; tiny, transparent fish that are delicately battered and fried. Fritters or omelettes made with this fish are an exquisite delicacy. Unfortunately, whitebait is so well-liked that it is in danger of extinction. Today, what is actually served under the name of *chanquete* is often the alevin of other types of fish, especially red mullet.

One of the most spectacular sights in Spanish fishing ports is the public auction of the catch. This is a great tourist attraction in the summer, and visitors gather in the fish markets to watch the piles of crates being auctioned off when the tide comes in. The wholesale dealers shout out the prices at such a dizzying speed that only the wholesalers and retailers who are used to it know how or when to interrupt them.

In Barcelona one can make a morning visit to the Mercat de la Boquería in the heart of the Ramblas. It is a nineteenth-century building with a metal structure and huge windows whose central section under the rotunda houses the fish market. The general uproar and merriment, the bustle and clamor — well-salted with the fish-sellers' good-humored swearing — and the fantastic variety of fish of every color and size, present an impressive picture. With produce like this it is almost impossible not to have a great cuisine.

But how did the Spaniards develop such an addiction to fish? The taste for sea produce would probably not have intensified to such a pitch were it not for the traditional Lenten fasting and abstinence from meat —

On the Mediterranean coast, calamars stuffed with ham and peas (above) have made many restaurants famous, including the Set Portas in Barcelona. This historic restaurant, which opened in 1896, has retained its old-world charm, and serves excellent rice dishes among its Catalan specialties. Lovers of marinated fish will enjoy these sardines in Spain's tapas bars and restaurants (facing).

more proof of the accuracy of Julio Camba's comment that Spanish cooking consists of garlic and religion.

At any rate, religious considerations enabled Ignacio Domenech, a famous Catalan chef of the beginning of the century, to write a book with the somewhat ironic title of *Ayunos y Abstinencias* (Fasting and abstinence), and publish it under episcopal authorization. The book, which is stamped with the *nihil obstat* of the archbishop of Madrid-Alcalá, has an interesting scholarly preface on Lenten fasting, as well as a judgement passed by Pope Pius X according to which "fishes large and small" may be eaten by the "Legionaries of Virtuous Publications" at the evening meal on fast days, in addition to a short description of the daily life of Pope Leo XIII, which praised him for his abstemiousness.

The recipes that follow are not quite in the same vein, however, and show that "fasting and abstinence" actually denoted sumptuous banquets of the finest fish to be had. Perhaps we should give the author some credit, however, for the recipes are named after abbots and saints.

Naturally, there are many salt cod recipes in the book, but one also comes across a "gilt-head bream, Spanish style," "prawns with two sauces," "Sicilian-style scalloped

hake," "modern-style whiting," "medallions of hake *a la romana*," a remarkable "salmon and prawns, with Father Guzman sauce," "Virgin of Guadalupe trout," "salmon medallions Marineta," "Andalusian-style oysters," "Reparadora nuns' salt cod loaf," the extravagant "Montserrat Monastery lobster," "perch in seaman's sauce," "eels *a la madres benedictinas*," "oyster soup Rachel," a "gilt-head bream in divine sauce," a "beggarwoman's sea bream" and "marinated sea bream," "sea perch grilled with sherry," and other delightful recipes to transform Lenten fare into anything but "fasting and abstinence."

Here, for example, is the "sea bream in divine sauce":

The "divine sauce" is prepared in the top of a double boiler with a glass of sherry, one and a half ounces of butter, the zest of one lemon, two tablespoons of milk, two egg yolks and two tablespoons of the bream fumet, salt and ground white pepper. The mixture is whipped until all lumps have disappeared and the sauce is thick and glossy.

The bream is placed whole in a dish and garnished with the potatoes, prawns and a little chopped parsley, and the sauce is served in a sauceboat.

For an ordinary day of strict Lenten penitence, the book recommends the following menu:
— Consommé with crab ravioli
— Lobster Samaritan
— Buckingham fillet of trout
— Cauliflower flan with cream
— Grilled hake-tail with anchovy
— Endive salad Almoraima
— San Honorato cake
— "Prioress" ice cream
— Chocolate-covered finger-biscuits
— Fruit

Spanish cooking may well be made of garlic and religion, but the sin of gluttony is the ecclesiastical transgression par excellence, and according to Ignacio Domenech, this failing is never so manifest as when fish is on the table.

106

Apart from salmon, trout, eel, shad, lamprey and one or two other species, freshwater fish is not especially popular in Spain, but some recipes featuring it are highly appreciated.

Eel, which is abundant in the delta of the River Ebro and the Valencian rice fields, is prepared in the truly splendid dish *all i pebre* (garlic and pepper), whose name comes from its accompanying sauce. Some rice recipes also use eel as their basic ingredient.

These curry-comb crabs (above), like all seafood, are highly appreciated in Spain, particularly in Madrid. In spite of its inland location, Madrid abounds in small bars specializing in seafood — gambas, shrimp, crabs, prawns. . . . Salsa verde, originally from Guipúzcoa, is a delicious sauce to accompany dishes of white-fleshed fish, such as hake with clams, a classic of Basque cuisine (facing).

TWO TYPES OF SAUCE FOR FISH

As already mentioned, the Spanish like fish prepared in the simplest, most straightforward way possible, with nothing to detract from its natural flavor. There are, however, several traditional fish casserole dishes and sauces that are extremely popular.

Among the most convenient and frequently used preparations are the *salsa verde*, a green sauce, and the *escabeches*, or marinades. There are innumerable variations on these favorites, of course, but the basic elements are always the same. Green sauces and marinades, which originated mainly in the northern Basque area and the Mediterranean, are used throughout Spain.

Salsa verde is to be eaten piping hot, while *escabeche* enables the fish to be kept fresh for several days and is usually served cold, as aperitif *tapas* or hors d'œuvre. The former is especially good with white fish such as hake, perch, and anglerfish, and the latter is best for dark fish like sardines, scad, tuna and mackerel. The preserving aspect of *escabeche* has made it a Castilian specialty, and today the finest such dishes are found in restaurants or *tapa* bars in Castile and La Mancha.

Salsa verde:

This sauce is easy to make, and the recipe below is one of the most common.

The first step is to make a *court-bouillon* with fish heads and bones. Fresh cod, whiting or anglerfish are best. A bay leaf and a sliced onion are added to a mixture of half water and half dry white wine.

While the stock is cooking, some chopped garlic and a lot of chopped parsley are softened in a saucepan with olive oil, without frying, over very gentle heat.

When the garlic is soft but not browned, a little flour is added. The amount of flour depends on how thick a sauce is desired. Personally, I prefer a light sauce, and put in only a teaspoonful of flour. To this is added a touch of white pepper and however much stock is required, and the mixture is left to reduce over low heat until it thickens into a smooth, gelatinous emulsion.

This sauce can be used to cook fish or clams, or the fish can be steamed and then napped with the sauce.

Escabeches:

There are dozens of ways to prepare *escabeche*, so marinated sardines might be as good a starting point as any.

Once the sardines have been gutted and the heads removed, they are dredged in flour and fried in hot oil (preferably deep-fried), then removed and left to cool while the marinade is prepared:

Put some oil into an earthenware pot and fry four cloves of garlic, without letting them burn. Add white wine and a glass of red wine vinegar (the exact amount is tricky to calculate, and depends on how sour you like the marinade — in Spain, it can be quite strong). To this is added aromatic herbs such as bay leaf, marjoram, oregano, parsley or fresh coriander, and mild or hot paprika, cloves and cumin. This is left to reduce until it barely covers the fried sardines, which are arranged in the pot when the marinade has cooled. This *escabeche* can be used with any type of fish.

A century ago, these marinades were prepared with sweet wines, but this custom has disappeared. Today, the most important point is that the vinegar is of the finest quality. The most delightful *escabeches* are made with sherry vinegar or vinegar made with Montilla or Moriles wines.

BASQUE TUNA AND POTATO STEW
MARMITAKO
Basque Country

Advance preparation: 2 hours
Preparation time: 15 minutes
Cooking time: 45 minutes
For 6 servings:
1 dried hot pepper
2 cloves garlic, peeled
6 tablespoons (3 fl oz/9 cl) olive oil
1 green bell pepper, seeded and cut into strips
1 onion, peeled and chopped
2 ripe tomatoes, peeled and chopped
2 1/4 lb (1 kg) potatoes, peeled and cut
    into pieces
1 tablespoon brandy
2 1/4 lb (1 kg) tuna fillet, cut into pieces

Method:
    Place the hot pepper in a small bowl
of tepid water and soak for 2 hours. Drain
the pepper, place in a mortar with the
garlic and grind to a paste with a pestle.
    Heat the oil in a Dutch oven. Add the
bell pepper, onion, and tomatoes and cook
over medium heat until tender. Stir in the
hot pepper/garlic paste.

Add the potatoes and brandy. Stir in
enough water to cover. Season with salt
and simmer until the potatoes are tender,
about 30 minutes.
    Add the tuna and cook for 3 minutes.
Remove the pan from the heat and let
rest for a few minutes before serving.

PORGY BAKED WITH PEPPERS AND BRANDY
URTA A LA ROTEÑA
Andalusia

Preparation time: 10 minutes
Cooking time: 30 minutes
For 6 servings:
1 large (2 1/4 lb/1 kg) porgy or sea bream
Salt
3/4 cup (6 fl oz/18 cl) brandy
2 oz (50 g) fat of cured ham, cut into
    thin strips
3/4 cup (6 fl oz/18 cl) olive oil
1 large onion, peeled and chopped
3 cloves garlic, peeled and chopped
2 1/4 lb (1 kg) very ripe tomatoes, peeled
    and chopped
1 1/2 medium green bell peppers, seeded
    and diced

Method:
    Ask your fishmonger to clean the fish,
leaving on the head and tail. Cut several
slits in the sides and place the fish in a
shallow baking pan just large enough to
hold it. Season with salt and drizzle the
brandy over the top. Insert the slices of
fat in the slits cut in the fish.
    Heat the oil in a skillet. Add the onion,
garlic, tomatoes and peppers, and cook
over low heat for 5 to 6 minutes. Spread
this mixture evenly over the fish.
    Place in a 375° F (200° C) preheated
oven and bake for about 30 minutes. The
fish is cooked when its flesh pulls easily
away from the bone.
    Serve immediately.

ZARZUELA OF SHELLFISH
ZARZUELA DE MARISCOS
Valencia

Preparation time: 20 minutes
Cooking time: 20 minutes
For 6 servings:
3/4 cup (6 fl oz/18 cl) olive oil
4 cloves garlic, peeled
2 onions, peeled and chopped
1 red bell pepper, seeded and cut into strips
1 green bell pepper, seeded and cut into strips
2 large tomatoes, peeled and chopped
2 bay leaves
8 saffron threads (see glossary)
7 oz (200 g) squid, cleaned and cut into
    rings (see glossary)
4 1/2 oz (125 g) smoked ham, chopped
3/4 cup (6 fl oz/18 cl) dry white wine
Juice of 1 lemon
Salt
6 grouper steaks, 3 1/3 oz (100g) each
7 oz (200 g) shrimp
7 oz (200 g) prawns
9 oz (250 g) jumbo shrimp
6 medium Dublin Bay prawns
12 mussels, washed and scraped

Method:
    Heat the oil in a large, shallow
earthenware casserole. Add the garlic and
onions and cook over medium-high heat
until tender. Add the red and green
peppers, tomatoes, bay leaves, saffron
and squid, and cook over low heat for
5 minutes.
    Add the ham, wine and lemon juice,
season with salt and cook for 5 minutes.
Add the fish and shellfish, and continue
to simmer for 5 minutes over low heat.
Correct the seasoning, if necessary.
Remove from the heat and let rest for
4 or 5 minutes before serving in the
casserole in which it cooked.

Zarzuela of shellfish (facing page).

GALICIAN-STYLE OCTOPUS
PULPO A FEIRA
Galicia

Preparation time: 20 minutes
Cooking time: 15 to 20 minutes
For 6 servings:
2 1/4 lb (1 kg) potatoes, peeled
1 large octopus, about 6 1/2 lbs (3 kg)
Coarse salt
2 tablespoons paprika
1 cup (8 fl oz/25 cl) olive oil

Method:
Cut the potatoes into pieces. Place them in a saucepan of salted water and cook over medium-high heat until tender.

Clean the octopus thoroughly, removing all waste, including eyes. Place in a large pan of boiling water and cook for about 15 to 20 minutes. Remove from the heat and let rest for 10 minutes.

Remove the octopus and drain. While it is still warm, cut it into strips using kitchen shears. Place the octopus on a wooden serving dish. Sprinkle with the salt and paprika. Drizzle the olive oil over the octopus.

Drain the potatoes, arrange them around the octopus and serve immediately.

STUFFED CRAB
TXANGURRO
Basque Country

Preparation time: 1 hour 30 minutes
Cooking time: 1 hour 15 minutes
For 4 servings:
4 crabs, about 2 1/4 lb (1 kg) each (see note)
10 tablespoons (5 fl oz/16 cl) olive oil
2 leeks, chopped
2 carrots, cut into thin rounds
1 medium onion, peeled and chopped
1 garlic clove, peeled and minced
2 cups (16 fl oz/50 cl) brandy
8 medium tomatoes (2 1/4 lb/1 kg), peeled and chopped
1 1/2 cups (12 fl oz/40 cl) dry white wine
2 cups (16 fl oz/50 cl) fish broth
2 tablespoons short-grain rice
1 small hot red pepper
Salt
Freshly ground pepper
3 tablespoons butter
1/4 cup (1 oz/30 g) breadcrumbs

Method:
Place the crabs in a large stock pot filled with boiling salted water, and cook over medium heat for about 12 minutes.

Drain the crabs. Crack them open, being careful to leave the top shell intact, and reserve the meat from the body and claws. Grind the claws and the undershell to a powder in a food processor.

Heat 1/2 cup (4 fl oz/12 cl) of the olive oil in a large Dutch oven. Add the ground shells, along with the leeks, carrots, onions, and garlic, and cook until the vegetables are tender.

Reserve 1 tablespoon of the brandy. Add the remaining brandy to the pan, heat it briefly, then ignite it with a match. Add the tomatoes, wine, broth, rice and hot pepper, and let simmer for 1 hour. Strain this mixture through a fine sieve, season with salt and pepper, and set aside.

Heat the remaining oil and 1 tablespoon of the butter in a skillet. Add the crab meat and mix thoroughly. Warm the reserved tablespoon of brandy, add it to the crabmeat and ignite with a match. Pour the strained sauce over the crabmeat and mix well.

Turn the crab shells bottom side up, and stuff the crabmeat into the cavities. Sprinkle the top of each stuffed crab with the breadcrumbs. Dot the top of each with the remaining butter.

Place in a 425° F (220° C) preheated oven and warm for 3 minutes.

Serve immediately.

Note: If you cannot find crabs this large, use 2 smaller crabs per person. The crabmeat may also be stuffed into scallop shells, sprinkled with breadcrumbs and butter, baked and served.

Stuffed crab (facing page).

GALICIAN-STYLE TURBOT AND CLAMS
RODABALLO A LA GALLEGA
Galicia

Preparation time: 15 minutes
Cooking time: 20 minutes
For 4 servings:
1 lb (500 g) potatoes, cut into pieces
2 cups (16 fl oz/50 cl) fish broth (see glossary)
Salt
1 turbot, about 2 1/4 lb (1 kg)
1/4 cup (1 oz/30 g) flour
3/4 cup (6 fl oz/18 cl) olive oil
3 cloves garlic, peeled and chopped
6 tablespoons (3 fl oz/9 cl) brandy
3/4 cup (6 fl oz/18 cl) white Albariño wine (see note)
Freshly ground pepper
16 littleneck or cherrystone clams
1 teaspoon paprika

Method:
In a medium saucepan, place the potatoes and 1 cup of the fish broth. Season with salt and cook over medium heat for 15 to 20 minutes, or until potatoes are tender. If necessary, add a little water during the cooking.

Rinse the turbot and pat dry. Cut it into pieces and dredge them in the flour. Meanwhile, heat the oil in a large Dutch oven. Add the garlic and cook over medium heat until it begins to color. Add the fish, searing on both sides. Warm the brandy in a small saucepan, then sprinkle it over the fish and ignite with a match. When the flames have died down, add the wine and season with salt and pepper.

Add the clams and the remaining fish broth, and simmer for 5 minutes.

Stir the paprika into the potatoes and add them to the pan with the fish. Continue to cook for 5 minutes.

Serve immediately.

Note: Albariño is a crisp, fragrant white wine from the Galician region of northwest Spain. It is particularly good with fish and seafood. If not available, substitute a Riesling wine.

OVEN-BAKED SEA BREAM
BESUGO A LA ESPALDA
Basque Country

Preparation time: 15 minutes
Cooking time: 35 minutes
For 4 servings:
1 large sea bream, about 2 1/4 lb (1 kg)
Salt
2/3 cup (5 fl oz/16 cl) oil
4 cloves garlic, peeled
1 large hot red pepper
1 tablespoon vinegar

Method:
Ask your fishmonger to clean and scale the bream. Season with salt, brush with 2 tablespoons of the oil, and place in a large shallow baking pan.

Bake in a preheated 375° F (190° C) oven for 30 minutes.

A few minutes before the fish has finished cooking, heat the remaining oil in a skillet. Add the garlic cloves and the hot pepper, and cook until the garlic is lightly browned. Remove the pan from the heat and stir in the vinegar.

Pour the pepper, garlic and vinegar over the bream and serve.

Sea bream baked in salt (above).

SEA BREAM BAKED IN SALT
DORADA A LA SAL
Andalusia

Preparation time: 15 minutes
Cooking time: 45 minutes
For 6 servings:
1 whole sea bream, about 3 1/3 lb (1 1/2 kg)
4 1/2 lb (2 kg) coarse salt

Method:
Thoroughly clean and scale the sea bream, being careful to make only a small slit in the belly when gutting it in order to prevent the salt from penetrating the cavity during cooking.

In a large shallow ovenproof casserole, prepare a bed of coarse salt about 3/4 inch (2 cm) deep, using half the salt. Place the fish on the salt, and cover completely with the remaining salt.

Place in a 375° F (190° C) preheated oven and let cook for 45 minutes. When the fish is done, the salt will have hardened and the top crust will crack.

Remove from the oven and remove the fish from the casserole, brushing off any excess salt. Place on a large serving platter, surrounded by steamed potatoes and accompanied by mayonnaise.

BASQUE-STYLE HAKE WITH ASPARAGUS TIPS
MERLUZA A LA VASCA
Basque Country

Preparation time: 10 minutes
Cooking time: 20 minutes
For 6 servings:
4 slices (9 oz/250 g each) hake
1/4 cup (2 fl oz/6 cl) olive oil
1 medium onion, chopped
1 tablespoon flour
3/4 cup (6 fl oz/ 18 cl) water
2 cloves garlic, peeled and chopped
Salt
6 tablespoons (3 fl oz/9 cl) white wine
2 1/2 cups (9 oz/250 g) fresh peas, cooked
2 cups (9 oz/250 g) asparagus tips (see note)
1 tablespoon chopped parsley
1 hard-cooked egg, sliced into rounds

Method:
Arrange the hake slices in a large, shallow earthenware casserole.

Heat the oil in a large skillet. Add the onion and cook for 5 minutes, or until transparent. Sprinkle the flour over the onion and mix thoroughly. Stir in the water and garlic, season with salt and cook over medium heat for 8 minutes, stirring constantly. Strain the sauce through a fine sieve and pour it evenly over the fish, adding a little more water if necessary to cover completely.

Place the casserole over medium heat and simmer for 6 minutes, shaking the pan and stirring gently to bind the sauce. Add the wine, peas, and asparagus tips and cook for 2 minutes longer. Correct the seasoning, if necessary, and sprinkle with the parsley.

Decorate with the sliced egg rounds and serve immediately.

Note: Though fresh asparagus is preferable, canned or frozen asparagus may be substituted if fresh is not available.

DOGFISH WITH SAFFRON
CAZON EN AMARILLO
Andalusia

Advance preparation time: 3 hours
Preparation time: 15 minutes
Cooking time: 20 minutes
For 4 servings:
1 1/3 lb (600 g) dogfish fillets
3/4 cup (6 fl oz/18 cl) olive oil
3/4 cup (6 fl oz/18 cl) dry white wine
1 tablespoon sherry vinegar
1 bay leaf
1 sprig thyme
Salt
Freshly ground black pepper
6 tablespoons (3 fl oz/9 cl) water
3 tablespoons flour
1 large onion, peeled and sliced into rounds
10 saffron threads (see glossary)

Method:
  Place the dogfish fillets in a large shallow earthenware casserole.

  In a bowl, combine 2 tablespoons of the oil with the wine, vinegar, bay leaf, thyme, salt and pepper. Stir in the water. Pour this marinade over the fish fillets and let marinate for 3 hours, spooning the mixture over the fish from time to time.

  Remove the fish fillets from the marinade and pat dry.

  Strain and reserve the marinade. Dredge the fish with the flour.

  Heat 1/2 cup of the remaining oil in a heavy skillet. When the oil is very hot, add the fish and cook until lightly browned on both sides. Remove fillets and drain on paper towels.

  Heat the remaining 2 tablespoons oil in a Dutch oven. Add the onion and cook until it is transparent. Add the strained marinade and let reduce over medium heat for 5 minutes.

  Remove 2 tablespoons of this sauce from the pan, place in a mortar with the saffron, and crush with a pestle. Stir this mixture back into the sauce. Add the fish and let simmer over low heat for 5 minutes.

  Serve immediately.

SARDINES GRILLED ON SKEWERS
ESPETONES DE SARDINAS
Cantabria

Preparation time: 35 minutes
Cooking time: 45 minutes for potatoes,
  5 for the sardines
For 6 servings:
2 3/4 lb (1 1/4 kg) potatoes
36 fresh sardines
2/3 cup (7 oz/200 g) coarse salt

Method:
  Prepare a wood fire well in advance so that the coals become red hot.

  Wrap the potatoes in heavy-duty foil, place over the hot coals and let cook for about 45 minutes, or until tender.

  Clean and scale the fish. Thread them onto metal skewers, three sardines to a skewer. Spear the point of each skewer into the floor of the fire so that the sardines are suspended above the coals.

  Sprinkle half of the salt evenly over the sardines and let grill for 2 minutes. Turn the skewers, sprinkle with the remaining salt, and cook for 2 minutes longer.

  Serve the sardines, accompanied by the potatoes.

CATALAN FISH SOUP
SUQUET DE PESCADO
Catalonia

Preparation time: 10 minutes
Cooking time: 35 minutes
For 6 servings:
14 oz (400 g) grouper
14 oz (400 g) rascasse or scorpion-fish
6 cups (48 fl oz/1 1/2 l) fish broth
  (see glossary)
6 tablespoons (3 oz/9 cl) olive oil
3 cloves garlic, peeled
1 large onion, peeled and chopped
1 tomato, peeled and chopped
1 tablespoon chopped parsley
4 potatoes, peeled
Salt

Method:
  Ask your fishmonger to scale the fish and cut them in large pieces. Rinse and pat them dry.

  Place the fish broth in a saucepan and bring to a boil.

  Meanwhile, heat the oil in a large earthenware casserole or deep skillet. Add the garlic, onion and tomato and cook for 5 minutes. Stir in the parsley. Add the fish and stir again.

  Pour the hot fish broth over the fish, add the potatoes, and let cook for 25 minutes over medium heat. Season with salt if necessary and cook for 3 minutes longer.

  Serve immediately.

At the fish market in Arenys de Mar, boats arrive loaded with sardines that were hauled from the sea only a few hours earlier.

OVEN-BAKED RED MULLET
SALMONETES AL HORNO
Asturias

Preparation time: 15 minutes
Cooking time: 27 minutes
For 6 servings:
6 red mullets, 5 to 5 1/2 oz (150 g) each
6 tablespoons (3 fl oz/9 cl) olive oil
2 large onions, peeled and chopped
2 cloves garlic, peeled and chopped
1 1/2 tablespoons chopped parsley
3/4 cup (6 fl oz/18 cl) dry white wine
2 tablespoons dry breadcrumbs
Salt
Freshly ground pepper

Method:
   Scale, clean and thoroughly rinse the mullet. Pat dry with paper towel.
   Pour the oil over the bottom of a shallow, earthenware casserole and sprinkle with the onions, garlic, and 1 tablespoon of the parsley. Place the vegetables in a 375° F (190° C) preheated oven and cook for 15 minutes.
   Remove the casserole from the oven and remove about half of the onion, garlic and parsley. Arrange the mullet in the casserole, and cover them with the reserved onion, garlic and parsley. Add the wine and sprinkle with the breadcrumbs. Season with salt and pepper.
   Return the casserole to the oven and cook for 12 minutes longer.
   Sprinkle with the remaining chopped parsley and serve immediately.

Oven-baked red mullet (above).
Venus clams with white wine
sauce (facing page).

VENUS CLAMS WITH WHITE WINE SAUCE
COQUINAS CARIHUELA
Andalusia

Advance preparation time: 4 hours
Preparation time: 5 minutes
Cooking time: 8 minutes
For 4 servings:
1 1/3 lb (600 g) venus clams or littlenecks
2 tablespoons olive oil
1 clove garlic, peeled and chopped
3/4 cup (6 fl oz/18 cl) dry white wine
Salt

Method:
   Place the clams in a large bowl filled with cold water and soak for 4 hours to eliminate all sand. Drain and set aside.
   Heat the oil in a large heavy pan. Add the garlic and cook until lightly browned. Add the clams and wine, and season lightly with salt. Cover the pan and let simmer over very low heat for 5 minutes, shaking the pan 2 or 3 times.
   Serve in a shallow serving bowl in the cooking broth.

FISH AND SHELLFISH MIXED GRILL
PARRILLADA DE MARISCO Y PESCADO
Valencia

Preparation time: 15 minutes
Cooking time: 6 minutes
For 6 servings:
3 garlic cloves, peeled
1 tablespoon chopped parsley
3/4 cup (6 fl oz/18 cl) olive oil
6 small cuttlefish
6 large Dublin Bay prawns
6 jumbo prawns
6 large shrimp
18 medium shrimp
11 oz (300 g) grouper, cut into 6 pieces
11 oz (300 g) monkfish, cut into 6 pieces
Coarse salt

Method:
   In a large mortar, combine the garlic, parsley and 2 tablespoons of the oil, and grind to a paste with a pestle. Stir in the remaining oil and set aside until ready to use.
   Rinse and thoroughly clean the cuttlefish, removing the ink sacs. Rinse the prawns and shrimp. Split the Dublin Bay prawns lengthwise down the center and set aside, until ready to us.
   Place a metal baking sheet on a grill over very hot coals.
   Brush the cuttlefish, prawns, shrimp, and fish generously with the garlic oil. When the baking sheet is hot, spread the shellfish and fish over it in a single layer. Sprinkle lightly with the salt. Turn the small shrimp and fish after 1 minute. Turn the larger shrimp, prawns, and cuttlefish after 2 minutes. (The largest prawns may require 3 minutes per side.)
   Brush again with the oil, sprinkle with salt, and cook each piece for the corresponding length of time on the second side.
   Serve hot, accompanied by a garlic mayonnaise or an aïoli (see glossary).

EXPENSIVE TASTES

Barnacles: *Pollicipes cornucopia*, class Cirripedia, sub-order Entomostraca, and an individual belonging to the noble and ancient family of Podocipodidos, according to Linnaeus's classification.

The barnacle has a rubbery aspect and texture, and is encased in a rough outer sheath that has what looks like a plastic coating of an infinite number of minute brown scales graduating into a calcareous gray color. The tip conceals the cirri, a kind of feathery arrangement of retractile organs.

The French name for *Pollicipes* is *poussepied*; in German they are called *seepocke*, *pico* in Italian and sometimes goose barnacle or limpet in English, but it is only in Spain that they are considered a gastronomic luxury, and people are willing to pay astronomical prices for them — at least those from the rocky coast of Galicia. There are Moroccan and Canadian varieties on the market that are far less expensive, but which seemingly bear no comparison to the Galician variety. And all it tastes of is sea water with a strong taste of iodine!

Like snails, these creatures are hermaphrodites. The larvae are hatched into the sea, where wild, stormy conditions suit them best, until they eventually tire, search for a rock and cement themselves to it with an extremely strong "glue" secreted by a special gland. And there, packed together, they spend the rest of their lives, until someone comes along and removes them.

Barnacles tend to attach themselves to rocks that are endlessly buffeted by violent seas, and gathering them is a perilous business that results in deaths every year. Sometimes the *percebeiros*, or barnacle-collectors, slide down the tall cliffs attached to a rope while the tide is out. The dangerous part comes when the tide rises, and unless great care is taken — and often despite all precautions — the waves can smash the *percebeiro* against the rocks. Because of the tremendous demand for these delicacies, they are becoming increasingly scarce and have to be fetched from more and more difficult places.

They are torn off the crags with a mace-like instrument called a *ferrada*, which resembles a long-handled rake with a triangular piece of iron on the end, and the limpets are scraped from the rock into a container. That is how it used to be, at least. Now that there are fewer and fewer barnacles, they must be fetched from deep waters, and the specialists use diving equipment. However, this technique tends to damage the rocks, because the divers use instruments that scrape the surface smooth. In addition, divers take small barnacles too young to have hatched their larvae into the sea. There is a regulated season (1 May to 30 September), but not everyone respects it, and *percebes* are being threatened with extinction along the Galician coast.

The best time for eating *percebes* is the month of April.

It is easy to prepare them. Bring some water to the boil, with salt and a bay leaf or two, then throw in the barnacles and cook them on high heat for five minutes. Remove from the water immediately and drain well. Serve on a tray or a large platter and cover with a white cloth to prevent the steam and flavor from escaping.

Eating them requires a certain amount of skill, for they sometimes squirt a reddish liquid that can stain. The technique is to take them by the tip with the left hand and, with the right hand, break the skin covering the peduncle, just at the base of the tip. The meat can then be carefully drawn upward until it slips free. The inside of the tip can also be eaten.

*The Hispania restaurant at
Arenys de Mar north of Barcelona
is famous all over the world.
The sisters Dolores and Paquita
Reixach and their families watch
over the cuisine and the diners
with impressive savoir-faire.
Cañaillas, or sea snails, are eaten
either as a first course or with
aperitifs. Cooked in salted or sea
water and served with a romescu,
aïoli, or vinaigrette sauce, they
often accompany a Fino wine
from Jerez, dry white wine or beer
(facing).*

Professional cooks with creative aspirations have tried many other ways of preparing *percebes*, with little success.

In the old days, even at the beginning of this century, people turned up their noses at barnacles; they were very cheap to buy, and only eaten locally where they were gathered. The fishermen's wives sold them cooked and ready to eat in the street, like hot chestnuts, in wooden bowls covered with a cloth. However, they never made their way to the big cities, where nowadays they are as sought-after as gold and cost as much as caviar.

Angula is baby eel, the leptocephalus, or first larva of eels. It is transparent, with a ribbon-like shape about two inches long. It turns white or white with a grayish-black streak along the back when cooked, or when it reaches adult stage.

They are usually caught in winter, at the mouths of rivers, estuaries and inlets along the Atlantic coast, the Bay of Biscay, and the delta of the Ebro — wherever the eels come to spawn.

Some years the catch is abundant, others less so. In either case, baby eels fetch scandalous prices, especially around Christmas.

The technique used to catch them is simple. A bucket is lowered to the bottom of river beds where they are known to gather,

and a thick mass of mud teeming with larvae is drawn up.

The baby eels must be rinsed several times to release them from the sticky mud before they can be killed. Traditionally, the latter process is done with a decoction of tobacco, made by boiling two to three and one-half ounces of tobacco fiber, or tobacco in any other form, in water. When it comes to the boil the tobacco is removed and the bag wrung to extract the juice. The liquid is left to cool and then poured onto the live eels in another recipient. They die very quickly.

Live baby eels are rarely found on the market — they are usually sold boiled or steamed.

There are a limited number of ways of preparing them. The most common method is *a la bilbaina* (Bilbao style), which consists of frying them in a small earthenware pot, in which they will afterward be served, with a little garlic and fried hot peppers. A more modern recipe is baby eels in a salad with oil, lemon juice and finely chopped garlic or onion. And, although this is debatable, they can also be prepared with avocado, endive or lettuce, in a filling for tomatoes, and in other fantasies of dilettante amateur cooks. I was even once served baby eels with pomegranate seeds.

When, for whatever reason, a product reaches the category of luxury fare, the only form in which it should be eaten is the one that brought it such popularity in the first place. This is the case with caviar and *percebes*, for example, and no one has yet invented a better way of preparing baby eels than fried in their little pot with garlic and hot peppers. Or cold, on their own, in a salad with a light sauce. The Harza restaurant in Pamplona prepares them very well this way.

In northern Spain, especially in the Basque region, a dish of baby eels is an absolute prerequisite for Christmas and New Year's Eve dinner. This is when their price is highest, and anyone who cares about maintaining social status, gastronomically speaking, must be ready for great financial

Expensive and highly prized seafood does not always reach the markets — it is often bought directly from the fishermen by restaurant owners. The famous restaurant La Dorada, located in Seville, Madrid, Barcelona and Paris, even has its own trawlers.

slightly before going into the pot, which can then contain considerably less oil. They are served as an hors d'œuvre.

Another culinary luxury that originated in the Basque country and has spread throughout Spain is hake *kokotxas*. *Kokotxa* is a Basque word that has been adopted by Spaniards in general, and, as mentioned earlier, it denotes the gelatinous triangular muscle that all fish have in the lower part of the jaw. It is considered particularly meaty and delicious in hake.

It is removed at sea as soon as the hake is caught, and sold separately from the rest of the fish — at a very high price, of course.

Less expensive, though also much appreciated, are the *kokotxas* and cheeks of salted cod.

Those from hake, however, are considered incomparably delicious. They are prepared essentially in two ways: in individual dishes, with a good *salsa verda*, or dipped in batter and sautéed.

They can also be served *pil-pil* style, but the garlic tends to overpower the subtlety of the fish. Like the baby eels, *kokotxas* are served as hors d'œuvre, and because of their gelatinous quality they should be eaten very hot.

sacrifice. The eels are traditionally presented in the earthenware pot they were cooked in, with its lid on, still boiling in their oil. The diner (or if it is in a restaurant, the waiter) lifts off the lid and stirs the eels with a small fork made of wood. In one of the many gastronomic associations in the Basque region, a recipe was recently invented that avoided the use of so much oil: the baby eels are wrapped in a linen cloth and steam-heated

The sea cucumber is a strange delicacy Catalans love to eat, whatever the price. It is commonly known as *espardenya* (espadrille) or *llonguet* because of its resemblance to the underside of a rope-soled shoe or to that type of small loaf. Its exterior consists of a long, slightly cylindrical cartilage of a white-blotched tawny color, surrounded by three rows of tubular feet in perpetual motion. The edible part is inside, and must be extracted with a knife or clam shell. This creature lives in deep waters and is snared with a trawl net. Nature has protected its delicate flesh by armoring it with a kind of tank that looks as though it could have been designed by Leonardo da Vinci.

The sea cucumber has a smooth, tangy sea flavor and is eaten grilled, with garlic, parsley and lemon juice, stewed with tomato sauce, with a sauce made of white wine and onions, or in a casserole with potatoes.

This Mediterranean creature, too, was disdained as inedible for centuries before it became the highly appreciated delicacy it is today. It is also abundant in the Andalusian area of the Atlantic, but nobody eats it there, whereas in the Mediterranean the demand is so high that the sea cucumber is thinning out to the point of extinction.

The sea also enriches Spain with products providing exquisite cold appetizers that are outside the budget of ordinary mortals, dishes such as *mojamas*, cured roe and salted, smoked or brine-cured fish from the Mediterranean, especially near Murcia.

Mojama is dried and salted tuna — the maritime equivalent of cured meat, in fact. A late nineteenth-century Spanish gastronomical dictionary defined it as "common, thirst-provoking food sold in the streets by vendors of pine nuts, almonds, etc." It has followed a similar pattern to that of *percebes* and *espardenya*: in 1992 *mojama* has become very expensive as well as difficult to find. No longer is it sold on the street, although it is still salty, and still provokes a thirst.

The liking for salty tastes has existed since time immemorial. Salt, it will be remembered, was an important element in an-

DWARF OCTOPUS

A fondness for sea creatures' fledgling populations is one of the more curious characteristics of Spanish cuisine. *Angula* is baby eel; *chanquete* is the young of whitebait, and its substitute is the young of any other type of fish; but the most amazing feature of this exotic and expensive tendency is surely the unbridled enthusiasm for the minute offspring of cuttlefish, squid and octopus.

The high season for amassing baby octopus is the end of winter and the beginning of spring. Before it begins, the female cuttlefish are caught in the Mediterranean just after they have spawned, which is when their white flesh is at its most tender and delicious. They should be tried cooked with potatoes at the Hispania restaurant in Arenys de Mar, a monument of Catalan cuisine.

The greatest preparation for the minute cuttlefish, the *chipirones*, or for dwarf octopus, is "in their ink," a recipe of Basque origin. The small octopus or baby cuttlefish are caught with hooks — a job requiring much time and infinite patience, and that can be accomplished only by very experienced fishermen. The sybaritism of wealthy Spanish gourmets is all that enables these incredibly patient fishermen to make a living at this job. An enormous quantity of baby cuttlefish are also caught in summer in the Galician Rías Bajas.

Dwarf octopus is really more of a Mediterranean creature. It is sautéed in olive oil with finely chopped garlic and parsley. This is the simplest, most traditional way of preparing it, but it is also greatly appreciated cooked with young broad beans, peas or white beans.

The recipe of the El Peixerot restaurant mentioned earlier is an ideal method as well: the baby octopus is cooked with potatoes and served in an earthenware terrine napped with an *aioli*.

cient barter economies and in the tax sytems imposed by European monarchies. Between the thirteenth and fifteenth centuries La Mata, in Murcia, was the principal Mediterranean salt-exporting center, and alongside this activity was a thriving salt-curing industry that dated from much earlier days.

At Raimundo Gonzalez's El Rincón de Pepe in Murcia, one of the best restaurants in Spain, a menu of biblical proportions features a wonderful selection of dried salt tuna and fish eggs. There are few things that accompany a glass of Fino sherry better than the almost transparently thin ruby slices of the finest *mojama* or the orange-colored eggs of red porgy, hake or mullet.

SEA LAMPREY A LA GALLEGA
LAMPREA A LA GALLEGA
Galicia

Preparation time: 30 minutes
Cooking time: 45 minutes
For 4 servings:
8 cups (64 fl oz/2 l) water
2 sea lampreys, about 1 3/4 lb (750 g) each
3/4 cup (6 fl oz/18 cl) olive oil
3 cloves garlic, peeled and minced
2 bay leaves
5 oz (150 g) Serrano ham, finely chopped
1 large onion, peeled and chopped
2 tomatoes, peeled and chopped
3/4 cup (6 fl oz/18 cl) red wine
7 slices (7 oz/200 g) bread, fried or toasted
1 teaspoon mustard
Salt

Method:
  Fill a large saucepan with the water and bring to a boil. Drop the lamprey into the boiling water and let cook for a few seconds.
  Drain the lamprey. When cool enough to handle, carefully scrape the skin. Hold the lamprey over a bowl and cut off their heads, letting the blood drain into the bowl. Then gut and clean the lamprey, removing the central nerves. Rinse and dry thoroughly, cut into 1 1/2 to 2-inch (3 to 4 cm) pieces and place them in the bowl with the blood.
  Heat the oil in an earthenware casserole or Dutch oven. Add the garlic, bay leaves and ham, and cook, stirring, for about 2 minutes. Add the onion and cook until it begins to brown. Add the tomatoes and cook over low heat for 5 minutes. Stir in the wine. Remove crusts and crumble the bread into the pan, and continue to cook for 5 minutes.
  Stir in the lamprey pieces and the blood. When the mixture begins to simmer, stir in the mustard and season with salt. Cook over medium heat for 25 minutes.
  Serve immediately, accompanied by white rice and fried bread croutons.

WHITEBAIT A LA MALAGUENA
CHANQUETES A LA MALAGUEÑA
Andalusia

Preparation time: 10 minutes
Cooking time: 6 minutes
For 4 servings:
1 lb (500 g) whitebait or fresh baby anchovies
1 1/4 cups (150 g) flour
3 cups (24 fl oz/75 cl) oil

Method:
  Carefully rinse and pat dry the fish.
  Place them in a colander. Sprinkle with the flour, coating the whitebait on all sides. Shake off excess flour.
  Heat the oil in a deep skillet. When the oil is very hot, add 1/3 or 1/4 of the fish and fry, turning gently, until lightly browned. Remove with a slotted spoon, drain, and keep warm. Fry the remaining whitebait in batches until all are cooked.
  Serve immediately, accompanied by a tomato, onion and bell pepper salad.

BABY EEL IN GARLIC SAUCE
ANGULAS A LA BILBAINA
Basque Country

Preparation time: 5 minutes
Cooking time: 30 seconds
For 4 servings:
1/2 cup (4 fl oz/12 cl) olive oil
4 cloves garlic, peeled and halved
1 hot red pepper, quartered
1 lb (500 g) baby eels

Method:
  Place 4 individual earthenware casseroles (about 5 inches/12 cm in diameter) over medium heat.
  Place 2 tablespoons of the oil in each casserole. When the oil is hot, add 2 halves of garlic and a piece of hot pepper to each casserole and cook until lightly browned and sizzling.
  Divide the baby eels equally among the 4 casseroles and cook briefly (about 1/2 minute), turning with a wooden spoon to coat the eels with the oil.
  Serve immediately.

SALTED MULLET ROE TORREVIEJA
HUEVAS DE MUJOL TORREVIEJA
Murcia

Preparation time: 10 minutes
Refrigeration: 30 minutes
For 4 servings:
2 very ripe tomatoes
8 thin slices fine white bread
6 tablespoons (34 fl oz/9 cl) olive oil
7 oz (200 g) salted grey mullet roe or tarama

Method:
  Cut the tomatoes in rings and arrange on the bread slices. Drizzle a little olive oil over the tomato.
  If the roe is intact, slice it very thinly and place on top of the tomato rings. If using roe from a jar, use a butter knife to spread a layer over the tomatoes.
  Place in the refrigerator and chill for 30 minutes before serving.

SAUTÉED BABY OCTOPUS
PULPITOS ENCEBOLLADOS
Catalonia

Preparation time: 10 minutes
Cooking time: 10 minutes
For 4 servings:
1 lb (500 g) baby octopus
1/4 cup (2 fl oz/6 cl) olive oil
1/2 onion, peeled and chopped
1 clove garlic, peeled and chopped
1 tablespoon chopped parsley
Salt

Method:
  Wash the octopus in cold water.
  Heat the oil in a skillet. Add the onion, garlic, and parsley and cook, stirring, until they begin to brown. Add the octopus. Season with salt and cook, turning, for about 3 minutes.
  Serve immediately.

Baby eel in garlic sauce (facing page).

A
MAN'S
WORLD

ROASTING
IS A MAN'S JOB

La Mesón Cuevas del Vino,
housed in a former oil mill in
Chinchón (Castile), is renowned
for its lamb and roasted kid.
Chops are served by the dozen,
generally grilled at the client's
table on small, elegant braziers
typical of Spanish grill restaurants
(above and at right).
The lamb is placed in the oven
in an earthenware dish partially
filled with water, which helps
degrease the lamb and preserve
the tenderness of its meat (facing).

Charles Lamb, who was a close friend of Samuel Taylor Coleridge, would have enjoyed Old Castile immensely if he had ever crossed the channel to visit Spain, as did so many of his compatriots in the nineteenth century.

Lamb was one of the most illustrious and subtle of British prose writers, and the author of a rare little work on roast suckling pig. In this essay he calls suckling pig *princeps obsoniorum*, the prince of victuals, and declares quite correctly that the charming progeny of the pig should only be eaten roasted.

Roast suckling pig and baby lamb have brought worldwide fame to the province of Segovia, but the whole of Castile practices this art with the timeless enthusiasm of amateur and professional roasters, or *asadores*. It has even given rise to rituals of a touristic rather than a gastronomical nature, such as those enacted in the spectacular Mesón de Cándido at the foot of the magnificent Roman viaduct in Segovia. The suckling pig is presented to the public, and the master-*asador* quarters it with a plate instead of a knife, as a demonstration of his affection for the beast. The master-*asador*'s chest is covered with so many medals and adornments that he looks like a Soviet general. Personal-

ly, I find the custom irreverent and unworthy of the infinite delicacy of the pig, which should be treated with the utmost loving care, not hacked about with a piece of crockery.

The annual sacrifice of roast suckling pig and lamb is an impressive sight. In towns like Sepulveda in Segovia, Aranda de Duero in Burgos and Peñafiel in Valladolid, a main source of wealth comes from the roasting establishments where crowds of people gather every weekend to devour roast suckling pig and baby lamb served with a simple lettuce salad. The fragrance of the roasting meat, which is one of the most mouthwatering smells on earth, fills the streets and squares, and mounds of stripped white bones pile up on the tables. Golden-crusted white bread is soaked in the luscious drippings, and wines from local vineyards are the ideal accompaniment to these friendly, family-style roasts.

Suckling pig should be the color of old gold, crispy on the outside, pinkish-white inside, and the meat should melt in the mouth. Lamb, preferably from a *churra* ewe, should be absolutely tender and have a lingering aftertaste of the aromatic herbs that flavored the mother's milk.

Obviously, as Confucius himself said, roasting came long before stewing in our culinary evolution. Writers of culinary treatises — including Brillat-Savarin — have claimed that "a roaster is born; a cook is made."

In Castile roasting is done in the oven, and the quality of the oven has an enormous effect on the final result. The meat, usually lamb, is put in the oven on long earthenware plates with a little water in them. The animal is placed on a rack or in such a way that it is above the water without touching

it. Thus the fat runs straight off the meat during the roasting process, while the steam rising off the water tenderizes the meat.

A sure hand, a keen eye and a sensitive nose are prerequisites in a good *asador*. The suckling pig or the lamb must be taken out of the oven at the exact point when it is cooked to perfection. According to Spanish taste, this point is when the meat is no longer raw but not overly cooked. People won't touch the meat if it is even slightly bloody, and if it is overdone it is rubbery and stringy.

Experience and intuition are other requirements. Traditionally, a man presides over the oven. This should not be viewed as anti-feminist, however. Roasting hundred of piglets and lambs is a physically demanding job, and a great deal of strength is required to re-move dish after dish of heavy earthenware from the oven.

The lamb- and pig-roasting *tostón* is an upright freestanding Castilian oven made of roofing or adobe bricks — never firebricks, which produce heat far too quickly and strongly — with a floor made of tiles on sand. The best firewood to use is ash, pine-tree branches or broom.

There are hundreds of *asadores* in Cas-tile, and enthusiasts never tire of discussing who is the best. Travelers will not be disap-pointed if they stop at the Virrey Palafox res-taurant in Burgo de Osma (Soria) for the suckling pig and the Mesón de la Villa in Aranda de Duero for roast lamb. *Asadores* from Aranda also prepare it wonderfully at the Mesón de Aranda in Barcelona.

However, as I mentioned in an earlier chapter, the person who brought suckling pig to glory was Cándido López. He is now retired, but his gastronomic titles and deco-rations rival those of the haughtiest Grandee of Spain: *Mesonero Mayor de Castilla* (Head Innkeeper of Castile), *Maestro Asador de la Chaîne des Rôtisseurs* (Master Roaster of the Roasters' Guild), *Consejero Culinario de la Cadena de Asadores por el Baílio de España* (Culinary Adviser to the Spanish Roasters' Guild), *Miembro Corresponsal Perpétuo de la Academia gastronómica Brillat Savarin* (Lifetime Member and Correspondent of the Brillat Savarin Gastronomic Academy), *Tastevin d'Honneur de la Gastronomie Lyonnaise* (Honorary Member of the Lyon Gastronomic Society), *Académico de la Academia Tastevins de Saint Humbert* (Member of Saint Humbert Academy of Wine Tasters), *Caballero de la Orden de Isabel la Católica* (Knight of the Order of Isabella the Catholic), *Medalla de la Orden de Malta* (Medal of the Order of Malta), et cetera.

Cándido won fame for his suckling pigs by following the method of a French adventurer-cook named Jean Botin, who fled France to find refuge in Madrid in the early seventeenth century. Botin established an eating-house where he served roast suckling pig and lamb. His Hostería Botin still exists today, a historic building next to the Arco de Cuchilleros, and is an obligatory halt in tourist visits to the Spanish capital. The suckling pig and the lamb are still excellent.

True lovers of roast lamb keep the head for themselves. It is usually roasted whole, but sometimes cut in two. The head is fairly well cooked, and the cheeks, neck, brains and tongue are delicate morsels to be extracted slowly and gently from the bones. Some people like to eat the head with no dressing at all, while others prefer it with a vinaigrette containing lots of olive oil, garlic, and oregano or marjoram or another aromatic herb. This is very much shepherds' food, and really very delicious, however uninviting a roast head of lamb might appear to the eye.

Everyday fare is generally reasonably priced food, especially in countries where means are limited. Everything has to be made use of, and prepared as flavorfully as possible. Animals' heads are scorned by the wealthy, but those of lesser means know that they contain delectable meat. Perhaps some of the poor feel that this is the part allocated to them by society. I shall never forget an experience I once had in the butcher's shop of a modest village in a sheep-farming area of Guadalajara.

I was returning to Madrid by car. It was a Saturday and there was nothing at home

for dinner, so I stopped to buy some lamb, which is of excellent quality in that region. It was customary there to sell lamb at a single price, whatever the cut desired — in other words, leg of lamb cost the same as neck or ribs.

An old lady in front of me asked for the head and neck. I asked her why she didn't take a piece of leg or chops, or shoulder, since it was all the same price, and she answered in a strangely resigned way that these parts of the animal were for rich people, and she was poor! Buying the cuts supposedly destined for the rich would have meant stepping out of her social class, which for her must have been unimaginable.

In Mediterranean cuisine a roast is a symbol of wealth and power, and is usually undertaken for a banquet, a celebration, or to impress. It almost seems to be an echo of the great medieval feasts in which whole roast cows were set before the guests. Even today, tourists in Spain are often given a "medieval-style" barbecue in doubtful taste and of worse quality.

But for rich and poor alike, it is still a typical weekend activity to go a few miles in a group by car and crowd into the inns and rotisseries of Castile in search of roast lamb or suckling pig.

The atmosphere and landscape of the Ribera del Duero provide a perfect setting for this kind of feast. The gently undulating valley with its great monasteries, its vineyards, and the Ribera wine itself all seem to have been intentionally created as a backdrop for the roasting ovens.

The practice of moving flocks to greener pastures, which often necessitates a lengthy walk, continues in Spain (below and facing).
In this unusual dining room in Chinchón, where wine is kept in huge earthenware jars, clients can order crisp, roasted lamb, a Castilian specialty (following double page).

FELICIDAD
LARGA VIDA
Mª LUISA
PACO LLATJOS
MARZO 1974
Stephen.
8/8/70
25-VI-69
IRLANDA
Exmo Sr. Embajador
CHINCHON QUE
ES MI PUEBLO!
Nuestro rec
es Co
Un homenaje
Buen pueblo Chinchón
lo mejor el Mesón
Manuel Vidrie
Rosalyn S. Yalow
Nobel Laureate 1977

OVER THE COALS

Some people think that the patron saint of Spanish cuisine should be Saint Theresa, because of her declaration that "God walks among the stewpots."

Others of us perhaps more accurately feel that if there must be a patron saint at all it should be Saint Lawrence, who is venerated in El Escorial, and whose martyrdom consisted of being roasted alive on a gridiron. He is said to have remarked to his torturers, "I am cooked on that side; turn me over." The author of such a delicate and considerate utterance obviously deserves to be revered by food-lovers everywhere, and Herrera, the architect who designed the famous San Lorenzo Monastery in the Sierra de Guadarrama, paid him homage by reproducing the structure of the gridiron in the plans of the church.

As the Spaniards conquered and colonized America, from Patagonia to Florida they discovered various techniques for roasting meat and fish — and vegetables as well — over a fire. Of course, this is the time-tested method for cooking food and they were already familiar with it, but the particular techniques of roasting-spits and racks were new to them.

Spits were used for large cuts of meat or carcasses, and racks over the fire for the smaller pieces. Of primary importance in both cases, though especially the latter, was the art of producing red-hot embers from the wood or charcoal and keeping them glowing constantly.

The Spanish are very fond of food grilled over wood embers or coals. A good gridiron is a utensil found in most household kitchens in Spain, although there is a tendency to replace them with barbecues — which was another of the techniques, of course, that the Spaniards learned in the Caribbean.

Grills are among the most popular eating establishments throughout the North, from Basque Country to Galicia. The more popular food for grilling is veal chops, rib of beef, and red sea bream. Lamb chops are more popular in Castile, Catalonia, and Valencia, and in the Balearic Islands, lamb and fish. In these regions the grilled dish is called a *parrillada,* and is a favorite attraction during the summer invasion of tourists.

In Galicia the enthusiasm for grills has its roots in ancient traditions and in the culinary exchanges brought about by the reciprocal migrations between Galicia and Latin American countries, especially Argentina and Uruguay. This type of cuisine is even now commonly known by the Argentinian name of *churrasco.*

Some roasting specialists acquire formidable reputations. "Rekondo," from San Sebastián in Guipúzcoa, is the undisputed master of grilled yearling lamb and veal chops.

To the Spanish palate the most delicious meat is veal from a calf that has already been fed on grass; in other words when it is just over a year old and the meat is red. White veal, which the French and the Italians prefer, has never had much impact on Spanish cuisine.

The best cattle for the Spanish type of veal come from Gerona, Avila, Galicia and Navarre.

Particularly in the Mediterranean, grilled meat and fish are often seasoned with herbs, especially thyme or rosemary, or accompanied by a sauce called *romescu.* Elsewhere they are preferred on their own or with hot peppers in vinegar. As a rule, the Spaniards are not keen on mustard, although early collections of recipes, particularly from the sixteenth and seventeenth centuries, do include several ways of preparing it.

In the Mediterranean *aioli* is the favorite sauce to accompany fish and snails, as well as one of the most popular dishes, *conill a l'ast,* which is spit-roasted rabbit. Nowadays, unfortunately, *conill a l'ast* is rarely cooked over red-hot coals, but almost invariably in a dreadful electrical appliance.

Experience and intuition are the two qualities demanded of a good Castilian grill chef (facing).

VEAL ROAST BRAISED WITH THYME
TERNERA ASADA AL TOMILLO
Castile-León

Preparation time: 30 minutes
Marinating time: 2 hours
Cooking time: 50 minutes
For 8 servings:
2 1/4 lb (1 kg) boneless veal roast
Salt
Freshly ground black pepper
3 1/2 oz (100 g) fresh pork fat or bacon, thinly sliced
1 tablespoon lard
6 tablespoons (3 fl oz/9 cl) olive oil
3/4 cup (6 fl oz/18 cl) dry white wine
Several sprigs fresh thyme
1 teaspoon cornstarch

Method:

Season the roast on all sides with salt and pepper. Wrap the fat or bacon slices around the roast and tie in place securely with kitchen string.

In a large Dutch oven, heat the lard and olive oil together over medium heat. Add the veal and cook over high heat until browned on all sides. Remove the pan from the heat and add the wine. Crumble the thyme evenly over the roast and set aside to marinate for about 2 hours.

Place in a preheated 450° F (230° C) oven and cook for 40 minutes.

Remove from the oven, set the veal aside to rest and let the cooking juices cool slightly in the pan before preparing the sauce. Dilute the cornstarch with a little cold water, then stir it into the pan juices. Warm over low heat, stirring, until the sauce thickens.

Carve the roast into thin slices and serve hot with the sauce.

Oven-roasted baby goat (facing page).

SEGOVIAN SUCKLING PIG
COCHINILLO A LA SEGOVIANA
Castile-León

Preparation time: 10 minutes
Cooking time: 1 hour 20 minutes
For 6 servings:
1 baby pig, about 7 3/4 lb (3 1/2 kg), cleaned
Salt
4 bay leaves
1 cup (8 fl oz/25 cl) water
3 1/2 oz (100 g) lard
5 cloves garlic, peeled and chopped

Method:

Ask your butcher to clean and prepare the pig, splitting it open along the ribs, leaving backbone and head intact and flattening it slightly, butterfly fashion. Sprinkle both sides with salt.

Place the bay leaves in a shallow earthenware casserole or baking pan large enough to hold the pig. Place the pig, skin side down, on the bay leaves in the casserole. Pour the water over it and cook in a preheated 400° F (200° C) oven for 1 hour.

Meanwhile, melt the lard in a small pan.

Turn the pig skin side up, brush with the melted lard and sprinkle with the garlic. If the meat seems dry, add a little more water to the pan before returning it to the oven to cook for 30 minutes longer.

When cooked, the pig should be crisp and a deep golden brown. Remove from the oven and present whole at the table. Carve and serve hot.

LAMB SEPULVEDA
CORDERO AL ESTILO DE SEPULVEDA
Castile-León

Preparation time: 10 minutes
Cooking time: 1 hour 45 minutes
For 6 servings:
1/2 small lamb, about 6 3/4 lb (3 kg)
Salt
1 1/4 cups (10 fl oz/30 cl) water
1 tablespoon lard

Method:

Ask your butcher to clean the lamb and cut it into two pieces. (If you can't find a lamb half, ask for 2 quarters.) Season the lamb on all sides with salt.

Place the water in a large shallow earthenware casserole or baking pan and add the lamb quarters, skin sides down. Place in a preheated 350° F (175° C) oven and cook for 1 hour.

Melt the lard in a small pan. After 1 hour of cooking, turn the lamb quarters, brush them with the lard, and cook for 45 minutes longer.

Serve hot, accompanied by a green salad.

OVEN-ROASTED BABY GOAT
CABRITO AL HORNO
Castile-La Mancha

Preparation time: 10 minutes
Cooking time: 1 hour 25 minutes
For 6 servings:
1/2 young goat, about 6 3/4 lb (3 kg)
1 garlic clove, peeled
Salt
3/4 cup (6 fl oz/18 cl) water
2 bay leaves
1/2 teaspoon oregano
3 tablespoons lard
3/4 cup (6 fl oz/18 cl) dry white wine

Method:

Ask your butcher to clean and quarter the goat. Halve the garlic clove and rub the cut sides thoroughly over the meat. Season with salt.

Place the water, bay leaves, and oregano in a large shallow earthenware casserole or baking dish. Add the goat pieces and cook in a preheated 375° F (190° C) oven for 45 minutes.

Melt the lard in a small saucepan. Remove the goat from the oven, turn the pieces and brush them with the melted lard. Add the wine and return the meat to the oven to cook 40 minutes longer.

Serve the meat hot, accompanied by fried potatoes and salad.

A MAN'S WORLD: BASQUE GASTRONOMIC SOCIETIES

Showing his pride in belonging to the Gaztelubide Society by wearing one of its aprons, this cook is ready to create Basque delicacies (above).
The Basque gastronomic societies, which render homage to the region's cuisine, accept only male members. Each society even has its own choir, and some are excellent. Nevertheless, humor is the main ingredient in the repertory of Basque songs (right and facing).

S peaking in relative terms — taking account of the area's size and population, that is — the autonomous community of Euskadi, the Basque region, must have more cooks per square yard than anywhere else on earth.

Some of them are professionals, but the vast majority are not. The Basque culinary trade union includes at least a dozen immensely talented cooks who are among the most respected in Europe. Amateur enthusiasts, who are members of a wide range of gastronomic societies, display their art — and at times their genius — in both traditional cuisine and with inventions that sometimes find their way to the menus of elite restaurants. The Basques are people who truly love to cook.

The phenomenon of gastronomic societies in the Basque region is unique in the world, and can only be understood if the history, idiosyncracies, and character of the people are taken into account. Basques say, correctly, that cooking is an absolutely essential part of their culture. It is an organic, communal activity that transcends class barriers and in which everyone participates — everyone, that is, except women.

Gastronomic societies are open only to men. Some associations have in recent times and on special occasions admitted women, and some women — though this is exceptional — have gotten together and founded women's culinary societies. These tend to be rather ephemeral, however.

This kind of exclusion has led some people to accuse the Basques of being macho and misogynist. In fact, Basques are no more macho or misogynist than anyone else, and they believe the accusations against them are a passing annoyance of modern ideology.

They simply enjoy spending a fraternal two or three hours a day at table in the company of other men.

These gastronomic societies were suppressed during the Franco era, though not because of their rigid entry policies. They were meeting places for Basques, and were therefore suspected of being hotbeds of nationalistic, anti-Franco activities. The Basques, however, discovered a way to keep them going legally by adding to their statutes a clause that necessitated getting together for a reason other than cooking and eating. It was therefore decided that the members would meet in order to organize and sponsor a sporting or cultural event that would take place once or twice a year. Somehow, this allayed the fears of the authorities, and so it was that bicycle races, fishing boat regattas and choral recitals enabled these societies to continue.

Paradoxically, this also cemented the societies even more solidly in the Basque social fabric.

A fairly typical meeting place for a society is a large (sometimes huge) room containing tables and benches, and decorated in characteristic Basque style. It is often adorned with antique Basque cooking utensils or sporting items, and artwork depicting regional customs or Basque symbols such as *laburus* and *ikurrinas*. At the end of the room is usually a kitchen fitted with the best equipment available: the finest ovens, pots and pans and utensils. The cooks work in full view of the members.

The society is administered by a board of directors financed by subscriptions. Each member of the board has a specific function: one keeps the cellar stocked with wine, cider, beer and liqueurs, another maintains the culinary equipment, another takes care of raw materials such as oil, salt, sugar, spices, seasonings, flour, and bread, while another handles day-to-day purchases according to market availability, and yet another deals with the accounts. Board members are elected by vote, and mini-campaigns are waged regularly. The presidency of a major society

is an office that carries considerable influence in a Basque city or town.

On the culinary front, the societies function in two ways: either they have an amateur cooking enthusiast who receives some payment or other for preparing a single dish for the assembly each day, or a member of the society buys whatever produce he needs to cook for a small group of member-friends.

The societies' cuisine is outstanding for the quality of its raw materials, and generally the associations are well managed. There are always members from the coast or the countryside who can procure excellent fish, vegetables, meat and fruit at extremely reasonable prices.

Basque cooking is down-to-earth, fairly unelaborate, and tends toward "winter" dishes, and the Basques are endowed with solid appetites. In the gastronomic societies the amateur cooks honor local cuisine, but this does not prevent them from indulging in sporadic incursions into non-Basque culinary territory, or deter them from inventing and experimenting.

José Castillo was a great Basque chef who established the Hostal Castillo in Beasain, and his son upholds his father's tradition in the Nicolasa in San Sebastián.

Fishing members of gastronomic societies sometimes contribute part of their catch, an occasion for some memorable dishes (following double page).

139

This attentive cook does not belong to a gastronomic society. A Benedictine monk, he is preparing a pan of migas for the vegetarian community of a monastery in Murcia (above).
This small village is in the heart of the Basque mountains, home of famous smoked cheeses (facing).

of things. Flour and cornflour are virtually absent from sauces, which are thickened and reduced through long slow cooking. By the same token, it resembles home-style cooking in that the cook has no compunction about using tinned products such as peas, green beans, asparagus, and artichokes, and humble sardines are cooked with the same attention and pleasure as the finest, most expensive hake.

The damp climate, the mountains, the rough sea, the rugged and peculiar sports of pelota, rock-lifting, rock-hauling with yoked oxen, fishing boat regattas, and rope-pulling, and many other aspects of life in this region, have all influenced the Basque cuisine, which is learned in childhood in family kitchens.

One of the strangest sports, and one that has no connection whatsoever with gastronomy, is eating competitions. Contestants can attain mythical heights as champions of boiled egg consumption or black pudding competitions, or whatever the particular challenge might be — in any case, a challenge to sensible eating and health. These fabulous, robust *tripasais* (gluttons) turn eating into a sport, like any display of unusual strength or physical ability in the Basque Country.

Castillo the elder traveled throughout the Basque region compiling hundreds of recipes, and published a great many books. One of them, *Recetas de 200 cocineros vascos* (Recipes from 200 Basque cooks), is of particular interest to scholars, cooking enthusiasts and dedicated eaters in general.

The societies' recipes are usually simple, rarely requiring more than five ingredients or any seasonings alien to Basque cuisine. There is absolute respect for the natural taste

TXOKOS, COFRADIAS AND BARZOKIS

In addition to the Basque gastronomic societies, there are parallel organizations called *txokos* (literally, "corners") and *cofradías*.

Txokos, of which the greatest number are in Viscaya, are groups of friends who meet to prepare and eat lunches and dinners together. They are totally informal, have no statutes, and no restrictions regarding the admittance of women. However, as the name suggests, these are intimate gatherings reserved for close friends, those with whom the host or hosts has the greatest affinities. There is a kitchen, a bar, a small storage area and a battery of kitchen utensils, as well as tables and chairs. Regular visitors to the *txokos* usually bring food or wine to share, or make a gift of their culinary talent in preparing the meal.

The *cofradías* sometimes group Basque gastronomic clubs from both the French and Spanish side of the border, and are usually more up-to-date than the societies

or the *txokos*. They have a proper structure and statutes, and are founded on the belief that cooking is a cultural affair.

The members of the *cofradías* do not always cook their meals themselves, although they have everything necessary for doing so on the premises. They pay a professional or invite a local or foreign cook to come and prepare dishes or whole menus, which are then commented on in the minutest detail. The *cofradías* are really more like associations of expert gastronomes.

Many of the *cofradías* are focused exclusively on a dish or a product characteristic of their locale, so that we find the Black Pudding Confraternity in Beasain (Guipúzcoa) and the Confraternity of the Knights of the Baby Eel in Hendaye (Atlantic Pyrenees), the Confrérie Ardi Gasna — named after a sheep's cheese — in Saint-Jean-Pied-de-Port (Atlantic Pyrenees) side by side with the European Wine

and Liqueurs Confraternity, whose headquarters are in Bilbao, and the Confrérie de la Garbure Angloye, from Anglet, France. These and other *cofradías* all belong to the Federación de Cofradías Gastronómicas, whose headquarters are in San Sebastián.

Does anyone know of another country in the world whose political parties' headquarters are located on the same premises as a public restaurant? This is the case in the Basque Country. *Batzokis*, or political party premises, all have a restaurant open to the public, where anyone can go and have a decent, inexpensive meal.

Of course, this is a means of contributing to the respective political parties (the Basque Nationalist Party is the greatest upholder of the custom), but it is also a forum for political meetings on a day-to-day basis. The cooking, which is simple and homely, is usually done on a volunteer basis or in return for some small remuneration by seasoned party members with years of social and political struggles under their belts.

Even the Basque parties' memorial celebrations and patriotic festivities involve huge culinary rituals. Meals for vast numbers of people are prepared all over the region under tremendous *txarpas*, or marquees. Party workers serve stews or sell specialties from their respective areas. These delights are consumed amid torrents of *sagardua* (cider) and *txakoli*, a light, sharp white wine with a low alcohol content — the only wine produced in the region.

No, there is no place in the world in which cooking and eating are as deeply ingrained in the social, political and cultural fabric as they are in the Basque Country.

MONKFISH WITH CLAMS
RAPE A LA DONOSTIARRA
Basque Country

Preparation time: 10 minutes
Cooking time: 35 minutes
For 6 servings:
6 tablespoons (3 fl oz/9 cl) olive oil
1 large onion, peeled and chopped
2 cloves garlic, peeled and chopped
2 teaspoons chopped parsley
6 tablespoons (3 fl oz/9 cl) tomato sauce
1 tablespoon paprika
3/4 cup (6 fl oz/18 cl) water
Small pinch saffron (see glossary)
14 oz (400 g) fresh peas, shelled
2 roasted red bell peppers, peeled and diced
2 1/4 lb (1 kg) monkfish, cut into 1-inch-thick slices
24 cherrystone or littleneck clams
Salt
Freshly ground white pepper

Method:
Heat the oil in a large earthenware casserole. Add the onions, garlic and parsley and cook over medium heat for 15 minutes. Add the tomato sauce, paprika, water, and saffron and cook for 5 minutes longer.

Stir in the peas and peppers, and cook 5 minutes longer. Add the monkfish and clams, season with salt and pepper and continue to cook over low heat for about 8 to 10 minutes, or until the clams open.

Serve hot.

Stuffed bell peppers (facing page).

STUFFED BELL PEPPERS
PIMIENTOS RELLENOS
Basque Country

Preparation time: 40 minutes
Cooking time: 1 hour 25 minutes
For 6 servings:
Stuffing:
1/3 cup (2 1/2 fl oz/8 cl) olive oil
1 onion, peeled and chopped
1 clove garlic, peeled and chopped
1 tablespoon chopped parsley
5 oz (150 g) Serrano ham, minced
7 oz (200 g) ground beef
1 tablespoon flour
Salt
Pepper

Sauce:
1 hot pepper, soaked in warm water
6 tablespoons (3 fl oz/9 cl) olive oil
1 large onion, peeled and chopped
5 medium tomatoes, peeled and chopped
3/4 cup (6 fl oz/18 cl) dry white wine
3/4 cup (6 fl oz/18 cl) chicken or beef broth
Salt
Freshly ground white pepper

Peppers:
12 round meaty bell peppers, roasted and peeled
1 2/3 cups (14 fl oz/32 cl) olive oil
1 1/2 cups (7 oz/200 g) flour
2 eggs, beaten

Method:
To prepare the stuffing, heat 1/3 cup oil in a skillet. Add the onion, garlic and parsley and cook for 10 minutes. Add the ham and beef and cook for 10 minutes, or until the meat is cooked through. Add 1 tablespoon flour, season with salt and pepper and mix well. Remove from the heat and let cool.

Meanwhile, prepare the sauce: Drain the hot pepper. Heat 6 tablespoons oil in a skillet. Add the onion and hot pepper and cook for 10 minutes. Add the tomatoes, wine, and broth, season with salt and pepper, and cook over low heat for 20 minutes. Strain through a sieve and set aside.

Fill the roasted peppers with the stuffing and secure them closed with wooden toothpicks. Heat the remaining 1 2/3 cups oil in a deep skillet until very hot. Dredge the peppers in the flour, then dip in the beaten egg. Carefully lower peppers into the oil and fry for about 15 minutes or until lightly browned.

Remove the fried peppers from the oil with a slotted spoon and place in a shallow ovenproof baking dish. Spoon the sauce over the peppers and cook in a preheated 350° F (175° C) oven for about 20 minutes.

GRILLED MARINATED VEAL CHOPS
CHULETON A LA BRASA
Basque Country

Preparation time: 10 minutes
Marinating time: 2 hours
Cooking time: 10 minutes
For 6 servings:
6 veal chops, about 1 lb (450 g) each
Salt
3/4 cup (6 fl oz/18 cl) olive oil
3 cloves garlic, peeled and chopped
2 tablespoons chopped parsley

Method:
Arrange the veal chops in one layer in a shallow earthenware or glass baking dish. Season them lightly on both sides with salt. Drizzle the oil evenly over them, and sprinkle with the garlic and parsley. Let marinate for 2 hours, turning once.

Meanwhile, build a wood fire long enough in advance to produce glowing hot embers for grilling the veal. Place a wire grill over the embers and, when hot, place the veal chops on the rack and grill for about 5 minutes on each side. (Reduce the grilling time for those who prefer their veal pink.)

The chops can also be grilled under a hot broiler or over an electric grill, but will not be as flavorful. In either case, the grill should be very hot before the chops are placed on it.

HAKE CHEEKS IN SALSA VERDE
KOKOTXAS EN SALSA VERDE
Basque Country

Preparation time: 10 minutes
Cooking time: 20 to 30 minutes
For 6 servings:
2 1/4 lb (1 kg) hake cheeks (see note)
Salt
3/4 cup (6 fl oz/18 cl) olive oil
2 cloves garlic, peeled and chopped
2 tablespoons chopped parsley

Method:

Carefully clean, rinse and pat dry the hake cheeks. Season lightly with salt.

Heat the oil in a deep, heavy skillet. Add the garlic and cook over medium heat until it begins to color, about 5 minutes.

Add the hake cheeks and parsley and continue to cook over medium-high heat until the oil begins to boil. Turn the heat to low, and, swirling the pan constantly, slide the pan on and off the fire until the hake cheeks give off their gelatin and the oil emulsifies, forming a thick sauce. (If the sauce does not emulsify, place the pan in a warm oven and heat briefly, making sure not to allow it to boil, as this would break down the emulsion.)

Serve immediately.

Note: The meaty tender cheeks of hake—at the base of the head just in front of the gills—are a delicacy in Spain. Ask your fishmonger to reserve them for you. If they are unavailable, substitute hake fillets or steaks.

RED BEANS A LA TOLOSA
ALUBIAS ROJAS AL ESTILO DE TOLOSA
Basque Country

Advance cooking time: 12 hours
Preparation time: 15 minutes
Cooking time: 2 hours 15 minutes
For 6 servings:
2 1/3 cups (1 lb/500 g) red kidney beans
1/3 lb (150 g) side pork or fresh, unsmoked bacon
3/4 cup (6 fl oz/18 cl) olive oil
1 large onion, peeled and chopped
Salt
11 oz (300 g) chorizo
2 1/4 lb (1 kg) cabbage
11 oz (300 g) morcilla de cebolla (see glossary)
1 clove garlic, peeled and sliced

Method:

A day in advance: Soak the beans in cold water for 12 hours.

The same day: Drain the beans. Place them in a large, heavy saucepan. Add the side pork, 6 tablespoons of the oil, about half of the chopped onion, and enough cold water to cover well. Season lightly with salt. Cook over low heat for about 1 hour, adding more cold water if necessary to keep the beans covered with liquid. Stir from time to time to help thicken the cooking liquid.

When the beans have cooked for 1 hour, heat 3 tablespoons of the remaining oil in a skillet, add the remaining onions and cook over medium heat until softened. Add the onions and chorizo to the beans, and cook for 1 hour longer, adding more water if necessary.

Core the cabbage and shred it into julienne strips. Place in simmering salted water and cook for 15 minutes. Pour off some of the water, add the morcilla and continue to cook for 25 minutes.

Shortly before the beans and cabbage have finished cooking, heat the remaining 3 tablespoons oil in a skillet. Add the garlic and cook over medium-high heat until soft. Drain the cabbage and morcilla. Pour the garlic and oil over both.

Transfer the beans to a large shallow casserole and arrange the meats on top. Serve hot.

BASQUE BEEF STEW WITH GLAZED PEARL ONIONS
ZANCARRON
Basque Country

Preparation time: 15 minutes
Cooking time: 2 hours 30 minutes
For 6 servings:
3 1/3 lb (1 1/2 kg) bone-in beef shank, cut into pieces
1 1/2 cups (200 g) flour
3/4 cup (6 fl oz/18 cl) olive oil
2 large onions, peeled and chopped
4 carrots, cut into pieces
3/4 cup (6 fl oz/18 cl) dry white wine
3/4 cup (6 fl oz/18 cl) chicken broth
Salt
Freshly ground black pepper
1 1/2 tablespoons butter
1 teaspoon sugar
24 small white pearl onions

Method:

Dredge the pieces of meat in the flour, gently shaking off the excess.

Heat the oil in a large skillet. Add the meat and cook over high heat, turning, until browned on all sides, about 10 minutes. (If necessary, brown the meat in 2 batches.) Remove the meat from the pan with a slotted spoon and set aside.

Add the onions to the hot oil remaining in the skillet, and cook over low heat for 10 minutes. Spread the onions in the bottom of a large Dutch oven. Add the pieces of browned meat, cover the pan and cook over low heat for 5 minutes. Add the carrots and the wine and let cook for 5 minutes longer. Add the chicken broth, season with salt and pepper, and simmer over low heat, covered, for 2 hours.

A few minutes before the meat has finished cooking, melt the butter in a skillet, add the sugar and onions and cook, shaking the pan, until the onions are nicely glazed.

Serve the meat with sautéed potatoes and the glazed onions.

Hake cheeks in salsa verde (facing page).

STUFFED SQUID
IN THEIR INK
CHIPIRONES EN SU TINTA
Basque Country

Preparation time: 30 minutes
Cooking time: 1 hour
For 6 servings:
2 1/4 lb (1 kg) small squid
6 tablespoons (3 fl oz/9 cl) olive oil
1 large onion, peeled and chopped
4 garlic cloves, peeled
9 oz (250 g) tomatoes, peeled and chopped
2 green bell peppers, seeded and chopped
3/4 cup (6 fl oz/18 cl) fish broth
**   (see glossary)**
Salt

Method:

Ask your fishmonger to clean the squid, reserving the ink sacs. Or clean them yourself (see glossary). Break the ink sacs into a cup and coarsely chop the tentacles.

Heat 2 tablespoons of the oil in a large skillet. Add about 1/4 of the chopped onion and 1 garlic clove and cook over medium-high heat for about 5 minutes. Add the tentacles, cook for 3 minutes, and season with salt. Remove the garlic clove.

Stuff the tentacles into the squid bodies. Close the squid with two wooden toothpicks. Heat the remaining 4 tablespoons oil in a skillet, add the stuffed squid and cook over high heat, turning. Remove from the pan and set aside.

Add the remaining chopped onion and garlic cloves to the hot oil remaining in the skillet. Add the peppers and tomatoes, and cook for 20 minutes.

Combine the fish broth with the squid ink, stir this mixture into the skillet and cook for 10 minutes. Strain the sauce through a fine sieve and return it to the skillet. Cook over low heat for 10 minutes. Remove the toothpicks and add the squid to the skillet with the sauce. Continue to cook until the sauce thickens, about 10 minutes longer.

Serve hot with white rice.

Country dwellers dry ripe tomatoes on cords, and use them in winter in sauces with garlic and herbs (above).
Stuffed squid in their ink (facing page).

FRIED FRESH ANCHOVIES
FRITADA DE ANCHOAS
Basque Country

Preparation time: 30 minutes
Cooking time: 6 minutes
For 6 servings:
2 1/4 lb (1 kg) fresh anchovies
4 eggs
1 3/4 cup (8 1/2 oz/250 g) flour
2 cups (16 fl oz/50 cl) olive oil
Salt

Method:

Carefully clean the anchovies, removing their heads, cutting them open lengthwise and removing the backbones. Rinse well and pat dry thoroughly with a kitchen towel.

Beat the eggs in a large bowl. Dredge the anchovies in flour, then dip them into the egg.

Heat the oil in a deep, heavy skillet until very hot. Add the anchovies in small batches and cook until lightly browned, 1 to 2 minutes per batch. Remove with a slotted spoon, drain, and season with salt. Serve immediately.

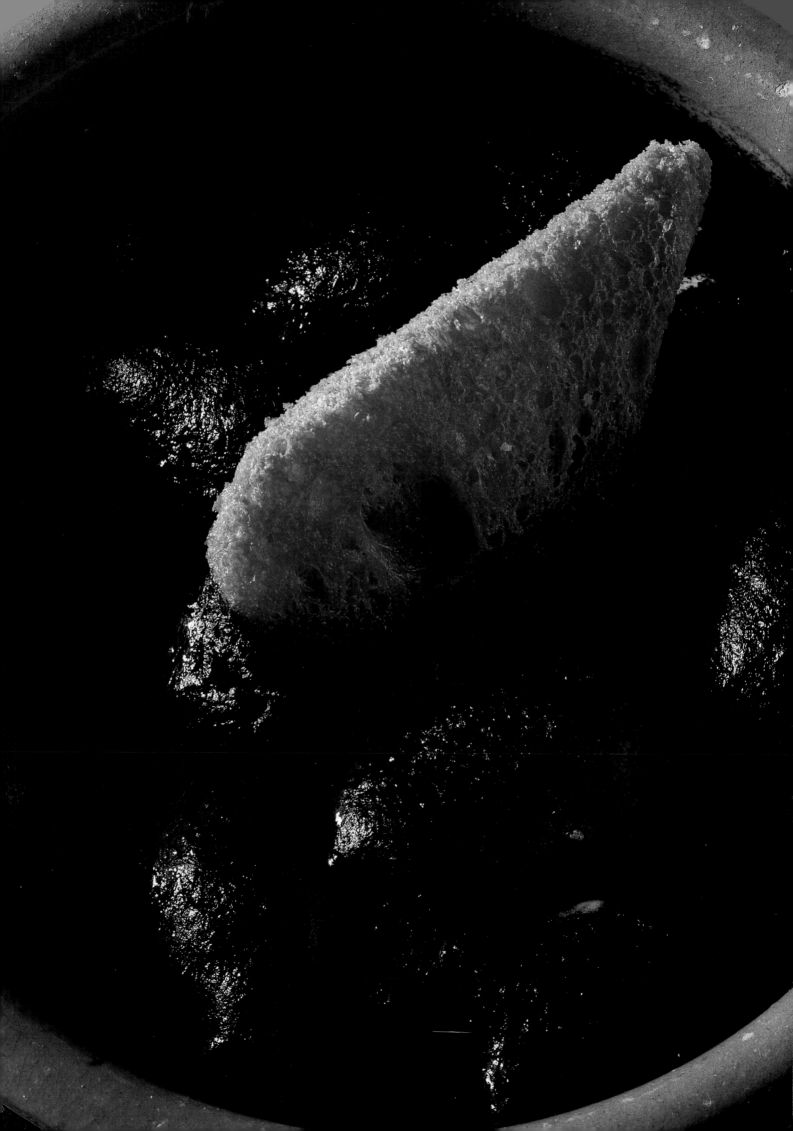

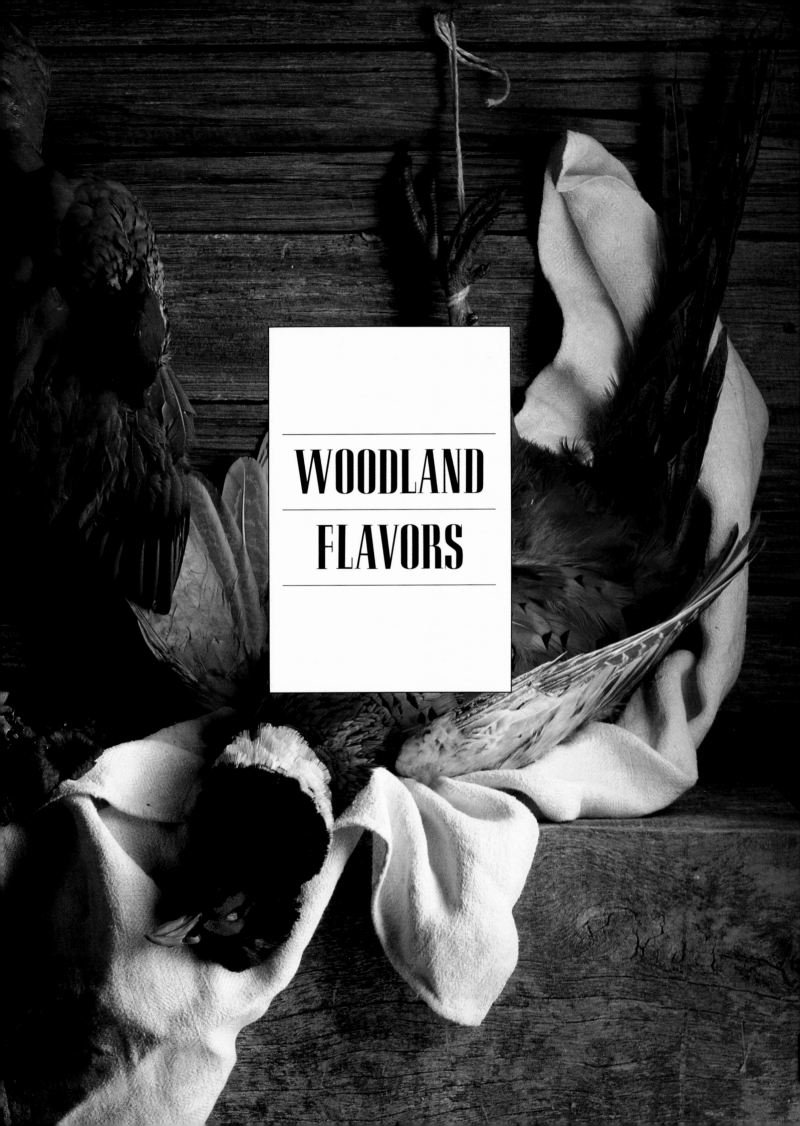

WOODLAND
FLAVORS

W hether practiced alone, with friends or as a social event facilitating informal but important meetings between politicians, financiers, press magnates, aristocrats or members of the jet set, hunting is the most popular sport in Spain. For many Spaniards, hunting is an enjoyable way to help fill the stewpot, while for others it is a "society" sport that confers status upon the practitioner, as caricatured by José Luis Berlanga in his film *La Escopeta Nacional*.

There is also a culinary dichotomy in hunting. European game cookery has descended from medieval court life. This type of cooking usually consists of stewed or roasted large game (venison, deer, wild boar, or mountain goat, for example), often accompanied by sweet or sweet and sour sauces. This cuisine is widespread throughout Europe, but especially in Spain, Germany, France and Italy, and is the perfect example of "class cuisine," according to the American culinary anthropologist Jack Goody in his book *Cooking, Cuisine and Class*.

This kind of game is served, in the proper season of course, in the better restaurants. The extraordinary roast venison ribs served at the Ampurdán restaurant in Salvador Dalí's home town of Figueras is an outstanding example, and attracts game lovers in droves. This restaurant was a favorite of the great painter, who was himself a confirmed gourmet. When he was hospitalized in Barcelona, he had his lunch and dinner sent to him every day from the Ampurdán. Dalí would accept food from nowhere else.

"Social" hunters tend to be people who have little interest in the sport itself and who slaughter the beasts merely for the pleasure of killing them — a fact that is of greater relevance to psychoanalysis than to the culinary arts. But hunting on a popular level, which puts the game to good use (namely eating), has, naturally and unpretentiously, inspired an original brand of cuisine.

The paradigm of the Spanish "social" hunter was the dictator Francisco Franco.

The photographs of him with his kill are famous: a fat little man posing stiffly over the bodies of hundreds of dead animals. Afterward he would go and eat a simple French-style omelette washed down with water (Franco was a teetotaler).

Hunters of this kind are beneath contempt, however, so let's leave them and get back to cooking.

According to the great Escoffier, in 1807 Napoleon's army sacked the monastery of Alcántara in Extremadura. Among the booty was a manuscript that contained recipes for a wide range of game birds such as partridge, woodcock and pheasant, all of which were absorbed into French *haute cuisine* under the general heading "Alcántara-style." The collection of recipes is said to have ended up in the hands of General Junot, who gave them to his wife Laura, Duchess of Abrantes, a woman with a refined palate who was herself a talented cook.

Unfortunately, nobody has seen the recipes since, but the tale nurtured a culinary chauvinism among Spanish food writers for decades. The anecdote probably indicates more of a mythomania on the part of the Duchess of Abrantes and her husband than historical reality, but it is certain that Junot discovered an interesting and delicious game cuisine in Extremadura.

The greatest number of recipes are devoted to partridge, quail, pigeons, squab, hare and rabbit. Apart from hare they are all domesticated animals, but even when they were wild they were an integral part of Spanish popular cuisine. Duck should also be on the list, although that relentless predator, man, is eliminating the natural habitat of wild duck and many other aquatic birds.

In his restaurant in the Valencian town of Alcudia de Carlet and in Valencia itself, Joan Galbis still makes his fabulous rice and chickpeas with greylag goose from the Albufera, a teeming marshland that is being gradually destroyed by industrial and urban development. This used to be an everyday dish among people living around the Albufera. The incomparably delicious

Hunters and gourmets both love the red partridge that frequents Andalusian vineyards. Its meat is particularly tender when braised and accompanied with lentils and beans (above).
In rural areas, the kitchen is the most important room in the house. In some regions, especially in the north, it is located in the center, and thus provides heating for all the other rooms built around the fireplace (facing).

meat gives the rice and chickpeas a flavor that is found nowhere else in the world. Nowadays the dish can be neither for everyday nor for everyone, as wild goose is becoming increasingly scarce and may one day disappear forever.

If I were asked what is the jewel in the crown of Spanish game cookery, however, I would undoubtedly say the partridge. Red-legged partridge is a handsome native bird found throughout Spain, particularly in the wine-producing areas of Andalusia, Castile, La Mancha and Extremadura. Those that inhabit the vineyards are especially tasty. The fat, big-chested birds gorge on the exquisite grapes used for making Jerez wine, and feature in wonderful dishes that are both sophisticated and extremely popular.

The king of all hors d'œuvre is *escabeche de perdiz*, marinated partridge. This is an ancient recipe that is often used for quail as well, and is designed for long-term storage. It is made throughout the dry areas of Spain from Castile and León to Andalusia.

The essential ingredients for the *escabeche* are good white-wine vinegar and top-quality olive oil. Bay leaf and peppercorns are usually added, followed by oregano, thyme or cumin, or other herbs and spices. The partridge may be browned lightly in the oil with some garlic or onion, then cooked in water or white wine. This stock is used for the marinade. When the partridges are tender they are put whole into a glass or earthenware jar, completely covered with their cooking stock and vinegar and left in a cool place until they reach the preserved stage, after which they can be kept for some time. The Castilian chef Seri prepares deservedly famous *escabeche*-marinated birds at her Mesón de la Villa in Aranda de Duero.

Today these game *escabeches*, especially those made with partridge and quail, are usually served only in fine restaurants, but they were originally an expedient dictated by necessity: meat was preserved for times of scarcity. However, there are many methods of preserving food, and *escabeche* particularly appeals to the Spanish liking for vinegar.

Edibles preserved in *escabeche* are served in their marinade, which after being in lengthy contact with the food acquires a jelly-like consistency, while the food in turn is tenderized by the vinegar. The red-legged and grape-eating partridges are ideal for marinating in *escabeche* because of the light, smooth

*Specialized butchers buy the bulls
that are killed in the corridas.
The meat is tender and flavorful,
and is often prepared like game.*

quality of their fat. An *escabeche* made with a good sherry vinegar can provide *haute cuisine* all year round.

Cecinas are dried or semi-preserved meats made from large animals such as deer, and, in very isolated regions, bear, goat and even donkey meat was commonly stored to help families survive the harsh winters. Today these meats are scarce, an expensive delicacy prepared with much care and served as an usual hors d'œuvre. The glacial winds of the mountains of northern Castile are particularly conducive to the preparation of these slightly dry meats, which are cured until they turn a deep red color.

Cecinas are no longer generally available on the Spanish market, but they can be found in many inns and restaurants. Like any other luxury item that is in fashion, the consumer must be prepared to pay dearly for it.

Partridge and hare go together extremely well in Extremadura (and elsewhere, of course), especially in autumn dishes. They are often accompanied by legumes such as white beans or lentils, and then simmered long and gently in earthenware casseroles. Spanish tastes do not favor food that is raw or *al dente*. These stews are cooked thoroughly in their flavorful juices, and fill not only the kitchen but the whole house with such a tantalizing aroma that they immediately give a hearty appetite to anyone who enters.

Shepherds, farmers, and other rural dwellers generally hunt for purely practical reasons. The Spanish culinary heritage has been enriched with an imaginative dish invented by them, the *gazpacho manchego*, which I mentioned in an earlier chapter. This heritage originated in the mountainous inland region of the provinces of Albacete and Alicante and southeastern Castile-La Mancha.

Gazpachos can be made with a variety of small game, including hare, rabbit, thrush, partridge, dove, pigeon and quail, and many kinds of large or small edible birds, even warblers and sparrows.

A cookbook appeared in Barcelona in 1892 that included a recipe for partridge *a lo torero*. It is not known who compiled the recipes, but this one is credited to a famous bullfighter of the time, José Redondo, known as El Chiclanero after his home town of Chiclana in Seville. Bullfighting legend has it that the master of the art of swordsmanship in the bullring was also an *aficionado* of the cooking range.

José Redondo's partridges are stuffed with giblets, anchovies, and strips of bacon finely chopped together. The stuffed birds are placed in a casserole with cooked, peeled tomatoes and bell peppers, and seasoned with salt, ground white pepper and parsley. They are cooked in oil for half an hour over a low heat, after which a glass of white wine is added and they are left for another half hour. The partridges are served with very thin slices of Serrano ham fried separately.

Spaniards in the North love to eat woodcock and other migrating waders when in season. Unfortunately, woodcocks have all but vanished from home cooking, and can be found almost exclusively in luxury restaurants. This delicious bird, which is a protected species throughout the rest of Europe, can still be hunted legally in Spain.

Apart from woodcock, however, Spanish game cooking belongs essentially to popular cuisine and country life, where game complements or enriches everyday food. In the country, a hunter shoots what he can, and whatever he gets goes straight into the stock pot, prepared according to family or local recipes, accompanied by vegetables that were grown in the garden.

The Canary Islands are practically overrun with wild rabbits, which are used in a dish that has become the symbol of the islands' cuisine: *conejo en salmorejo*. It is often served on Santa Cruz de Tenerife, at the El Coto de Antonio and at the El Drago, two restaurants that feature the best of traditional local cuisine. Nevertheless, *salmorejo* rabbit is originally a home-style dish. A true Canary Islander will swear that there is no *conejo con salmorejo* anywhere in the Canaries better than the one his mother or grandmother makes.

How about stretching the list of popular dishes to include lizard? *Lagarto* is served at feasts and banquets in Extremadura, especially in the spring, which is the best season for catching and eating the reptile. It is prepared in little pots with tomato sauce, with hot peppers or *salsa verde.* Lizard meat is very white, somewhere between frog and young rabbit in taste. The *entomatá de lagarto* from Jaraiz de la Vega and the *lagarto en salsa* of Campanario somewhat resemble Mexican dishes prepared with iguana.

Mention was made earlier of the bullfighter cook; bulls, too, should be included in this chapter on game. These are wild bulls and, though obviously not hunted, neither are they slaughtered in the usual way. They die fighting in the bullring, in combats that are strictly regulated. Their meat is delicious, and *rabo de toro,* one of the classic Spanish stews, is made from their tails (definitely worth trying at the Caballito Rojo in Córdoba). They also make good sirloin cuts and stewing meat, and the testicles, which used to be reserved for the matadors, can be dipped into batter and fried.

Restaurants such as the Bermeo in Bilbao and the Florian and San Leopoldo in Barcelona have all the bulls that are killed during the *Ferias* reserved for them, and for weeks will feature different fighting bulls on the menu.

Caballito Rojo in Córdoba and Florian and Leopodo in Barcelona are the best restaurants for tasting this delicacy of corrida bulls. The great specialty in Andalusia is rabo de toro, a stew made with the bull's tail.

155

MUSHROOM HUNTING

Spain is not a great mushroom-eating country compared to France, Italy, Switzerland or some of the Eastern countries like Poland or the former Soviet Union, but two of the Spanish autonomous communities are: Catalonia and the Basque region.

Spain, like all Mediterranean countries, has an abundance of mushrooms, and many German, French and Italian companies come to Spain for the fungi that they subsequently process in their own countries.

The damp Galician woods of ash and oak produce many varieties of mushrooms, but the Galicians neither pick nor eat them. They seem to have an almost superstitious distrust of them, which can perhaps be explained by ancient ecclesiastical prohibitions, particularly on the *Amanita muscaria* variety that was used in religious ceremonies by the Celts.

Basques and Catalans compensate for this irrational fear. There are many societies and clubs that organize mushroom-hunting expeditions, and thousands of individuals who, basket and knife in hand, explore woods and mountains in search of carpophores to be cooked and eaten at home. The Catalan word for seeking out mushrooms is *caçar*, which means "hunting," and Catalonian cooking in spring and autumn features mushrooms of all kinds, the most highly prized being the *moixarnó* (*Marasmius oreades*), indispensable in the *fricandó*, a characteristic Catalan dish, morels (*Morchella conica*), chanterelles (*Cantharellus cibarius*), *robelló* (*Lactarius deliciosis*), cepes (*Boletus edulis*), *llanega*, *fredolic* and, of course, truffles. The king of mushrooms in Catalonia is *Amanita caesarea*, known in Catalan as *ou de reig*, which, being rare, is extremely expensive.

In Basque Country spring mushrooms, *perretxiko* (*Tricholoma georgii*), are the favorites. They are tiny, very flavorful and extremely costly. They are usually prepared with scrambled eggs or sautéed.

Castilians prefer the *Pleurotus* known as *seta de cardo*; the favorite mushroom in Extremadura is the *criadilla de tierra*, which is a member of the Tuberaceae family, although it lacks the subtle flavor of the white Piemonte truffles; and in Andalusia people like the *gurumelos*, a large, fleshy *Agaricus* mushroom that is usually grilled.

Barcelona boasts many restaurants that offer mushroom specialties in the autumn, but the best is the Florian, whose owner-chef, Rosa Grau, has an exceptional talent for this woodland delicacy.

The robello mushroom is considered an autumn delicacy in Castile and Catalonia. Cooked with ajillo (garlic and hot peppers) or simply with a parsley garnish, it is a wonderfully refined dish.

HARE A LA ZAMORANA
LIEBRE A LA ZAMORANA
Castile-León

Advance preparation time: 24 hours
Preparation time: 10 minutes
Cooking time: 2 hours 30 minutes
For 6 servings:
2 cups (14 oz/400 g) large white beans
1 hare, about 4 1/2 lb (2 kg)
1 tablespoon chopped parsley
8 cloves garlic, peeled and chopped
1 green bell pepper, seeded and cut
    into pieces
1 large tomato, peeled and chopped
2 bay leaves
1 large onion, peeled and chopped
6 tablespoons (3 fl oz/9 cl) olive oil
1 tablespoon flour
1 teaspoon paprika
Salt
Freshly ground black pepper

Method:

A day in advance: Place the beans in a bowl filled with cold water and let soak for 24 hours.

Thoroughly clean and rinse the hare, pat dry. Cut it into pieces and place in a bowl. Sprinkle with the chopped parsley and half of the chopped garlic and let rest at least 12 hours, turning the meat once or twice to coat thoroughly with the seasoning.

The same day: Drain the beans. Place them in a large earthenware casserole along with the hare, bell pepper, tomato, bay leaves, onion and 3 tablespoons of the oil. Add enough cold water to cover, cover the pan and cook over low heat for 2 hours and 15 minutes.

Meanwhile, heat the remaining oil in a skillet. Add the remaining chopped garlic and cook until it begins to color. Add the flour and paprika, stirring rapidly. Stir this mixture into the pan with the hare. Season with salt and pepper and cook for 5 minutes longer.

Serve hot, accompanied by boiled potatoes.

RAGOUT OF VENISON WITH RAISINS AND PINE NUTS
RAGU DE CIERVO CON PASAS Y PIÑONES
Aragon

Advance preparation time: 12 hours
Preparation time: 15 minutes
Cooking time: 2 hours
For 6 servings:
3 1/3 lb (1 1/2 kg) venison
6 cups (48 fl oz/1 1/2 l) milk
6 tablespoons (50 g) raisins
1/2 cup (4 fl oz/12 cl) brandy
3/4 cup (6 fl oz/18 cl) olive oil
2 onions, peeled and chopped
4 cloves
4 sprigs thyme
1/2 teaspoon oregano
10 black peppercorns
Salt
10 cups (80 fl oz/2 1/2 l) chicken broth
6 tablespoons (50 g) pine nuts
12 small white pearl onions, peeled
1 tablespoon butter

Method:

A day in advance: Cut the venison into pieces. Place them in a large bowl with the milk and soak for 12 hours.

The same day: Place the raisins in a small bowl with 3 tablespoons of the brandy and let soak. Drain the meat, pat dry, place in a large earthenware casserole and warm over low heat to dry. Add the remaining brandy, heat briefly and ignite with a match.

When the flames have died down, add the oil, chopped onions, cloves, thyme, oregano, and peppercorns. Season with salt and simmer over low heat for 5 minutes. Add the chicken broth and cook over low heat for 1 3/4 hours.

Drain the raisins, add them to the venison with the pine nuts and continue to cook for 10 minutes.

Meanwhile, melt the butter in a skillet, add the pearl onions and cook for 10 minutes, shaking the pan frequently.

Remove the venison to a serving platter. Strain the juice in which it cooked through a sieve, if desired, and pour it over the meat. Surround with the onions and serve.

HARE AND PARTRIDGE STEW
MORTERUELO
Castile-León

Preparation time: 40 minutes
Cooking time: 2 hours 30 minutes
For 10 servings:
1/2 hare or wild rabbit, cleaned
1/4 chicken, or 1 thigh and 1 leg
1 partridge, cleaned
9 oz (250 g) Serrano ham (see glossary)
9 oz (250 g) pork liver
9 oz (250 g) smoked slab bacon
Salt
6 tablespoons (3 fl oz/9 cl) olive oil
1 tablespoon paprika
1/2 teaspoon ground cumin
1/2 teaspoon ground cloves
1/2 teaspoon ground cinnamon
1/2 teaspoon freshly ground black pepper
2 1/3 cups (11 oz/300 g) breadcrumbs

Method:

Rinse and pat dry the rabbit, chicken, and partridge. Place them in a large stock pot with the ham, liver, and bacon. Add enough cold water to cover, season with salt and cook over medium heat for 2 hours.

Remove the meats from the pan, reserving the cooking liquid. Skin and bone the meats and chop coarsely with a knife.

Heat the oil in a large saucepan. Add the paprika, stirring rapidly. Add the reserved cooking liquid, along with the cumin, cloves, cinnamon and pepper. Bring to a boil and stir in the breadcrumbs. Cook for 5 minutes and add the meats. Let simmer over very low heat for 20 minutes, stirring frequently to keep ingredients from sticking.

Correct the seasoning, if necessary, and serve with slices of toasted country bread.

MARINATED PARTRIDGE
PERDIZ ESCABECHADA
Castile-La Mancha

Marinated partridge (above). Spaniards are not aficionados of the mushroom except in Catalonia and the Basque Country, where mushroom-lovers rush to the woods to pick morels, chanterelles, amanites and St. George's agaric, which are among the most appreciated varieties (following double page).

Preparation time: 15 minutes
Cooking time: 1 hour 30 minutes
For 6 servings:
3 large or 6 small partridges
2 large onions, peeled and sliced
     into thin rounds
1 2/3 cups (13 fl oz/40 cl) dry white wine
3/4 cup (6 fl oz/18 cl) wine vinegar
6 tablespoons (3 fl oz/9 cl) olive oil
2 sprigs thyme
2 bay leaves
8 black peppercorns
3/4 cup (6 fl oz/18 cl) chicken broth
Salt

Method:
    Clean the partridges. (If wild, pluck and gut the birds, then singe over a flame to remove pin feathers.) Rinse thoroughly with cold water inside and out, pat dry and truss.

    Place the birds in a large Dutch oven along with the onions, wine, vinegar, oil, thyme, bay leaves, peppercorns and chicken broth. Season with salt.

    Cover the pan and simmer over low heat for 1 1/2 hours or until the partridges are tender and juices have greatly reduced.

    Remove the pan from the heat and let the birds cool in the sauce. Cut into pieces before serving.

PARTRIDGE A LO TORERO
PERDICES A LO TORERO

Preparation time: 35 minutes
Cooking time: 1 hour 15 minutes
For 4 servings:
4 small partridges or 2 large partridges
3 anchovies
3 1/2 oz (100 g) side pork or fresh,
    unsmoked bacon
Freshly ground black pepper
Salt
6 tablespoons (3 fl oz/9 cl) olive oil
4 large ripe tomatoes, peeled and chopped
3 medium bell peppers, seeded and chopped
1 tablespoon chopped parsley
3/4 cup (6 fl oz/18 cl) dry white wine
4 very thin slices Serrano ham
    (see glossary)

Method:
Clean the partridges, reserving the livers. (If wild, pluck and gut the birds, then singe them over a flame to remove pin feathers.) Rinse thoroughly with cold water and pat dry. To prepare anchovies, remove their backbones, rinse under cold water and pat dry.

Finely chop the livers, anchovies and bacon, season with pepper and mix thoroughly. Stuff the partridges with this mixture. Stitch their cavities closed and truss with needle and kitchen string. Season the birds with salt.

Heat 3 tablespoons of the oil in a large Dutch oven. Add the partridges and cook over high heat until browned on all sides.

Heat 2 tablespoons of the remaining oil in a skillet, add the tomatoes, bell peppers and parsley, and cook until tender. Season with salt and pepper. Add the vegetables to the pan with the partridges, cover and cook over very low heat for 30 minutes. Add the wine and continue to cook for 30 minutes.

Just before the partridges have finished cooking, heat the remaining oil in a skillet, add the ham slices and cook briefly.

Remove the partridges from the pan, remove the string and arrange them on a serving platter with the sauce from the pan. Arrange the ham slices on a separate platter and serve.

QUAIL WITH OLIVES
CODORNICES CON ACEITUNAS
Andalusia

Preparation time: 20 minutes
Cooking time: 50 minutes
For 4 servings:
12 quail
Salt
Freshly ground black pepper
4 cups (32 fl oz/1 l) chicken broth
6 tablespoons (3 fl oz/9 cl) olive oil
2 cloves garlic, peeled and chopped
1 small onion, peeled and chopped
5 oz (150 g) Serrano ham, diced
3 large carrots, diced
2 tablespoons flour
1 teaspoon crumbled thyme leaves
1/2 tablespoon chopped parsley
2 bay leaves
1 1/3 cup (7 oz/200 g) pitted olives

Method:
Clean the quail, singe off pin feathers, if necessary, and tuck the wing tips under the birds. For the legs, cut a small slit on either side of the cavity, cross the legs and slip the tip of each leg through one of the slits to prevent quail from losing their shape. Season with salt and pepper.

Bring the chicken broth to a boil in a small saucepan.

Heat the oil in a large Dutch oven. Add the quail and cook over medium-high heat until browned on all sides. Remove the quail from the pan and set aside.

Add the garlic and onion to the oil remaining in the pan and cook until lightly browned. Add the ham and cook until lightly browned. Add the carrots and cook for 5 minutes longer. Sprinkle the flour over all and let cook, stirring, for a few minutes. Add the hot broth. Let cook for 20 minutes.

Return the quail to the pan, add the thyme, parsley, and bay leaves, and cook over low heat for 15 minutes longer, stirring frequently, and adding more broth if necessary.

Just before serving, add the olives and bring the sauce to a boil for several seconds. Remove the quail, arrange them on a large shallow platter and spoon the sauce over them. Serve very hot.

ALCANTARA PHEASANT
FAISAN AL MODO DE ALCANTARA
Extremadura

Preparation time: 15 minutes
Marinating time: 3 hours
Cooking time: 40 minutes
Ingredients:
1 large or 2 small pheasants
2 tablespoons lard
2 duck livers
Salt
Freshly ground black pepper
3/4 cup (6 fl oz/18 cl) Rancîo or port wine
12 small black truffles (see glossary)
To serve:
2 1/4 lb (1 kg) mashed potatoes
1 tablespoon chopped parsley

Method:
Remove any gristle from the duck livers. Melt 1 tablespoon of the lard in a skillet. Add the livers and cook over medium-high heat until lightly browned. Transfer the livers to a mortar. Season them with salt and pepper and grind to a paste with a pestle. Force the livers through a sieve. Let cool completely.

Place 3 of the truffles in a pan with the wine and simmer briefly. Remove the truffles, reserving the wine. Pat the truffles dry and chop coarsely. Add them to the livers and mix well.

Stuff the liver and truffle mixture into the pheasant and truss. Place it in an earthenware casserole, add the reserved port and let marinate for 3 hours in the refrigerator.

Remove the pheasant from the wine, reserving the wine, and pat dry. Season the pheasant and spread it with the remaining tablespoon lard. Place it in a shallow earthenware casserole or roasting pan and cook in a preheated 350° F (175° C) oven for about 25 minutes per pound, turning and basting occasionally.

Shortly before the pheasant has finished cooking, place the reserved wine in a saucepan with the remaining truffles, bring to a boil and let reduce briefly. Pour over the pheasant and cook over medium-high heat for 5 minutes longer.

Serve with the sauce, accompanied by mashed potatoes and chopped parsley.

HOME-STYLE PIGEONS
PALOMAS A LA CASERA
Catalonia

Preparation time: 25 minutes
Cooking time: 40 minutes
For 4 servings:
2 large or 3 medium pigeons
Salt
6 tablespoons (3 fl oz/9 cl) olive oil
2 tablespoons lard
1 head garlic, peeled and chopped
1 onion, peeled and chopped
1/2 tablespoon chopped parsley
3/4 cup (6 fl oz/18 cl) wine vinegar
2 slices toasted or fried bread, shredded
    into pieces
3 tablespoons toasted almonds
3/4 cup (6 fl oz/18 cl) dry white wine

Method:
Clean the pigeons. (If wild, pluck and gut the birds, then singe over a flame to remove pin feathers.) Rinse thoroughly with cold water inside and out, pat dry, and cut the birds into quarters. Season with salt.

Heat 3 tablespoons of the oil and the lard in a Dutch oven. Add the pigeon quarters and cook over medium-high heat until browned on all sides. Add enough warm water to half fill the pan. Cook over very low heat for 35 minutes.

Meanwhile, heat the remaining oil in a small skillet. Add the garlic, onion and parsley and cook, briefly. Transfer ingredients to a mortar and grind to a paste with a pestle while adding the vinegar and a little water. Add this mixture to the pan with the pigeons, and continue to cook over low heat until the pigeons are tender, 10 to 15 more minutes.

When the pigeons are cooked, add the bread pieces, almonds, and wine to the pan. Bring to a boil and cook over medium heat for 5 minutes.

Serve hot.

CEPE MUSHROOM CAPS STUFFED WITH CATALAN SAUSAGE
CAP DE CEP FARCIT DE BUTIFARRA
Catalonia

Preparation time: 15 minutes
Cooking time: 10 minutes
For 4 servings:
1 1/3 lb (600 g) fresh cepe or porcini
    mushrooms
3 1/2 oz (100 g) cooked butifarra
    blanca (see glossary)
1/4 cup (2 fl oz/6 cl) virgin olive oil
Salt
Freshly ground white pepper
Chopped parsley

Method:
Brush off any dirt or mud from the mushrooms, rinse them carefully and dry thoroughly with paper towels.

Separate the caps from the stems. Only the caps are used in this recipe; reserve the stems for another use.

Cut the sausage into slices thin enough to be tucked into the mushroom caps; about 1/8 to 1/4-inch (1/2 cm) thick.

Brush the mushroom caps on both sides with the oil, and season lightly with salt and pepper. Arrange the mushrooms on an oiled wire grill or baking sheet and cook over a medium-strength wood fire or in a 350° F (175° C) oven, brushing again with the oil and turning the mushroom caps to cook them evenly all over. The cooking time will depend on the size of the mushrooms.

When the mushrooms are tender, remove from the heat and insert a slice of sausage into each cap.

Serve hot, decorated with the chopped parsley.

MARINATED CHANTERELLE MUSHROOMS
MARINADO DE ROSINYOL
Catalonia

Preparation time: 30 minutes
Cooking time: 6 minutes
Marinating time: 6 hours
For 4 servings:
1 lb (500 g) chanterelle mushrooms
1 large lemon
1 shallot, peeled
Salt
Freshly ground white pepper
1/4 cup (2 fl oz/6 cl) olive oil

Method:
Brush off any dirt or mud from the mushrooms, rinse them carefully and dry thoroughly with paper towels. Cut any large mushrooms in half.

Rinse and dry the lemon. Remove the zest from about 1/2 of the lemon. Squeeze and strain 2 tablespoons of the juice. Place the zest and juice in an earthenware bowl.

Crush the shallot and add it to the bowl. Season with salt and white pepper and add the olive oil, stirring with a fork to bind the sauce.

Place the mushrooms in a large non-stick skillet and cook, without any fat, over low heat until the water they give off in cooking has completely evaporated.

Add the hot mushrooms to the marinade in the bowl and toss gently. Let cool, toss again and place in the refrigerator to chill for 5 to 6 hours.

Remove the mushrooms from the refrigerator 30 minutes before serving.

POTATO AND WILD MUSHROOM CASSEROLE
OUS DE REIG CON PATATAS
Catalonia

Preparation time: 15 minutes
Cooking time: 35 minutes
For 4 servings:
1 1/3 lb (600 g) Amanita caesare
    mushrooms (see note)
6 tablespoons (3 fl oz/9 cl) olive oil
2 cloves garlic, peeled and chopped
1 tablespoon chopped parsley
1 teaspoon oregano
Salt
Freshly ground white pepper
1 lb (500 g) potatoes, thinly sliced
6 tablespoons (3 fl oz/9 cl) chicken broth

Method:
    Brush off any dirt or mud from the mushrooms, rinse them carefully and dry thoroughly with paper towels. Separate the caps from the stems and chop the stems.
    Heat the oil in a large ovenproof casserole. Add the garlic and parsley and cook until softened. Add the mushroom caps and sprinkle the chopped stems over them. Sprinkle with a little of the oregano and season lightly with the salt and pepper.
    Layer the potato slices over the top and season with salt, pepper and the remaining oregano.
    Place the casserole in a preheated 350° F (175° C) oven and cook for 30 minutes, adding enough of the chicken broth to moisten the potatoes.
    Serve hot.
    Note: Amanita caesare, or Caesar's mushroom, belongs to the Amanitas family, which includes some extremely poisonous varieties. Amanita caesare is often eaten while the cap is still hidden within its delicate sheathlike "veil." The mature mushroom is also excellent, but it is most prized in its egglike younger form. If unavailable, substitute another variety of wild mushroom.

WILD MUSHROOMS SIMMERED IN RED WINE
LLENEGUES AL VINO TINTO
Catalonia/Basque Country

Preparation time: 10 minutes
Cooking time: 12 minutes
For 4 servings:
1 1/3 lb (600 g) Hygrophorus or other
    wild mushrooms
2 tablespoons olive oil
Salt
2 cups (16 fl oz/50 cl) good red wine
1 clove garlic, peeled and chopped
1 sprig parsley, chopped

Method:
    Clean the mushrooms carefully and dry thoroughly with paper towels.
    Heat the oil in a large skillet. Add the mushrooms, season them with salt and cook over high heat until the water they give off during cooking evaporates.
    Add the wine and continue cooking until it has almost completely evaporated. Sprinkle with the garlic and parsley, toss briefly over high heat and serve very hot.

CEPE MUSHROOM SALAD
ENSALADA DE CEPS
Catalonia

Preparation time: 20 minutes
For 4 servings:
12 small cepe mushrooms
4 artichoke bottoms or 3 Belgian endive
6 tablespoons (3 fl oz/9 cl) olive oil
Salt
Freshly ground white pepper
1 tablespoon fresh lemon juice

Method:
    Choose small, firm cepes in good condition. Brush off any dirt or mud from the mushrooms, rinse them carefully and dry thoroughly with paper towels. Using a sharp knife, trim off the stem ends. Slice the mushrooms into thin vertical slices so that each slice retains the shape of the mushroom.
    Slice the artichoke bottoms or endive into thin julienne strips and arrange them on a serving platter. Arrange the mushroom slices over the bed of vegetables. Drizzle the oil evenly over the mushrooms, season with salt and pepper and sprinkle with the freshly squeezed lemon juice.
    Serve immediately.

WILD MUSHROOM FLAN
EL PASTEL DE LAS 1000 SETAS
Catalonia

Preparation time: 15 minutes
Cooking time: 1 hour 15 minutes
For 10 servings:
2 1/4 lb (1kg) mixed wild mushrooms,
    such as cepes, chanterelles, or moixernons
3/4 cup (6 fl oz/18 cl) olive oil
1 1/2 tablespoons butter
2 medium onions, peeled and chopped
2 cloves garlic, peeled and chopped
2 sprigs parsley, chopped
1 teaspoon salt
Freshly ground white pepper
1 cup (8 fl oz/25 cl) heavy cream
6 eggs, beaten
1 tablespoon breadcrumbs

Method:
    Clean the mushrooms carefully and dry thoroughly with paper towels. Peel and trim, if necessary, and cut any large mushrooms in small pieces.
    Heat the oil and 1 tablespoon of the butter together in a skillet, add the onions, garlic and parsley, and cook until they begin to brown. Add the mushrooms, season with salt and pepper and cook over medium-high heat until the water given off during cooking has evaporated.
    Bring the cream to a boil in a saucepan. Remove from the heat and let cool briefly before stirring in the eggs. Add the mushrooms and mix well.
    Use the remaining butter to coat a large, high-sided mold, then sprinkle evenly with breadcrumbs. Turn the egg and mushroom mixture into the mold, and place it in a pan filled with enough water to come about halfway up the outside of the mold. Place in a 350° F (175° C) oven and cook for about 1 hour. Do not let the mixture boil.
    Serve tepid.

GIFTS FROM THE GARDEN

To working-class Spaniards, and sometimes to people from the middle classes as well, the word *huerta* has a magical aura to it: it means a kitchen garden. *La caseta i l'hortet* — a house and a plot of land — often represents a Spaniard's greatest dream.

It reflects the human desire to own a piece of land to cultivate, and above all, to have delicious vegetables fresh every day to put into the cooking pot. Many people work and save money all their lives so that they can spend their retirement with a hoe in their hands, growing their own tomatoes, leeks and peas.

Huerta also connotes an expanse of fertile irrigated land, which in Spain is famous for the quality of vegetables it produces: specifically, the cultivated farmlands of Murcia, Valencia, Aragon and Navarre and the plains of Castile, Extremadura and Andalusia. Here the slightest drop of water is used to maximum advantage.

The love of gardens and the strict husbandry of water is inherited from the sons of the desert, the Arabs, whose ingenious channelling and irrigation systems are still much admired today. They understood that water is rare and precious. Even today its use is regulated in Valencia, where a Water Tribunal, a very ancient body, has jurisdiction over water matters. Donkeys toiling round and round the pump or propelling the water mill are still an everyday sight in these riverless areas, where water has to be drawn from deep underground.

A *huerta* is more than a simple plot of land. It is a place for spending relaxed and contemplative hours in the shade of a climbing grapevine, cooled by a jug of white wine and a sweet melon from the garden. It is a place where family and friends are invited for meals cooked over fires of vine shoots and olive branches: rice with rabbit and home-grown vegetables such as artichokes and green beans. Orange and lemon trees fill the air with their sweet, dense perfume.

The first of the vegetable dishes to appear on Spanish tables are salads. Among the simplest are Tudela lettuce-hearts, compact little greens known in Murcia by the evocative name of *perdices de la huerta*, or "garden partridge." These are cut lengthwise in half, dressed simply with oil and vinegar and eaten with one's fingers. Sometimes they are served with anchovy or tuna fish, salt, a little lemon juice and a few rings of sweet white or spring onions.

There is, nonetheless, a love-hate relationship between the Spanish and vegetables. In a tragic vein, Antonio Machado spoke of the "two Spains" perpetually divided and at war. To apply the concept to more trivial, culinary terms, it can also be said that Spaniards are divided into those who love vegetables and those who hate them, or who eat them solely because they feel they should.

Other salads are identified with a particular district or region, such as the *xató* from southern Garraf, the Penedés and the Vendrell in Catalonia.

Xató is a salad made when endives are in season, and is a specialty that provides a multitude of excuses for festivals, contests, lectures and debates. There are even academies that monitor its orthodox preparation, investigate its origins and so forth. It is

a complicated, substantial salad that is a meal in itself.

The basis of the dish is the juicy white and yellow endive, to which is added anchovies, tuna fish either tinned or marinated in *escabeche*, green onions, olives and other ingredients. These are napped with a special sauce made with chopped almonds or hazelnuts, garlic and *ñoras*, round reddish peppers dried in long strings. In the Garraf, these are cooked in water, then the pulp is scraped out with a knife and added to the mortar with the rest. In the Vendrell, on the other hand, the *ñoras* are fried in oil before being ground with the almonds and other ingredients. This is one of the many differences between the various regional versions of *xató*.

But the dish has another original feature: *xató* is served with tiny vegetable omelettes, stacked one on top of the other, made with young artichokes, red or green bell peppers, peas, broad beans, spinach, or onions.

Xatonadas are held in which the public participates in *xató* demonstrations and contests, and the streets and squares of participating towns are filled with tables replete with platters and bowls of the salad. Everyone from housewives to restaurateurs tries to give the dish his or her distinctive touch. All

this, of course, takes place in a wine-producing area — where the Catalan sparkling wine, *cava*, is produced. During *xatonada*, this wine, which has begun to compete with champagne on international markets, flows in torrents. It marries extremely well with the *xató*.

At the end of the last century, one of the best Spanish romantic writers, Pedro Antonio de Alarcón, wrote a beautiful book based on a visit to Granada. He called it *La Granadina* (Women of Granada), in homage to the women of that town.

Alarcón devotes an enthusiastic chapter to the art and skill with which the Granada women create salads. He believed that this skill reflected the enormous respect and love the people of Andalusia in general, and Granada in particular, have for green things, and for everything that needs water to sprout, grow and thrive. He lists a series of Granada salad variations, each more subtle and delicious than the next. Almost all are a harmonious combination of salad vegetables and fruit: lettuce and pomegranate seasoned with oil and lemon juice; grated carrot with endive and slices of orange or tangerine; melon or watermelon salads with garden purslane or romaine lettuce; strawberry vinaigrettes, and many other home recipes

An inhabitant of Navarre heads to the market to sell produce from his vegetable garden (above). Raimundo, owner of the Rincón de Pepe restaurant in Murcia, proudly shows off fresh home-grown lettuce, the perdices de la huerta. Only the inner leaves are eaten, accompanied by a simple dressing (right).

characterized by the clean and fresh flavors so sought after by modern cuisine.

Three basic herbs are used to flavor salads: fresh mint; coriander, which is a strong parsley-like herb; and the sensual, aromatic sweet basil. Sometimes the salad greens are enhanced with a sprinkling of paprika, and in Castile, in particular, a lettuce or endive salad is often served with tinned peas.

An item that belongs on the list of vegetables discovered in the New World, along with tomatoes, peppers, and potatoes, is the avocado — a relative newcomer to Spanish cuisine.

It has been most successfully integrated into Spanish cooking in Andalusia, in the form of a gazpacho. This resembles a guacamole, except that it is more liquid. It contains the same ingredients as the tomato gazpacho, apart from the bread: finely chopped onion, a little garlic, bell pepper and cucumber, and sometimes small pieces of ham.

Asparagus is very popular in Spain. Among the white varieties, those from Aranjuez, Ribera de Navarra and Cordoba are the favorites. Large, fat and juicy asparagus is preferred, and curiously enough, tinned asparagus is more popular than fresh. The latter is called *pericos*, and is served with a vinaigrette sauce or mayonnaise.

Asparagus is eaten not only as an hors d'œuvre in Spain, but also as an accompaniment to cooked dishes, especially fish.

The most sought-after and expensive kind of asparagus, however, is the green *triguero*. This is not the ordinary cultivated green variety, but grows wild in the fields and vineyards in springtime. It has an incomparable taste, with a subtle, appealing bitterness. It is eaten with a vinaigrette sauce, in scrambled eggs, and in many other preparations.

Triguero is not the only wild plant that is prized in modern Spain. When the winter snows begin in the Pyrenees, people look for *xicoia* (*Taraxacum dissectum*), a tiny dandelion (the French call it *pissenlit*) with in-

tensely green leaves that is eaten in salads, preferably dressed with a truffle vinaigrette. In Extremadura and Andalusia, people also search for cardoons (*Scolymus hispanicus*), a small thistle-like plant with a delicious taste not unlike artichoke, of which only the blanched inner leaves and stalk are eaten. And then there are edible fungi and mushrooms, of course, which we mentioned in the preceding chapter.

The annual seasonal demand for these plants provides a welcome source of income

Wild asparagus, or triguero, is popular in Andalusia. Extremely delicate, it is either grilled or served with scrambled eggs.

169

La Huerta, Castile's big, fertile plain, is also the word for garden. Here Spaniards lovingly cultivate vegetables used in the surtido de verduras—prepared with cardoons, artichokes, borage and peas (above).
La huerta is also a delightful place for meeting friends and for enjoying, under the shade of an olive tree, grilled vegetables and lettuce hearts, asparagus, tomatoes, artichokes, chicory and spring onions (facing).

for many people of small means. This is, of course, a small underground economy that, fortunately for food lovers, is as yet untrammeled by VAT and the taxman.

Which does in fact present a small but interesting fiscal problem. Restaurants make no invoices when they buy these wild-growing crops, some of which, like certain varieties of mushrooms or wild strawberries, net high returns. They do, however, have to bill the client for them. This explains why they have completely disappeared from the table in every one of the state-run Spanish *Paradores Nacionales*: the state is a strict and vigilant manager.

Despite the general Spanish fondness for vegetables, it is unthinkable to have nothing but greens on the table. There is always meat in one form or another.

Menestras are winter and spring vegetable soups, and they always include small pieces of ham. A Navarrese garden is the best place in which to enjoy them: the pleasure is doubled by the fact that not only are the quality and freshness of the ingredients first-rate, but the surroundings too are lovely and green. Ham is also added to the Basque *porrusalda* soup, which is made with leeks and potatoes mashed into a purée (rather like a vichyssoise, but without cream, and served

hot). *Habas a la catalana* (Catalan-style broad beans), the Catalan vegetable dish par excellence, is cooked with black or white Catalan sausages and bacon.

At the beginning of the season, raw broad beans are eaten as appetizers to accompany an aperitif or in salads, but later they are usually served with other tasty ingredients such as ham or fish eggs.

Red *Lombarda* cabbage is cooked with apples in a typical dish from Madrid, and is also used for the special garnish of the traditional Christmas sea bream. The dark-green, flavorful mountain *berza negra* cabbage is cooked with potatoes, which are mashed with it into a purée, then fried in lard like an omelette to make the Pyrenean *trinxat*. It is always served with a crisp-fried slice of streaky bacon.

Spaniards like starchy foods, particularly potatoes, chickpeas, kidney beans and lentils. Spanish cuisine includes many dishes in which these are the basic ingredient, but like vegetables they are rarely served alone.

The most typical meal in Rioja is a first course of *patatas a la Riojana*, followed by ribs of baby lamb broiled over vine shoots. For the centenary of the Bodegas CVNE, one of the most prestigious establishments in Rioja, Paul Bocuse was asked to prepare a banquet for the invited press and the authorities. The master chef from Lyon revved his culinary genius into full gear for the banquet, and it was an unforgettable event for everyone there.

Bocuse himself, however, lunched on Rioja-style potatoes prepared by the modest *bodega* cook. He said to me, "I'm delighted that you liked my cooking. But I can't see why you asked me to come, when you have food like this! I've had three servings — this is *real* cooking!" What he had was simply potatoes cooked with some good chorizo sausage — the potatoes soak up the wonderful flavor of the chorizo. This is a substantial dish that was originally served during grape harvests, and which has become the culinary symbol of this famous grape- and wine-producing region.

Legumes make good, solid winter food. In Spain (except for Catalonia) dishes made with legumes are eaten with a spoon. They are eaten as a first course in a kind of thick, heavy soup.

Three are particular favorites: *alubias con morro y oreja* (broad beans with pig's snouts and ears), which is typically Castilian; *alubias negras de Tolosa* (Tolosa black broad beans), which takes its name from the Guipúzcoan town that is famous for, among other things, the quality of its beans; and *lentejas a la castellana* (Castilian-style lentils).

The first features pig's snout and ears cut into small pieces and cooked for quite some time, which produces a luscious jelly. The black or speckled broad beans are cooked in an earthenware pot with chorizo blood sausage and small pieces of bacon. This is accompanied by green or white cabbage, which is cooked separately, and is customarily eaten with red-hot green or yellow peppers in vinegar. The lentils are cooked thoroughly in enough liquid to make a hefty gravy, along with chunks of chorizo and blood sausage.

In Catalonia, and especially Barcelona, the industrial revolution gave rise to a commercial activity that still characterizes the area today. This is the sale of dried beans and chickpeas that have been pre-cooked by the tradesmen the night before. People either buy them in paper cones and eat them on the job, or take them home for the evening meal. They must be heated up, however, and since they disintegrate if they are boiled a second time, another solution was found: the chickpeas or kidney beans are fried in oil or animal fat. This is not easy to do, as the peas or beans almost have to be fried individually — kept well separated, in any case — and should come out golden and crispy but not burnt. They are served with a slice of fried bacon or, more often, in one of the most typical dishes of Barcelona: *butifarra amb seques* — fried white sausage with white kidney beans. The quality of the pre-cooked vegetables is guaranteed, and they contain no preservatives or other artificial ingredients.

Chickpeas have a long tradition in Spain, and are a basic element in the cuisine of the two Castiles, La Mancha and Andalusia. Boiled with spinach or Swiss chard to make *potaje*, the Castilian soup par excellence, they can be cooked with pieces of meat, or with salt cod during Lent.

The first crop of each season is awaited with impatience. The arrival of spring garlic signals the appearance on restaurant menus of a much-loved dish: scrambled eggs with new garlic. The tender Liliaceae is picked before the clove segments have formed, and inspires a prodigious rise in egg consumption. Scrambled eggs are made with tomatoes, bell peppers, wild asparagus and a variety of vegetables, but garlic is the long-time favorite.

At the Mesón de la Villa in Aranda de Duero, the wonderful local produce is given its due in a refined dish consisting solely of vegetables. These are grilled seasonal vegetables, and include new garlic, wild *triguero* asparagus, and halved lettuce. Seri, the owner-cook, prepares this dish with supreme elegance, while her husband Eugenio, a former *Guardia Civil*, demonstrates his talent at oven-roasting: his shoulder of baby lamb with grilled vegetables is extraordinary.

An important festival in Catalonia honors the arrival of *calçots*, a kind of elongated onion resembling a leek. During the *calçotada* these vegetables are cooked over open fires by the thousands. When they are done, they are taken in the fingers, dipped into a dish of *romescu* sauce, then with the tips between the teeth, the *calçot*'s soft white middle is gently sucked out. People tend to get spattered with sauce from head to toe during the process, but with liberal helpings from the wine jug, nobody seems to mind. In Galicia the first crop of *pimientos del Padrón* is the occasion for a no less impressive or crowded fiesta. Eating these small, sometimes minuscule peppers can be a suspenseful undertaking. Generally, they have a

Cauliflower with garlic is one of the most popular vegetable recipes. Cooked and drained cauliflower is added to oil with fried garlic and chopped red peppers (above). This charming store in Barcelona's Boqueria market sells many kinds of chickpeas, lentils and beans, which are the basis of numerous hot and cold dishes (facing).

Candied, boiled or raw onions are used in everyday Spanish cooking. The Catalans even have an onion festival, the calçotada, which takes place at the annual calçot harvest. The calçot is a small, elongated, extremely flavorful variety (above and facing).

cooked with ham or in the finest *menestra* soups. They can also be chopped, coated with batter and fried, a technique that is used with many vegetables.

Also from Navarre, and from Aragon as well, is wild or cultivated borage (*Borago officinalis*), whose almost transparent leaves appear in the springtime. Anyone who wants to taste one of the most delicious, subtle dishes to be had in this world should try the borage prepared at the Príncipe de Viana in Madrid, cooked with chicken stock and diced ham.

mild, sweetish taste, but occasionally a glossy, dark green *Padrón* pepper turns out to be diabolically hot, sending the victim dashing for water, bread or wine. *Padrón* peppers are eaten fried in oil or as a garnish for meat or fish. Tons of them are consumed at the harvest celebrations every year, to the sound of music and flowing rivers of wine.

A long-awaited arrival for those with subtler palates is the cardoon, especially the variety from Navarre. The thick, velvety green leaves, stripped of their skin and veins, reach the markets in late winter, and are

When the best Catalonian restaurants announce the arrival of the tiny, sweet, and infinitely tender peas from Maresme or Baix Llobregat, the tables have already been reserved for some time. At the Hispania in Caldetas, about twenty miles north of Barcelona, the first of these peas to reach the kitchens of Paquita and Dolors Rexach are put away as though they were priceless green pearls, and kept for food-loving friends who are informed by telephone. Legend has it that some people eat them kneeling in reverence. . . . The peas arrive straight from the garden, gathered one by one into a Catalonian worker's apron before sunrise. They are covered with dew when they are picked, and that is how they reach the famous kitchens. And on the plate, they are pure pleasure.

ASPARAGUS WITH FRESH PEAS

ESPARRAGOS A LA TUDELANA

Navarre

Preparation time: 20 minutes
Cooking time: 1 hour 20 minutes
For 6 servings:
4 1/2 lb (2 kg) fresh white asparagus
6 tablespoons (3 fl oz/9 cl) olive oil
2 small white onions, peeled and chopped
2 1/4 lb (1 kg) fresh peas, shelled
5 oz (150 g) Serrano ham, diced
1 teaspoon sugar
2 cups (16 fl oz/50 cl) chicken broth
Salt
Freshly ground pepper
1 hard-cooked egg, sliced into rounds
1 tablespoon chopped parsley

Method:

Peel the asparagus, trimming off and discarding the tough stem ends. Cut the spears into 1 1/2-inch (3 cm) lengths. Place in a saucepan filled with boiling salted water and cook until tender, about 20 minutes. Drain and set aside.

Heat the oil in a shallow, earthenware casserole. Add the onions and cook for 6 minutes. Add the peas, ham, sugar, and broth and cook over very low heat for 45 minutes or until the peas are tender, between 30 and 45 minutes, depending on their size. Add the asparagus and season with salt and pepper. Increase heat and bring to a boil.

Serve immediately, decorated with the egg slices and parsley.

Vegetables are displayed with art and refinement in a dazzling array of color at the Spanish market (facing).

FRUIT ORGEATS AND ICE DRINKS

Chufa, or the earth almond, is a member of the family Cyperaceae. It is cultivated in Valencian market gardens and grows wild in the Spanish Mediterranean and in North Africa, from whence the Moors brought it to Spain.

It produces a small tuber that is extremely rich in oil. The milky substance derived from it is used to make the famous orgeat, *horchata de chufas*, a delicious regional summer drink.

The word *horchata* comes from the French *orgeat*, which was a medieval barley-water that is still made in homes in Provence as well as produced industrially. Made of barley (*orge*) or oats (*avoine*), it was originally called *hordeate* in Spanish and is still known as *ordi* in Catalonia and Valencia. Some forms of the drink are still known as *avenate* in Valencia — a name that was used in Rupert de Nola's recipe for the drink in the fourteenth century.

Orgeat was very popular in the Middle Ages, and earth almond, or chufa, which is rich in oils and natural sugars, considerably improved the beverage.

Today it is short of miraculous to find pure, unadulterated chufa orgeat. It would be far too expensive to produce as a popular drink. These refreshments are often made with other fruits such as almonds and hazelnuts, but more often than not they are based on a common cereal such as rice. *Horchata* is also made using a variety of other ingredients, including chufa itself.

The *horchaterías* where one buys orgeat usually also sell *granizados*, a kind of crushed-ice drink that is easy to make at home with a variety of ingredients, including wine.

To make a wine *granizado*, red or white wine is placed in a glass recipient and sugar is added until the liquid becomes thick and homogeneous. It then goes into the freezer or the coldest part of the refrigerator until it begins to freeze and take on a slushy consistency. It can be served immediately, preferably with a straw. *Granizados* can be made with fruit juices as well, or with coffee. One of the most delicious of these iced drinks is blended coffee and lemon.

The industrious and enterprising Valencians sell their *horchatas* and *granizados*, as well as nougat and ice cream — the latter they market throughout Spain and also export. In this field they rival the Italians.

GIFTS FROM THE GARDEN

ESCAROLE SALAD WITH FRIED GARLIC
ENSALADA DE ESCAROLA CON AJOS FRITOS
Valencia

Preparation time: 5 minutes
Cooking time: 2 minutes
For 4 servings:
1 head escarole lettuce
6 tablespoons (3 fl oz/9 cl) olive oil
3 cloves garlic, very finely chopped
1/2 tablespoon sherry vinegar
Salt

Method:

Trim, separate and carefully rinse the escarole. Drain and dry thoroughly.

Heat the oil in a skillet. Add the garlic and cook until it begins to color. Remove from the heat and let the garlic continue to brown lightly in the pan's residual heat.

Place the greens in a salad bowl. Scrape the oil and garlic from the skillet into the salad bowl. Add the vinegar, season lightly with salt, and toss the salad gently to coat the leaves thoroughly with the seasoning.

SPINACH A LA CATALAN
ESPINACAS A LA CATALANA
Catalonia

Preparation time: 10 minutes
Cooking time: 16 minutes
For 4 servings:
3 1/2 tablespoons (1 oz/30 g) seedless raisins
2 1/4 lb (1 kg) spinach leaves
6 tablespoons (3 fl oz/9 cl) olive oil
3 1/2 oz (100 g) Serrano ham, minced
3 1/2 tablespoons (1 oz/30 g) pine nuts
Salt
Freshly ground black pepper

Method:

Place the raisins in a bowl filled with warm water and soak for 30 minutes.

Carefully clean the spinach leaves, removing stems and rinsing in several changes of cold water. Drain. Plunge the spinach into a large saucepan of boiling salted water and cook for 10 minutes. Drain thoroughly.

Drain the raisins. Heat the oil in a large skillet. Add the ham and cook for 1 minute. Stir in the raisins and pine nuts. Add the spinach leaves, season with salt and pepper, and cook over medium heat for 5 minutes.

Serve hot.

NAVARRESE MIXED VEGETABLES
MENESTRA DE VERDURAS REBOZADAS
Navarre

Preparation time: 25 minutes
Cooking time: 1 hour
For 4 servings:
4 medium (2 1/4 lb/1 kg) artichokes
1 lemon
1 tablespoon flour
Salt
2 1/4 lb (1 kg) fresh peas, shelled
2 1/4 lb (1 kg) fresh fava beans, shelled
1 small bunch (9 oz/250 g) baby carrots
12 fresh white asparagus
6 tablespoons (3 fl oz/9 cl) olive oil
4 slices Serrano ham (see glossary)
1 onion, peeled and chopped
2 hard-cooked eggs

Method:

Break the stems from the artichokes. Trim off and discard most of the leaves, reserving only the hearts. Halve the lemon and rub the cut side over the artichoke hearts. Place them in a large saucepan and cover generously with cold water. Squeeze the juice from the lemon into the saucepan, and add the flour. Bring to a boil and cook over high heat until tender, 30 to 45 minutes.

Meanwhile, fill a separate saucepan with water, season with salt and bring to a boil. Add the peas, fava beans, and carrots and cook until "al dente," or slightly firm, about 15 minutes.

Peel the asparagus, trimming off the tough stem ends. Tie them into a bundle with string and place, stem ends down, in a saucepan of boiling salted water. Cook until "al dente," about 15 minutes.

Drain the artichoke hearts and remove the chokes, using a small spoon. Drain the remaining vegetables and set aside.

Heat the oil in a large shallow pan. Add the ham and cook until lightly browned. Add the onions and cook until tender. Add the drained vegetables to the casserole and cook over low heat until lightly browned. Season with salt.

Cut the eggs in half, add them to the casserole and continue to cook until they are warm. Serve hot.

ANDALUSIAN SUMMER SALAD
ENSALADA DE VERANO
Andalusia

Preparation time: 25 minutes
For 6 servings:
1 large head lettuce
2 cloves garlic, peeled
3 firm tomatoes, peeled and quartered
7 oz (200 g) asparagus tips
7 oz (200 g) tuna packed in oil
1/2 onion, peeled and sliced into rounds
3 1/2 oz (100 g) cucumber, peeled and sliced
   into rounds
1/3 cup (2 oz/50 g) pitted black olives
3 gherkins or small dill pickles, sliced
3/4 cups (6 fl oz/18 cl) olive oil
4 tablespoons sherry vinegar
Salt
2 hard-cooked eggs, sliced into rounds

Method:
Separate and rinse the lettuce leaves, drain them thoroughly and cut them into strips.

Rub the garlic cloves over the bottom and sides of a salad bowl.

Place the leaves in the salad bowl along with the tomatoes, asparagus, tuna, onion, cucumber, olives, and gherkins.

In a small bowl, combine the oil and vinegar, and season with salt. Drizzle the dressing over the salad and toss until thoroughly mixed.

Decorate with the egg slices and serve immediately.

CARDOONS WITH RAISINS AND PINE NUTS
CARDO CON PASAS Y PIÑONES
Catalonia

Preparation time: 40 minutes
Cooking time: 2 hours 25 minutes
For 6 servings:
3 1/3 lb (1 1/2 kg) cardoons
2 tablespoons flour
3 1/2 tablespoons (1 oz/30 g) seedless raisins
6 tablespoons (3 fl oz/9 cl) olive oil
1 garlic clove, peeled and chopped
2 cups (16 fl oz/50 cl) chicken broth
3 1/2 tablespoons (1 oz/30 g) pine nuts
Salt
Freshly ground white pepper

Method:
Carefully trim and pare the cardoons of any fibrous parts, leaving only the tender portion of the ribs. Rinse and cut them into uniform pieces.

Stir 1 tablespoon of the flour into a large saucepan filled with salted water, add the cardoons, bring to a boil and cook until the cardoons are tender, at least 2 hours. Meanwhile, place the raisins in a bowl of warm water and soak for 30 minutes.

Heat the oil in a skillet. Add the garlic and cook for about 2 minutes, or until lightly browned. Stir in the remaining tablespoon flour, and quickly add the broth, stirring constantly. Add the pine nuts and cook for 10 minutes. Remove from the heat, and, if desired, strain the sauce through a sieve.

Drain the cardoons and arrange them in a large earthenware casserole. Drain the raisins and sprinkle them over the cardoons. Pour the sauce evenly over all and simmer over low heat for 10 minutes.

Season with salt and pepper and serve.

CATALAN-STYLE GRILLED VEGETABLES
ESCALIVADA CATALANA
Catalonia

Preparation time: 10 minutes
Cooking time: 25 minutes
For 4 servings:
2 eggplants
2 red bell peppers
1 onion
6 tablespoons (3 fl oz/9 cl) olive oil
Several drops sherry vinegar
Salt
Freshly ground white pepper
1 teaspoon chopped garlic (optional)
1 teaspoon chopped parsley (optional)

Method:
Wrap the onion in aluminum foil and cook over hot coals or in a preheated 400° F (200° C) oven for 25 minutes.

Rinse and pat dry the eggplants and peppers. Grill them over hot coals or in a preheated 400° F (200° C) oven for 15 minutes.

When the vegetables have cooled enough to handle, remove their skins. Seed the peppers and cut them in strips. Cut the eggplant into strips. Slice the onion into rounds.

Arrange the vegetables on a serving platter. Season them with olive oil, sherry vinegar, salt and freshly ground white pepper. Add garlic and parsley if desired.

Place in the refrigerator to chill.

Catalan-style grilled vegetables (facing page).

Water can be a major problem in fruit- and vegetable-producing countries. Spain is no exception, and where there is a lack of canals, orchards are watered by hand. Many vegetables of the gourd family such as melons and pumpkins grow on secano, or non-irrigated land, moistened only by rainfall.

PISTO MANCHEGO
RATATOUILLE
PISTO MANCHEGO
Castile-La Mancha

Preparation time: 15 minutes
Cooking time: 40 minutes
For 6 servings:
6 tablespoons (3 fl oz/9 cl) olive oil
1 large onion, peeled and chopped
2 small green bell peppers (9 oz/250 g),
    seeded and coarsely diced
2 small zucchini (11 oz/300 g), peeled
    and coarsely diced
2 1/4 lb (1 kg) ripe tomatoes, peeled
    and coarsely diced
Salt

Method:
Heat the oil in a large earthenware casserole or Dutch oven. Add the onion and cook for 5 minutes. Add the green pepper and zucchini and cook over low heat for 5 minutes.

Add the tomatoes and simmer over very low heat for 30 minutes, stirring from time to time to prevent vegetables from sticking to the pan.

Season with salt and serve hot with poached, fried or scrambled eggs.

This dish can also be served chilled.

ARAGONESE STUFFED ZUCCHINI
CALABACINES RELLENOS
Aragon

Preparation time: 20 minutes
Cooking time: 55 minutes
For 4 servings:
4 medium zucchini
6 tablespoons (3 fl oz/9 cl) olive oil
1 medium onion, peeled and chopped
2 very ripe tomatoes, peeled and chopped
5 oz (150 g) ground pork
5 oz (150 g) ground beef
Salt
Freshly ground black pepper
1 teaspoon oregano
1 tablespoon flour
2 tablespoons breadcrumbs
2 tablespoons grated cheese
3/4 cup (6 fl oz/18 cl) chicken broth

Method:
Rinse and thoroughly dry the zucchini. Cut them in half lengthwise, scoop out the center flesh with a tablespoon, chop the scooped-out flesh and set aside.

Heat the oil in a skillet. Add the onion and tomatoes and cook over medium heat for 15 minutes. Stir in the chopped zucchini flesh and cook for 5 minutes. Add the ground pork and beef, season with salt, pepper and oregano, and cook over high heat for 5 minutes. Stir in the flour, mix well and remove from the heat.

Stuff this mixture into the zucchini halves. Place them in a baking dish. Sprinkle with the breadcrumbs and grated cheese. Pour the broth into the baking dish, place in a preheated 350° F (175° C) oven and cook for 30 minutes.

Serve hot.

OYSTER MUSHROOMS SIMMERED IN WINE
SETAS DE CARDO ESTOFADAS
Cantabria

Preparation time: 15 minutes
Cooking time: 30 minutes
For 6 servings:
2 1/4 lb (1 kg) oyster mushrooms
6 tablespoons (3 fl oz/9 cl) olive oil
1 clove garlic, peeled and chopped
1 small onion, peeled and chopped
6 tablespoons (3 fl oz/9 cl) hearty red wine
Several leaves fresh tarragon
Salt
Freshly ground black pepper

Method:
Carefully clean the mushrooms of any grit or dirt. Dry thoroughly and cut them into pieces.

Heat the oil in a large skillet. Add the garlic and onion and sauté for 5 minutes. Add the mushrooms and cook over high heat for 5 minutes.

Stir in the wine and tarragon, and season with salt and pepper. Simmer over low heat for 20 minutes or until the mushrooms are tender.

Serve accompanied by toast or bread sautéed in olive oil.

MUSHROOMS WITH SERRANO HAM
SENDERILLAS AL ESTILO DE SORIA
Castile-León

Preparation time: 15 minutes
Cooking time: 33 minutes
For 6 servings:
2 1/4 lb (1 kg) cultivated mushrooms
6 tablespoons (3 fl oz/9 cl) olive oil
3 garlic cloves, peeled and finely chopped
3 1/2 oz (100 g) Serrano ham, diced
1 tablespoon chopped parsley
Salt
Freshly ground black pepper

Method:
Clean the mushrooms and dry thoroughly.

Heat the oil in a large skillet. Add the garlic and cook for 2 minutes. Add the ham and cook for 1 minute. Add the mushrooms and parsley and season with salt and pepper. Cook over low heat for about 30 minutes, or until most of the water given off by the mushrooms during cooking has evaporated.

These mushrooms are frequently served with scrambled eggs.

WILD MUSHROOMS WITH GARLIC AND SAUSAGE
ROVELLONS A LA AMPURDANESA
Catalonia

Preparation time: 15 minutes
Cooking time: 25 minutes
For 4 servings:
14 oz (400 g) Lactarius (see glossary)
  or other wild mushrooms
2 tablespoons water
2 fresh butifarra blanca sausages
  (see glossary)
1/4 cup (2 fl oz/6 cl) olive oil
2 cloves garlic, peeled and chopped
1 tablespoon chopped parsley
Salt

Method:
Remove the stems from the mushrooms and reserve for another use. Wipe the caps clean with a damp towel.

Place the water in a saucepan. Add the mushrooms, cover, and cook over low heat for 10 minutes, shaking the pan from time to time. Drain the mushrooms in a colander. Wipe the saucepan clean.

Coarsely chop the mushrooms and return them to the saucepan. Remove the sausage meat from the casing and add it to the saucepan. Add the oil, garlic, and parsley, season with salt, and cook over low heat for 12 minutes.

Serve immediately.

The humble potato was cultivated in the Canary Islands on its way to Europe from the New World. Here potatoes are harvested in a huerta in Andalusia.

FRUIT COUNTRY

Spain's climate makes it an ideal country for growing fruit. There is an abundance of every imaginable variety of Mediterranean fruit, as well as those that grow in an Atlantic climate, and fruit is a major Spanish export on the European market.

Among the most popular Spanish summer fruits are Castilian melons, especially those grown in Villaconejos. These are famous for being extraordinarily tender and sweet, and this is probably due to their being cultivated in dry conditions, with no irrigation other than an occasional light rain.

In Madrid, particularly in its less residential districts, the streets fill during the melon season with improvised stalls laden with huge piles of the fruit. Lizard-green, shaped like rugby balls, they can be bought whole or cut in slices to be eaten on the spot. There are watermelons too, among which the favorite variety is grown in market gardens in the Mediterranean; these are irrigated with brackish water that is unsuitable for drinking, but which according to popular belief gives the watermelons a special flavor and, paradoxically, makes them sweeter.

As summer in Spain is associated with melons, winter evokes roasted chestnuts. Eating chestnuts is not exclusively Spanish, but certainly is a popular and deeply entrenched custom here. The arrival of winter is hailed by the sudden emergence in the streets of metal drums containing hot coals and a rack. The best chestnuts are from Galicia and northern Castile-León, and are just as useful for warming one's hands in an icy north wind as they are for eating. A popular way of preparing them at home is to slit the shell and cook the chestnuts in boiling water with a few grains of aniseed or a glass of aniseed liqueur. Chestnuts were once the basic foodstuff in the isolated mountain areas of Galicia and Atlantic Spain as far as the Hurdes. This chain of wild mountains south of Salamanca stretching to the Portuguese border was the site of wretched poverty, as Luis Buñuel demonstrated in his famous documentary *Las Hurdes* (Land without Bread). Its virtually exclusive use as the staple food gave rise to serious illnesses.

Raisins and sultanas are indispensable ingredients in many Catalan and Valencian recipes. They are usually accompanied by another fruit, wild-growing pine nuts, in Catalan-style spinach, salt cod, and other regional specialties. They create a very unusual blend of flavors that can become rather complicated and over-elaborate, like the chicken stuffed not only with raisins and pine nuts but also plums, peaches and dried apricots, which is a very popular Christmas dish in Mediterranean communities. In the North, capons are stuffed with whole apples and quinces.

Fruit and fruit derivatives are not widely used in Spanish cooking. However, eating cheese with quince or quince jelly is a time-honored tradition. Spaniards tend not to like cheese after a meal, preferring it as a snack or appetizer accompanied by an aperitif, but they will eat it if it is served as a dessert with quince. In some areas of the Mediterranean coast, especially in southern Catalonia, this fruit is replaced by *cabello de ángel* ("angel-hair"), an intensely sweet, agreeably textured concoction of the syrup and fibrous pulp of pumpkin or melon.

A favorite dessert in Spain is chilled Rioja peaches, which are preserved in syrup in big glass jars. Although these huge and delightful-looking peaches are also handled on an industrial level, they are mainly produced by small cottage industries.

Almonds and hazelnuts are used a great deal in sauces under the heading of *picadas*

Dry fruit such as prunes, apricots, raisins, pine nuts, and especially almonds and hazelnuts are favorite ingredients in desserts. For the Catalan postre de musico (musician's dessert), they are served with naturally sweet wine. They are also used in sauces like the romescu, made with crushed almonds and hazelnuts. The fruit stalls at the entrance to Barcelona's Boqueria market are an amazing cornucopia of colors and smells (facing).

These succulent and fragrant winter pears are an incomparable delight. The best are from the village of Puigcerdá in the Catalan Pyrenees mountains (above).
The small shops of old-fashioned charm sell fruit and vegetables, baskets for picking mushrooms and even straw fans that are perfect for reviving embers (facing).

a country that is one of the world producers of citrus fruit. It certainly does not help the declining prestige of Spanish hotels at a time when tourism is still one of the country's greatest sources of foreign exchange.

Orange and lemon production is highest in Valencia. A range of varieties enables the region to produce oranges year round, and one of the most sensual experiences in Spain is a walk among flowering orange trees, the air laden with the heady perfume of the orange-blossoms. Under the starry sky at night one has the impression of being transported into the gardens of caliphs and sultans, symbols of love and femininity. Not surprisingly, brides traditionally carry orange-blossoms to the altar in Spain.

An unusual superstition observed throughout the country consists of eating twelve grapes at midnight on New Year's Eve while the twelve bells of the Puerta del Sol in Madrid sound the end of the old year and the arrival of the new. Before the advent of television this was a custom exclusive to Madrid, and took place at the Puerta del Sol itself, where festive crowds celebrating the New Year would gather. With television coverage of the event, however, the ritual has spread to the whole of Spain. The superstition claims that if the twelve grapes are eaten in time with the bells, without any mistakes or omissions, it will be a lucky year. The origin of the ritual is uncertain, but I suspect that since the clock that rings the hours is in the building that used to house the Ministry of the Interior, this is just another ploy for political centralization in Madrid, which wants the rest of Spain to eat and dance to the rhythm it dictates.

Madrid is "the city of the bear and the arbutus tree." Its coat of arms features this tree with a bear scrambling up to reach the delicious wild fruit. Perhaps once upon a time there were bears and arbutus trees in and around Madrid, but apart from the bears in the zoo and the arbutus fruit occasionally seen in luxury shops, both of which come from anywhere but Spain, those on the city's coat of arms are the only ones left.

and the Taragonese *romescu*, and give an original flavor to meat and fish. The fresh or toasted nuts are ground in a mortar with garlic and parsley, emulsified with olive oil and thinned with white wine, and served with fish stews or ragouts made with rabbit, chicken or beef.

European markets are inundated yearly by Spanish strawberries, which are cultivated extensively in the Andalusian province of Almería and in the Catalan Maresme area. Strawberries were among the fruit introduced from America — Peru, to be exact — but they were called *fresas* after the French botanist Fraize. The best-known and finest strawberries in Spain are probably those from Aranjuez, an extremely fertile plain near Madrid, which is also famous for its asparagus. In late summer the Pyrenean woodlands yield large quantities of wild strawberries, redcurrants and blackberries, which are picked for home use or taken to the better restaurants, where they are often served with a sauce of orange juice.

Oranges are such a symbolically Spanish fruit that it might seem superfluous to mention them. It is, however, worth pointing out that there are few hotels in Spain in which the breakfast orange juice is natural and freshly squeezed, which is scandalous in

Tiny pomegranate seeds sprinkled over lettuce delight both the eye and the palate (above).

In late summer, the cool and humid undergrowth of the Pyrenees forest invites explorers to hunt for redcurrants, mulberries and wild strawberries, which are also served in the best restaurants with a sauce of fresh orange juice (right).

Levant is huertas country, bordered by the Mediterranean and graced with olive and orange groves. Their powerful scent can make you drift momentarily to the era of the caliphs of Muslim Spain (facing).

thing of an industry exists, which produces the liqueur in varying degrees of quality.

The taste for *pacharán* corresponds to the Spanish liking for aniseed — in fact, it actually belongs to the same family. The success of the drink, which is rather sickly-sweet, may well be due as much to its attractive pinkish-purple hue as to its taste. Whatever the case, there is no doubt that it has a characteristic flavor unique to Spain, and has to a large extent replaced brandy as an after-dinner drink.

Symbolically speaking, reference must also be made to the *granada* — pomegranate. This fruit, which is on the Spanish coat of arms, commemorates the conquest of Granada by the Catholic Kings, whereby the Arabs were put to flight from Spain in the same year as the discovery of America. The 500th anniversary of this event will be celebrated in 1992. Pomegranates are typically Andalusian, and were often eulogized by Arab poets, particularly the Sufis, who saw in its tightly packed ruby seeds the symbol of the harmony of the universe and the unity and splendor of the heavens.

An extraordinary wild fruit that grows extravagantly in Spanish territory north of Madrid is the sour biennial sloe, from which a liquor called *pacharán* is made. This fashionable ice-cold digestive results from macerating the fruit with aniseed or reducing it to a syrup that is dissolved in brandy. The fruit is native to Navarre, and until recently *pacharán* was prepared only at home or for local consumption. Today, however, now that it is better known, some-

Pomegranates are eaten not only as a dessert, but also mixed with lettuce and onion in salads. With a dressing of lemon juice, the contrast of flavors is delicious.

SPANISH

CHEESES

When it is made in these conditions Manchego cheese is one of the finest in Europe, and it is certainly the most popular in Spain. The abundance of *churra* ewes in La Mancha enables the cheese to be produced in great quantity, but its excellent quality and reputation have given rise to many imitations throughout Spain.

Before it became popular, Manchego was essentially a shepherd's cheese, and with white bread was the shepherds' staple food during the long seasonal migrations to new pastures. The literature of the Golden Age, especially Cervantes, is full of allusions to this delicious cheese, curdled with rennin from the fourth stomach of a ewe, and redolent of wonderful country flavors.

It is usually eaten in one of three ways: fresh, while it is still a soft and moist curd; ripe, when it becomes semihard and slightly resistant, at which point it has a pleasant, parmesan-like piquancy; and cured, after macerating in good virgin olive oil for some time.

Picón de Cabrales is usually known simply as Cabrales, the town in Asturias where almost all of its artisan production takes place. It is a strong blue cheese made of various kinds of milk and family secrets. The method used is similar to that of Roquefort, for Cabrales is also cured in caves, although Roquefort is aged in the warm Mediterranean region of the Hérault, whereas Cabrales matures in an Atlantic climate in the damp caverns of the mighty Picos de Europa. Another difference is that it is wrapped in oak or chestnut leaves, which in time give it a grey or reddish tint in addition to the blue of the penicillium.

The fiercely individualistic character of the mountain people who make this cheese has so far prevented any standard definition of Cabrales, a cheese that has made its way to fame in conditions of total anarchy. Cabrales was reportedly the favorite cheese of Clémenceau, who had it brought to Matignon from the vicinity of the terrible Naranco de Bulnes.

A good-quality Cabrales, therefore, is

Ignacio still makes sheep cheese in the traditional manner on his farm in Idiazabal. This Basque specialty is also entered in a major competition organized by the city (facing).
Torta del casar is a rare sheep cheese made in Extremadura. It is unique in Europe and a favorite of cheese-lovers (above and following double page).

Cheese is not served in Spain as it is in France or Italy. It is usually eaten as an appetizer or a snack; rarely is the cheeseboard brought to the table at the end of a meal.

Several of the Spanish autonomous communities produce excellent cheeses, most of which, however, are unknown even in Spain. There are only half a dozen that are widely popular: *Manchego*; *picón de Cabrales*, a strong blue cheese from Asturias; Galician *tetilla*; *Burgos*, a white cheese made with ewe's milk, which is eaten fresh; *Idiazabal*, a smoked ewe's-milk cheese from the Basque region, and *Mahón* from Minorca, which is also made with ewe's milk.

On the other hand there is a widespread liking for many dairy products such as *cuajada*, *mato*, particularly in Catalonia, and *recuit*, all of which are soft-curd cheeses. These appear on the table in the form of a dessert, usually sweetened with honey.

It is obvious from its name that Manchego cheese comes from La Mancha. According to a recent law on guarantees of origin it must be made by specified methods and solely with milk from ewes of the coarse-wooled *churra* breed, with no admixture of any other type of milk.

A small cheesecake amid other traditional Spanish pastries. The quesada pasiega was a favorite of gourmets back in the fourteenth century (above). Cider, the ideal drink to serve with cabrales, the famous blue cheese of Asturias, is made in huge factories in the mountains of northern Spain (right).

unique, and cannot be compared with other members of the family. In order to find it at all, one has to follow one's intuition and information gleaned from reliable sources in the area. Generally, the best Cabrales-makers have contracts with quality restaurants all over Spain.

Cider is probably the best drink to accompany this cheese. It should be poured from as high as the arm can reach, so that it splashes hard into the bottom of the glass, which is held as far down as possible in the other hand. This way of "drawing" cider is a skill that the Asturians have mastered to perfection. The liquid should describe a perfect arc and land hard in the bottom of the tumbler, which is specially made of very fine glass, without spilling a drop. Only a finger or two of it is put into the glass at a time, and the cool, cloudy cider must be drunk quickly, before it loses its sharpness. When the blue cheese is well cured and at the peak of its strength, with no hint of dryness, its piquancy goes wonderfully well with the fresh-tasting fermented juice of reinette apples, drunk in the welcoming, intimate atmosphere of the mountain cider bars. Everything here contributes to a moment of supreme pleasure — the all-pervading aroma of the cider, the merry, epicurean mood of

the clients, the singing, and the fascinating sight of the people serving the cider with a grace and gravity that never fails to astonish even the regular customers.

Galician cheeses are made of cow's milk, and the best known are the *país*, *tetilla*, and *San Simón*. People much prefer the farm-produced variety of the first two. Galicia is an autonomous community with many small holdings; farmers usually own only three or four cows, sometimes even less, from whose milk they make their cheese. *Tetilla* ("nipple") cheese is so called because of its resemblance to the female breast. These farm cheeses are usually sold discreetly very early in the day, as their production transgresses the arbitrary labeling laws imposed under vague pretexts of hygiene.

Tetilla and *país* cheese are at their best in spring, when the cattle feed on fresh turnip leaves: these greens give the milk an exceptional creaminess and a distinctive aftertaste. A similar phenomenon occurs in the ewe's milk cheese *torta del Casari*, which is made in Extremadura. Damp spring pastures produce bacteria that give the milk a buttery creaminess, resulting in a cheese that is unlike any other in Europe. It is a thin, round cheese that looks rather like a pie. Unfortunately, the bacteria that give it its

special texture do not appear every year, so that when they do, the cheese is doubly appreciated.

The San Simón, another Galician cow's-milk cheese, is produced in a tall cone shape and is slightly smoked. It is cut horizontally instead of vertically, in round slices from the top to avoid its drying out. This is originally a mountain cheese, and despite the fact that its production has become largely industrialized, it is not difficult to find good ones in the better shops and restaurants of Galicia.

From the Basque Country comes Idiazabal cheese, which is made of ewe's milk and can be smoked or not. This is a favorite cheese in Spain, and is eaten either fresh, when the rind is still soft, or dry, which is how the true devotees prefer it. It is produced both by hand and industrially. Every year the town of Idiazabal holds a contest for making the cheese in the traditional farmhouse way. I was once a judge in this contest, and it was a memorable experience to sample the entries under the intense scrutiny of the shepherds with their crooks and staffs. The winning cheese is put on auction and fetches a high price. It is usually carried off by some well-known restaurant in San Sebastián. The Basque shepherds make their cheese in huts high in the mountains, and say that its quality depends greatly on the direction of the winds blowing the smoke from their fires.

It is probably due to the different quality of the pastures and variations in humidity that the Basque and Navarrese ewe's milk cheeses (*Roncal*, in this particular instance) are milder and more unctuous than those from Castile and La Mancha. The cheese from the coarse-wooled sheep of the Navarrese valley of Roncal is so popular with the French on the other side of the border that they cream the best off the top every year, and unfortunately it is becoming increasingly difficult to find in Spain.

A typical Spanish Mediterranean cheese is the Minorcan *mahón,* made from ewe's milk. Its flavor evokes the island pastures on which the ewe feed, which are buffeted

by sea winds and therefore slightly salty.

The finest goat cheeses in Spain are produced in Andalusia and especially in Extremadura. Among the former, the cured, blue-veined cheese from the Sierra de Aracena, Málaga and Grazalema deserve special mention. The most noteworthy of the Extremaduran cheeses are the Ibores and Plasencia, which are also among the best in Europe. They are usually white and very creamy. The Canary Island goat cheeses are also very good.

Besides Cabrales, Asturias is home to many other remarkable specialties. One of them is called *Afuega el pitu,* which in the local *bable* language means "throat-suffocating," because of its astringent dryness. This is a cow's-milk cheese that is produced in different varieties, one of which is reddish because of the powdered red pepper mixed with the curdled milk. Without this attractive addition, the cheese is white, but whatever its color, it is extremely strong.

An interesting curiosity among Castilian cheeses is the *pata de mulo* — "mule's leg." It is a ewe's-milk cheese made primarily in Villalón that is strong-smelling, rich and creamy, and shaped just as its name suggests.

The Catalan *recuit* is a fresh ewe's-milk cheese from the Ampurdán region in

Rennin is used to curdle milk in several varieties of sheep cheese; the fermentation is watched carefully.

In spite of more than 100 varieties of cheese, Spain does not yet enjoy the reputation it deserves. The cabrales from Asturias is worthy of the most discerning palates in the world.

Gerona that is usually eaten with honey. *Montsec* is the most popular goat cheese in Catalonia, where people also love *tupi*, a paste of ewe's milk and aged ewe's-milk cheese that is fermented in brandy or aniseed. It is very strong.

Famous throughout Spain is the Basque *cuajada*, which is similar to the Catalan *recuit* but made from cow's milk to which curds are added when it is heated. This is also served with honey.

In the exceptional cases when Spaniards eat cheese at the end of a meal, it is usually served with a piece of jellied quince, or *codoñate*. This is a very old tradition, especially in the center of Spain. The contrast of the two flavors can be quite agreeable.

There is a Spanish proverb about the pleasure of eating something sweet with the salty taste of cheese: "grapes with cheese: like a kiss are these" — "*uvas y queso, saben a beso.*"

An official Ministry of Agriculture catalogue recognizes over one hundred varieties of Spanish cheese. There are in fact more than that, but many are lesser variations of the more familiar ones. This ambiguity is a result of the anarchy reigning at the artisan level in this food sector. The anarchy arises from legislation born of a purely bureaucratic mentality and incompetence and the individualistic attitudes of small-scale cattle- and sheep-farmers who are hostile to any standardization or regulation. Because of this, the only cheese that has managed to obtain an official Label of Origin is the Navarrese Roncal.

Antiquated and absurd labeling laws have slowed the production of artisanal cheese-making and prevented the blossoming of small local industries. These laws have favored an inundation of bland cheeses produced on an industrial scale by European cheese "factories," assisted by European Community regulations that have completely overlooked the Spanish cheese industry. A movement is afoot today to revive traditional Spanish cheese-making, but the small output of these companies, their high prices and the chaos that exists in the food sector makes these cheeses vulnerable to the flood of commercially processed cheeses arriving from Europe.

Authentic Spanish cheeses have also been undermined by their numerous imitators, who take shortcuts to make an inferior, cheaper product. It is nonetheless possible to find quality cheeses, either where they are produced or in the better restaurants.

It seems strange to say that Spain is the third greatest cheese producer of Europe after France and Italy, when Spanish cheeses are so little known, even in Spain. If it were left to the administrative authorities, this treasure would be completely lost within a short time, but fortunately, cooperatives and small-scale private businesses have been producing and marketing high-quality local cheeses for some time now.

CANTABRIAN CHEESECAKE

Quesada pasiega (Pasiega cheesecake) is one of the few dishes in Spanish cuisine that are based on cheese. *Pasiegos* are the day-laborers or cattle farmers in the valleys of Cantabria. This dish, which has become popular throughout Spain, has many variations and is very easy to make.

Here is a popular method: take one-half pound of cheese curds, eight ounces of flour, eight ounces of sugar, three and one-half ounces of butter, three eggs, the grated zest and the juice of half a lemon, a glass of rum, two tablespoons of cinnamon and a pinch of salt. Mix the ingredients well and cook in a greased tin in a hot oven for half an hour.

This *quesada* (or *quesadilla*) is a very old dish, and one that the Spanish brought to Latin America, where it is still prepared in many different versions. Nowadays cheesecake is eaten all year round, but it was once a purely Lenten dish, with powdered or very finely chopped mint instead of cinnamon.

One late sixteenth-century recipe gives it a truly Lenten slant by adding spinach or Swiss chard to the cheesecake mixture along with the mint.

DESSERTS

MOCTEZUMA'S GIFT

The Spaniards brought back from the Americas many new foods that irrevocably changed the course of European cuisine: potatoes, tomatoes, peppers of all kinds, strawberries . . . and, above all, chocolate.

Curiously enough, the only one of these foods that the Spaniards immediately adopted was the latter — the thick black drink served hot and fragrant at the table of Moctezuma. Could its swift popularity at the court of his conquerors have had something to do with the aphrodisiac properties attributed to this substance in ancient Mexico, a virtue that drew Hernán Cortés's army like a magnet? Its consumption became the object of intense Inquisitorial suspicion, and gave rise to heated arguments among theologians over the legitimacy of its use during Lent. Was chocolate a solid or a liquid? If the former, then it should be forbidden in times of fasting and abstinence; if the latter, then it

was permissible. The controversy faded away when the clergy itself adopted chocolate as its favorite breakfast drink.

Bernal Díaz del Castillo, who unlike some of Cortés's chroniclers was a first-hand observer, wrote that "they brought vessels, goblets of fine gold filled with a drink made from the cacao bean. They said that this drink gave them success with women, and at first, we took no heed of it. But then I saw that more than fifty large pitchers were brought, containing good cacao, with its foam, and that Moctezuma did drink of it, and the women did serve him with great willingness." The Spaniards also observed how the cacao harvest was a time of wild orgies, and heard the Aztec noblemen claim that they never went to bed with a woman without drinking chocolate beforehand. It was only logical that the Spaniards hurled themselves into drinking chocolate with abandon, and none more so than Hernán Cortés, who afterward never let a day go by without drinking a cup. What was less easy for the Conquistador to understand was that the cacao beans were used by the Aztecs as money. Frankly, he preferred gold.

In Moctezuma's palace the task of preparing chocolate for the ruler was the exclusive domain of specially skilled women. The lord of the Aztecs had approximately twenty women in his service for this purpose alone.

Moctezuma's chocolate was a very different beverage from the one we know today; it contained numerous spices, the ground petals of flowers, and other vegetable and even animal substances, such as amber and musk. And no sugar at all, for sugar cane was not indigenous to the Americas, but was brought by the Spaniards.

On his return from Mexico in 1631, Antonio Colmenero de Ledesma, a doctor of

The churro, a long, hollow fritter that originated in Madrid, is served warm and crisp, with a cup of hot, creamy chocolate.

medicine, wrote a *Curioso Tratado de la naturaleza y calidad del chocolate* (A curious treatise on the nature and quality of chocolate), containing a recipe recommending its preparation with "several very hot chili peppers, a handful of aniseed and *orejabala*, one or two vanilla flowers, six powdered Alexandria roses, two drachmas of cinnamon, a dozen chopped almonds and hazelnuts, sugar, and whatever quantity of *achiote* necessary to obtain the red color desired." *Achiote* is the red annatto seed, a delicious seasoning and colorant basic to Mexican cuisine.

Earlier, in 1590, the Jesuit theologian José de Acosta wrote in his *Historia natural y moral de las Indias* (Natural and moral history of the Indies) that "the principal use derived from cacao is a beverage called chocolate, which is a drink of madmen that in those lands is prized highly, although those who are not accustomed to it are sickened by it. . . . And it is the prized drink offered to personages who traverse their lands by Indians and Spaniards, and most especially Spanish ladies accustomed to those parts of the world, who would die for this black chocolate. It is said that chocolate is made in a variety of ways and drunk at various temperatures: hot, cold and barely warm. They put into it spices and much chili pepper. Also they make it into flat tablets and call it *pectoral*, which is beneficial for the stomach and for warding off colds."

So the chocolate discovered and adopted by the Spaniards was a spicy, strong drink to which, aided by medical beliefs of the period, interesting aphrodisiac properties were attributed. This may explain why it was not accepted in the puritanical Austrian court, but did enter, albeit at a later date, the court of the French Bourbons. Some poets and intellectuals, among them Francisco de Quevedo, were by that time using the substance more or less clandestinely, and spoke about it in much the same way that intellectuals of the 1980s might have referred to hashish or cocaine. The greatest disseminator of chocolate propaganda in seventeenth-

century Europe was undoubtedly the extravagant Madame de Sévigné — despite the fact that she was later to disavow all she had ever said or written about the drink of the Aztecs and Spanish colonizers.

In Spain people prefer their drinking chocolate thick, almost the consistency of a purée. This is reflected in the popular saying, "Accounts should be kept transparent, and chocolate thick."

The first creators of recipes for chocolate-based confectionery were the Spanish cloistered and missionary nuns who arrived in Mexico with the colonizers. Spanish convents in Mexico amassed fortunes in a short time through the sale of their confectionery, so great was popular demand for anything with the taste of chocolate.

Perhaps it was for this reason that for centuries the people of Spain associated chocolate with the well-being of the clergy. According to certain documents, this well-being was an indisputable fact, at least for many of the higher ecclesiastics. In one of his best books, *La jornada del Inquisidor* (The Inquisitor's working day), the anthropologist Julio Caro Baroja uses such documents to describe the Inquisitor's breakfast, which consisted of *picatostes* with an impressively large cup of thick chocolate prepared by nuns in his service.

Chocolate cups were made of silver or fine porcelain and filled with the fragrant liquid lovingly prepared by nuns' hands, hands of the Brides of Christ, who saw the nuncio or cardinal as God's ambassador. To the Aztec *chocolateras*, Moctezuma was God himself, the direct incarnation of Quetzalcoatl, the Gardener of Paradise, creator of the cacao-producing *cacahuatl* tree.

Picatostes are thin slices of fried or toasted bread spread with shortening and sugar, but these are simple, abbreviated versions compared to their seventeenth-century counterparts. Martínez Montino, Philip IV's chef, gives us the older recipe: in those days, *picatostes* were heifers' udders that were cooked and coated with breadcrumbs, then fried in cow's fat or toasted in the oven. The udders eventually disappeared from the preparation, and the word *picatoste* was applied only to fried or toasted bread sprinkled with sugar.

Nowadays, *picatostes* have been supplanted by *churros* and *porras*, and what was once the breakfast of the Grand Inquisitor has become that of the general populace. It is also the first sustenance taken in the early morning in *churrerías* and *chocolaterías* by night owls and inveterate drinkers, when they greet the dawn from the wrong end of the day. Even in these circumstances, the most tradition-conscious among them accompany their chocolate and *churros* with a small glass of aniseed liqueur.

Churros are also among the *fruta de sartén* (frying-pan fruits), as ancient culinary treatises called confectionery that was fried in oil or shortening. They are made with a light batter and boiled in deep fat in a frying pan with the help of a gadget that gives them their special shape — a kind of ridged, spiral tube. Once they are fried, the *churros* are cut into pieces the size of the palm of the hand, and sprinkled with sugar. They should be eaten hot, and are a marvelous accompaniment to chocolate.

Nowadays *churros* are popular throughout Spain, but they were originally a Madrilenian dish. In the old days, *churro*-sellers would walk at the break of dawn through the working-class streets of Madrid, with a basket of *churros* that they would sell to the workers on their way to the factories.

There is a huge annual chocolate festival held in Barcelona on Easter Monday. Many enormously talented chocolate "artists" participate. The ancient European rite of chocolate Easter eggs is observed everywhere, but in Barcelona you can find more than mere eggs. There are chocolate statues that reach gigantic proportions, representing anything from an aircraft carrier to an enchanted palace.

Some people agree with the early twentieth-century essayist Angel Moro in believing that, along with bulls, chocolate is the symbol of Spain. Of course, from

Mexico via Spain, chocolate spread like wildfire throughout Europe. In terms of comestibles, it was the greatest cultural shock in the collision between two worlds. Spanish queens married French kings and launched the vogue for chocolate that overwhelmed Paris and all of France. It became not only a fashionable delicacy but also the universal panacea for all ills, from melancholia to rheumatism.

Although chocolate triumphed in confectionery, its entry into cooking proper took place much more cautiously.

The cuisine of Ampurdán includes a decidedly baroque dish: *langosta con chocolate* — lobster with chocolate. It is a curious variant of *mole*, the Mexican national dish, although this is made with a variety of meats, often turkey or pork. Interestingly, *mole* was created by Spanish nuns (or daughters of Spanish families) in Puebla, in homage to Don Tomás de la Cerda y Ragón, viceroy of Spain, according to Paco Ignacio Taibo. My own research has led me to conclude that it was invented in honor of Monsignor Don Manuel Fernández de Santa Cruz y Sahagún, bishop of Puebla and native of Palencia in Spain — a dismal poet who signed his work with the peculiar pseudonym "Sor Filotea." Not that it really

The magnificent "Samuel de los Santos" patio is one of the treasures of Córdoba. Spilling over with flowers, the inside gardens of Andalusian houses are ideal for breakfast in the cool hours of the morning or for enjoying pastries with a glass of sweet wine.

matters — the fact is that *moles* (from the Nahuatl word *molli*, meaning "concoction" or "sauce") existed before this, but the nuns from Santa Rosa in Puebla were the first to add chocolate to the sauce, thereby creating the greatest dish to emerge from Hispano-Mexican culinary crossbreeding.

Lobster with chocolate, also known as "Catalan lobster," is much less complicated than the Mexican *mole* — the similarity is due to a few ingredients, such as chocolate, that are common to both.

The lobster is cooked on a bed of lightly fried onions, garlic and tomatoes to which chopped almonds and a teaspoonful of ground chocolate are added. These ingredients also go into a *mole*, but in far greater quantities. In any case, lobster with chocolate is delicious.

Another chocolate recipe, from Galicia this time, features lamprey eel; it is made along the lines of game civets, and is a delectable dish.

Nevertheless, good chocolate is becoming a thing of the past in Spain, especially the higher-quality product, although it can still be found in the better confectioneries or restaurants that make a specialty of it.

Chocolate was once the preferred Spanish breakfast or children's afternoon drink. Unfortunately, it is now being ousted in favor of instant products that children love, but that bear no comparison with those wonderful cups of thick chocolate that the *picatostes* and the *churros* could stand up in and emerge coated with a delicious creamy paste that smelled like heaven! Moctezuma and Hernán Cortés would never understand this modern world, and sometimes, neither do I.

JUAN DE LA MATA'S CHOCOLATE

Toward the end of the eighteenth century and for the first twenty-five years of the nineteenth, Don Juan de la Mata, native of Matalavilla in the province of León, owned a confectionery and fine food shop in Madrid. The fame and prestige it enjoyed was comparable to that held today in Paris by Fauchon or Hédiard.

Juan de la Mata wrote a book in 1786 entitled *Arte de la Repostería* (The art of confectionery). The important thing about Juan de la Mata was that he was also a chocolate-maker, who produced and sold chocolate in liquid form and in tablets, and whose products acquired a wide reputation for their excellent quality.

He wrote, "Everyone knows the composition of chocolate, the solidified paste composed of cacao (whose varieties are numerous, the best of which is from Caracas), sugar and cinnamon. The proportion of each of these ingredients, to give an example, is eight pounds of sugar to a similar quantity of cacao and one pound of cinnamon. Since the manner of treating this mixture is common knowledge, I shall omit its description here. If one wishes to make the mixture even more delightful, when the paste is formed, a few drops of essence of orange-blossom or vanilla are added and the paste well whipped and put through the sieve. This being said, despite its improvement in taste and fragrance, neither can such a concoction be kept for the same length of time, nor is it of such healthful gain; for which reason it should be avoided as a harmful thing: vanilla has overheating qualities and no other function than to introduce inflammation into the body. Orange-blossom water, which possesses none of these defects, may be used in moderation; however, a judicious and prudent man will despise all effeminate delights, whose only use is the destruction of nature, and will take his chocolate composed only of sugar, cinnamon and cacao, with the admission of no other adjunct; for in this manner, besides being perfect, it has the further virtue of being wholesome. This virtue is not unknown to foreign persons, for which reason the French, in particular, call it *chocolat de santé*, which in our own tongue is the equivalent of 'health chocolate.'

"It is of the greatest benefit, when made with the necessary purity of ingredients, for the stomach and the chest; it maintains and restores the natural warmth of the body; it nourishes; it dissipates and destroys malignant humors; and fortifies and sustains the voice.

"Chocolate must be kept in a dry place and well wrapped in paper."

A common dessert on Spanish restaurant menus is "mousse au chocolat." Confectioners in Spain are unaware that Juan de la Mata prepared this recipe long ago, and called it — as it should be in Spain — *espuma de chocolate*. The recipe for it is simple and delicious: "A pound of best chocolate is crumbled with a half pound of sugar, a few sticks of cinnamon and a little zest of lime. The chocolate is made in the ordinary manner, and when it is somewhat thickened it is taken from the flame and put through a fine cloth or sieve into a recipient where it is left to cool, with a little melted ice added before beating it; it should finally resemble a milky foam."

EGGS, FLOUR, HONEY AND A NUN'S TOUCH

In his splendid biography of the great Mexican poet and nun, Sor Juana Inés de la Cruz, Octavio Paz recounts that the Spanish colonial nuns amassed fortunes baking pastries that they sold to the wealthy hidalgos of the viceroyalty.

The Mexican Revolution did away with the practice, but it continued in Spain for centuries, and even today gourmets avidly search out convents renowned for their candies, jams or fruit preserves. The sisters also produce many other varieties of sweets whose ingredients seem simple enough, but that nobody seems to have the knack of making as well as these ladies well practiced in contemplation and patience. Their products are often the culmination of centuries of tradition, and are made from jealously guarded recipes transmitted from one abbess to another in secret handwritten notebooks.

However, Doña María Luisa Fraga Iribarne, the sister of the Spanish conservative leader Manuel Fraga and a lover of good food, won the confidence of the confectionery-making nuns in convents in the diocese of Seville, and wrote a fascinating guide to the delicacies they produce: the *Guía de dulces de los conventos sevillanos de clausura*. The book is tremendously useful to scholars of the culinary arts, and it is indeed the only Spanish book on convent confectionery in existence. The cloistered nuns are deeply reluctant to open their convent doors to outsiders; the rule is applied rigorously.

Confectionery-making religious communities exist all over Spain, but they are especially numerous in Andalusia, Extremadura and the two Castiles. Their cakes and candies have some characteristics in common, such as crossing regional and local boundaries. The same cakes, biscuits and *pestiño* fritters can be found at a good many convents, although the recipes may vary somewhat. They are always of excellent quality.

These cloisters are communities of women from a wide range of social and regional origins. This has always been so. For centuries the sisters have brought with them traditional family or village recipes, and a naturally conservative attitude as well as the public's appreciation ensured that they would never change. The nuns may come and go, but their cakes and sweetmeats live forever.

Saint Theresa of Avila, that spiritual mystic, coined the down-to-earth phrase, "the Lord walks among the stewpots," thereby becoming the patron saint of Spanish cooks. The confectioner-nuns are firmly convinced of the truth of Saint Theresa's phrase, and this may explain why they avoid altering their recipes, which are like articles of faith to them.

Sor Juana Inés de la Cruz, who so beautifully combined metaphysics and poetry, was the author of a manual of convent cooking that was re-edited by my friends Guadalupe Pérez San Vicente and Josefina Muriel, both Mexican culinary anthropologists. Sor Juana transcribed what she considered the best recipes from her San Jerónimo convent, and she herself prepared cakes and dishes for her friends among the clergy and the colonial aristocracy. Her little book is a priceless document on the Golden Age intermingling of Spanish and native Mexican cuisines. Some of the methods for making cake mentioned by Sor Juana are

Spaniards love sweets, and willingly travel many kilometers to savor specialties found only in distant villages.

The nuns at the San Leandro monastery in Seville have no contact with the outside world, and still use a revolving door to deliver pastry ordered by clients (above).

Spanish convents are renowned for their cakes and jams, especially in Andalusia, where the nuns are excellent pastry cooks. The recipes have been kept secret for centuries (facing page).

still used in Spanish cloistered convents today: *huevos hilados* (eggs beaten with sugar and thrown into hot syrup; this makes threads that are then pulled into different shapes), *buñuelos de requesón* (cottage-cheese puffs), *buñuelos de viento, hojuelas* (pancakes), *ante de nuez* (walnut macaroons), *bienmesabe* (a meringue dessert), *leche frita* (a paste made with flour cooked with milk, cut into squares, coated with egg and fried), *arroz con leche* (rice pudding), *mancha manteles, alfajores* (honey cakes) and *huevos reales.*

How many Sor Juanas are cloistered in the confectionery-making convents described by María Luisa Fraga Iribarne? In any case, the tour she takes us on is fascinating.

The most famous of the Sevillian convent desserts are the *yemas de San Leandro* (San Leandro egg yolks), made by the Augustine nuns of the convent of that name. They are made to an ancient recipe, and consist of a ball of *huevo hilado* with a coating of sugar, called a *crosta de azucar.*

Doña María Coronel founded the Santa Inés Convent in Seville in the fourteenth century, after an unfortunate encounter with King Peter the Cruel. To rid herself of the king's relentless amorous pursuit, the beautiful Doña María burned her own face with boiling oil.

Doña María bequeathed her worldly goods to the convent she had founded, and among these was a recipe for *bollitos de Santa Inés* (Santa Inés bread rolls), which are as well-loved as the San Leandro egg cones, though far less elaborate. They are a simple dessert made of bread dough and sugar fried in oil.

The Dominican nuns of Santa María la Real, in the outskirts of Seville on the road to Huelva, produce a number of different specialties, including exquisite *pestiño* fritters made with wheat flour, frying oil, red and white wine, salt, sesame seeds and ground toasted aniseed.

The Purísima Concepción Convent in Carmona, a lovely Andalusian town north of Seville, is famous for its ancient recipe for *bollos de azucar* (sugar rolls). These are made with lard, eggs, flour, sesame seeds, cinnamon and lemon; once they are cooked, the still-hot *bollos* are dipped into syrup, drained, and powdered with sugar. They are fabulous.

In Ecija is situated a convent whose nuns were known as *las marroquíes,* but although the word means "the Moroccans," the name derives from its sixteenth-century founder, Francisca Marroqui. Today it is inhabited by Franciscan Conceptionist nuns. A sister who in the outside world had been the

The spiral-shaped ensaimada and the coca de llardons are specialties of the Argentona bakery near Barcelona. These pastries are popular both for breakfast and for afternoon tea (above). The flour and sugar tarta from Santiago is branded with the cross of the monastic and military order. The best come from Monforte de Lemos, in the province of Lugo (facing).

Marquesa de Valdetortas, a Navarrese aristocrat, shut herself in the convent with four of her servants in 1751, and died there in 1772. She had brought with her the recipe for a tremendously elaborate *bizcocho* cake famous in her region.

The founding statutes of the Order of Saint Clare pronounced in 1597 that the nuns would make confectionery to earn their living. Then, as now, their specialties were *suspiros* (little meringues) and *ganotes*. The latter are made with a dough of egg yolk and finely ground flour, which is set in molds about four inches long and then fried, coated with syrup and rolled in powdered sugar.

Delicious *corazones de almendra* are made by nuns of the same order in their convent in Zafra, in Extremadura. These are heart-shaped cookies made with almonds, sugar and egg yolks on a wafer base, baked in the oven and coated with syrup. They are among the most popular of all convent confectionery.

In Osuna there are four convents, of which two subsist on the proceeds of their sweets: the Mercedarian nuns' Convento de la Encarnación, and the Dominican Santa Catalina convent.

The former, beautifully decorated with eighteenth-century Sevillian glazed tiles, makes a delicious *arroz con leche* (rice pudding), and the latter produces a number of specialties, including a recipe with medieval origins: *capiruletas*. This is a thick, rather heavy uncooked custard cream made with egg yolks, sugar and ground almonds and laced with cinnamon. It is extremely difficult to make, for the mixture must be beaten by hand for two hours without stopping! Not surprisingly, the nuns make it only to order.

The town of Estepa is well worth a visit, not only for its exceptional beauty, but for the *mantecados de Estepa* produced at the Santa Clara convent. This is made according to the most ancient recipe in existence for this sweet, which is a favorite in Spain. Only cinnamon and sesame seeds are used to fla-

vor the simple mixture of lard, flour and sugar. The nuns also make a highly appreciated *rosco de vino y mazapan* (wine and marzipan ring), also made to a very old recipe. And both are still cooked in a wood-fired oven — quite unusual nowadays — which imparts a special flavor to these delicacies.

I have mentioned only a few convents and specialties, and if my references have centered mostly on Andalusia, it is because this region is paradigmatic of this kind of cooking. Examination of Spanish convent and cloister confectionery and pastry shows that the preparations are generally based on the same simple ingredients: eggs (often from the convents' own hens), flour, sugar or syrup, oil or lard, and predominantly cinnamon and sesame seed for flavoring. Customers of the confectionery-producing cloisters never see the makers of the products. One rings a bell, which is answered by the voice of a sister taking the order: the money is placed on a revolving table, and it spins back with the package of sweets.

The nuns often prepare traditional recipes found throughout Spain, such as *tocinillos de cielo* (egg and syrup custard), *alfajores* and *mazapanes* (marzipan), *bienmesabe*, and many others. The origin of *alfajores* was a subject of tremendous public debate among nineteenth-century specialists. Don Mariano Pardo Figueroa, who under the pen name of "Doctor Thebussem" wrote some of the most important treatises on Spanish culinary arts, resolved the discussion by demonstrating that *alfajores* originated in ancient times in Medina Sidonia (Córdoba). Some say their source is purely Arabic, but I find much about them that is reminiscent of Roman confectionery. They are still made today in Mazagán, Fez and other places in the Maghreb, in exactly the same way that they were made in Medina Sidonia.

Alfajores are made in other parts of Spain, but the Medina Sidonia version differs from these in shape and presentation. Elsewhere, they are sandwiched between two wafers,

The pastry specialties of the provinces are all devilishly tempting: the Mesón de la Villa in Castile offers leche frita, a kind of milk fritter (above), and a delicious Catalan panellet, marzipan coated with grilled pine nuts (right).
It is almost impossible to resist the confections of Escribá in Barcelona—his braç de gitano (gypsy's arm), for example, stuffed with whipped cream, his tortells with Catalan cream, and his assortment of pannellets (facing).

whereas in Medina Sidonia they are a roll or croquette coated with cinnamon and sugar, and wrapped in a spiral of paper elegantly folded at one end. *Alfajores* have a strong taste and an intense aroma that need some getting used to. Once the taste for it is acquired, however, it can be almost addictive.

The connection between confectionery and religion goes beyond the convent walls. Virtually all important church feast days and local religious celebrations in Spain feature some kind of special cake, custard, sweet, or marzipan proper to the particular saint being honored. An infinite variety of local bakery products are named after saints whose birthdays appear on the Christian calendar. *Huesos de Santo* (saint's bones) are eaten on All Souls' Day, *panellets* (marzipan cakes) are baked in Catalonia for All Saints' Day, and throughout Spain nougat *turrón* is associated with Christmas and Epiphany.

The confectionery of ancient Rome included many sacrificial dainties for offering to the temple gods at different times of the year. Spain's "Saints' Days" baking probably grew from these pre-Christian Roman roots. Many people attribute it to Muslim sources, although here they are forgetting —

or are unaware of — the Roman and later Visigothic cooking that the invading Arabs (who, being nomads, had no established cuisine) found in the Iberian peninsula and adopted as their own. In all likelihood, in fact, much of North African cooking descended from Roman Spain conquered by the Arabs, and not the opposite. In Roman Iberia, for example, people were already eating couscous and *pastela* when the Arabs arrived. There is even a recipe still being prepared in Murcia that uses methods that existed in Augustan Roman times. Of course, the Arabs modified and enriched the cooking tradition they found in Spain, but they did not bring it with them, nor did they originate it.

In this chapter, the reader will find two of the most interesting of the Spanish home-style desserts: *tocinillos de cielo* and *crema catalana* (Catalan custard). Both of these egg-based recipes are easy to make at home.

Although the most expert confectionery-making hands are found behind convent doors, there are many regional and traditional recipes that are prepared by local people: All Saints' Day *panellets* in Catalonia and the eastern Mediterranean, for example; Lenten fritters in Barcelona; aniseed *pestiños* throughout Spain; and *torteles* and *brazos de gitano* ("Gypsy's arm" rolled sponge cake), a favorite dessert of bourgeois and proletarian alike on feast days in Barcelona. These are filled with cream, often the Catalan variety.

Crema catalana is another of the few Spanish recipes that are currently acquiring a reputation in international circles, although the orthodoxy of the original recipe is rarely respected outside Catalonia itself. It should be made only with the freshest egg yolks, sugar, and flavored with stick cinnamon. Catalan cream is served in an earthenware dish, caramelized and seared with a special branding iron, or left plain, as the customer wishes.

Flor de sartén, a sugary batter fried in oil, is popular in Castile. This ancient home-style dessert (it appears in medieval cookery books), is made to perfection at the La Villa

restaurant in Aranda del Duero. The compact almond *polvorón* "crumble cakes" dusted with powdered sugar are also a Castilian specialty.

The Spanish are known for having a sweet tooth, and although each area, region, and village has its own typical cakes and desserts, there are three communities that enjoy a particularly good reputation for their excellent confectionery: Madrid, Valencia and Catalonia.

Torreznos, leche frita, arroz con leche, picatostes (sugared French toast), the Catalan *carquinyolis, tejas* and *neulas* and an infinite number of homemade specialties add to a long list of desserts and sweets in which cinnamon, vanilla and aniseed recur constantly, as do almonds and hazelnuts.

Spanish children are fond of afternoon snacks of jellied quince, *dulce de membrillo* (this is also served with cheese as a dessert), and *pan de higo*, fig loaf, which is delicious when made with figs from Fraga in Aragon, on the boundary with Lérida. This is unmistakably a dessert of Arab origin.

Five hundred years ago the Conquistadores brought sugar cane to America. To them sugar was an absolutely essential ingredient, and perhaps more important, it enabled them to reproduce in those faraway lands the cakes, desserts and sweets to which these incorrigible sweet-lovers were accustomed.

The authentic turrón, made with honey and almonds (or hazelnuts), is the traditional Spanish Christmas dessert (facing page).

HONEY AND ALMONDS

The most popular of all Spanish candies is *turrón* (nougat), a sweet that is traditionally associated with Christmas.

There are only two true *turrónes* with absolute and exclusive rights to the name: those from Alicante and Xixona, both in the autonomous community of Valencia and the province of Alicante.

Although their textures are very different, both consist of the same basic and simple ingredients: honey and almonds. These two essentials give weight to the conviction that *turrón* existed a good deal earlier than is indicated in written sources, some of which go back to the fourteenth and fifteenth centuries. We might even consider it a pre-Roman product, if we read Lévi-Strauss's studies on the role of honey in the mythological/culinary structures of primitive peoples. This would lead us to look at *turrón* as a legacy of Iberian cultures, and might also explain its time-honored association with a religious feast day; today it is Christmas, and in the past, probably the feast of an Iberian divinity.

Alicante *turrón* is hard, and is made with white honey and almonds (and sometimes hazelnuts). *Turrón* from Xixona is soft and pliable, and a lovely ocher color. Both are marketed in rectangular bars in boxes of black poplar wood.

There are many other varieties of *turrón*, including one made with marzipan and crystallized fruit, one with chocolate, another with egg yolks, and the "coal" nougat, made with black-dyed sugar, that the Three Kings leave on the night of 6 January for children who misbehaved during the previous year. These varieties are often very good, but they are a spin-off of the genuine *turrón* rather than the real thing.

Turrón is a winter product. In the summer, nougat-makers in Xixona turn to the production of ice cream. Not surprisingly, one of their most popular flavors is the exquisite Xixona *turrón*.

HONEY FRITTERS
PESTIÑOS
Andalusia

Preparation time: 20 minutes
Cooking time: 25 minutes
For 4 servings:
2 cups (16 fl oz/50 cl) oil
Peel of 1 orange
1 tablespoon sesame seeds
1 tablespoon aniseed
4 cups (1 lb/500 g) flour
1 tablespoon ground cinnamon
Grated zest of 1/2 lemon
1 2/3 cup (13 fl oz/40 cl) white wine
1/2 teaspoon salt
2 cups (16 fl oz/50 cl) water
1 1/2 cup (12 fl oz/40 cl) honey

Method:

Heat the oil in a large, heavy skillet. Add the orange peel, sesame seeds and aniseed and simmer over low heat for 10 minutes. Remove from the heat and let the oil cool before straining through a sieve.

Place the flour in a mixing bowl. Add the cinnamon, lemon zest, wine, salt, and 1 2/3 cups of the water. Mix the ingredients together and knead lightly into a smooth ball. Roll the dough out on a lightly floured surface to a 1/8-inch thickness. Cut into 1 by 2-inch rectangles.

Return the strained oil to the skillet and heat to the smoking point.

Meanwhile, combine the honey and water in a saucepan and bring to a simmer.

When the oil is hot enough, add as many of the dough squares as will fit in the pan without crowding and fry, turning once, until puffed and golden. Drain on paper towels and keep warm while frying the remaining dough.

Dip the fritters in the honey and place on a wire rack. Arrange them on a round serving tray.

MADRID-STYLE HONEY FRITTERS
OREJUELAS
Madrid

Preparation time: 20 minutes
Cooking time: 20 minutes
For 8 servings:
1 1/2 cups (7 oz/200 g) flour
1 egg
2 tablespoons sugar
1/4 cup (2 oz/60 g) butter
1 teaspoon ground cinnamon
Pinch salt
3/4 cup (6 fl oz/18 cl) anise-flavored liqueur
1 cup (8 fl oz/25 cl) honey
6 tablespoons (3 fl oz/9 cl) water
2 cups (16 fl oz/50 cl) olive oil

Method:

Combine the flour, egg, sugar, butter, cinnamon, salt and 6 tablespoons of the anise liqueur, and knead into a smooth dough. Roll it out thinly on a lightly floured surface. Cut the batter into large diamonds.

Combine the honey, water and remaining anise liqueur and stir. Pour half of this mixture in a large platter, reserving the second half.

Heat the oil in a deep, heavy skillet. When the oil is hot, but not smoking, add the dough diamonds a few at a time and fry, turning, for about 5 minutes. Remove fritters with a slotted spoon, shaking off excess oil, and place them on the platter with the honey. When all the fritters have been fried, pour the remaining honey mixture over them.

Cakes and biscuits come in various shapes — like this delicious cake from the Basque region (above) or the flores de sartén (pan flowers), a Castilian delight that requires special utensils in its preparation (facing).

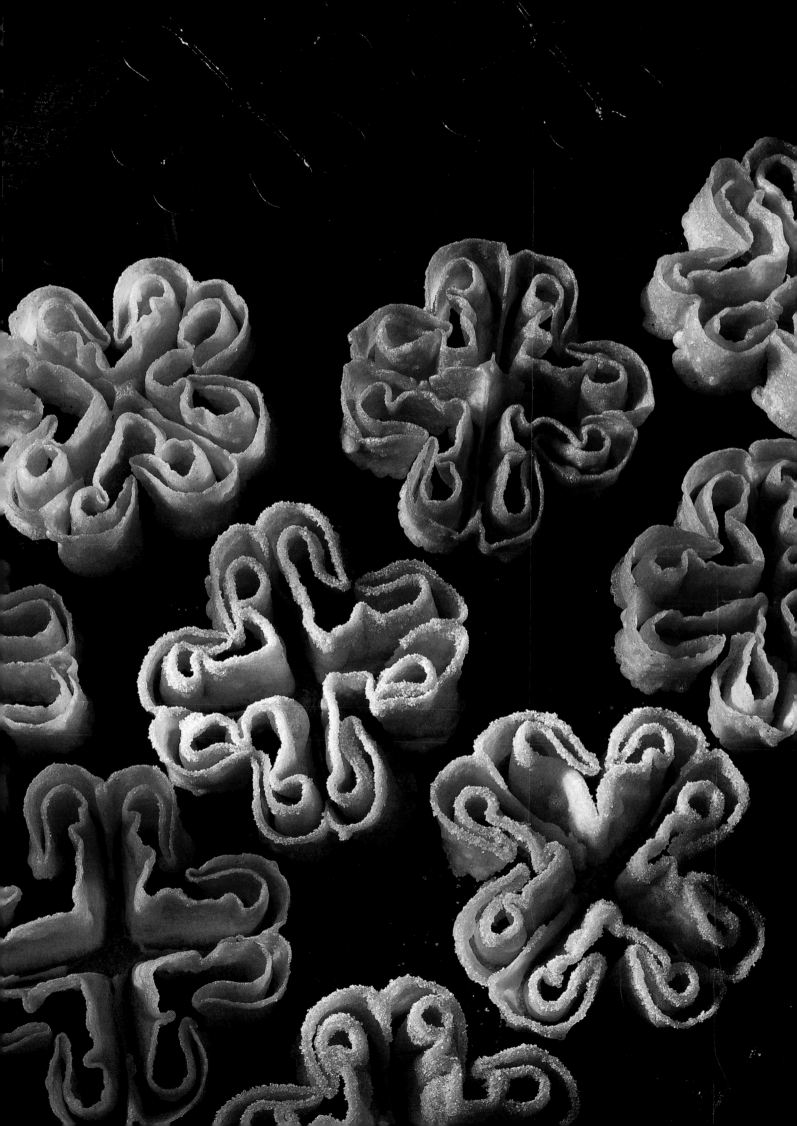

*In Casar, Extremadura, Teodoro
Perez and his daughters make
rosquilla, a dry, ring-shaped
biscuit that is a favorite in
the region. It is prepared in
exclusively artisanal fashion
(above and top, facing).*

ALMOND MERINGUE COOKIES
ALMENDRADOS
Andalusia

Preparation time: 10 minutes
Cooking time: 15 minutes
For 8 servings:
1 1/3 cups (8 oz/250 g) granulated sugar
1 cup (8 oz/250 g) ground almonds
1 egg white
1/2 cup (3 1/2 oz/100 g) whole almonds

Method:
Mix the sugar, ground almonds and egg white into a smooth dough. Form into a ball and flatten the dough with a rolling pin. Cut into small rounds.

Place the rounds on a well-buttered baking sheet, placing a whole almond in the center of each cookie.

Bake in a preheated 325° F (160° C) oven for 15 minutes. Transfer to a wire rack and let cool.

GALICIAN DESSERT CREPES
FILLOAS
Galicia

Preparation time: 10 minutes
Resting time: 30 minutes
Cooking time: 12 minutes
For 6 servings:
2 cups (16 fl oz/50 cl) milk
2 cups (9 oz/250 g) flour
6 eggs
Grated zest of 1 lemon
Melted butter
Powdered sugar

Method:
Combine the milk, flour, eggs, and lemon and beat thoroughly. Set aside for 30 minutes.

Brush a little of the melted butter in a skillet or crepe pan and add a small ladle of the batter, tilting the pan to distribute the batter evenly. Cook until lightly browned, turn the crepe and brown the second side, about 1 minute per side.

Serve the crepes hot, sprinkled with powdered sugar. Or, if you wish, fill the crepes with jam or pastry cream.

ARAGONESE SPICE COOKIES
CANTOS DE BARBASTRO
Aragon

Preparation time: 30 minutes
Cooking time: 30 minutes
For 4 servings:
6 tablespoons (3 fl oz/9 cl) olive oil
1/2 cup (3 1/2 oz/100 g) granulated sugar
13 tablespoons (3 1/2 oz/100 g) flour
1 tablespoon baking powder
1/2 tablespoon ground cinnamon
3 eggs
Zest of 1 lemon
2 tablespoons powdered sugar

Method:
Place the oil in small saucepan and warm over very low heat.

Combine the granulated sugar, flour, sugar, baking powder, and cinnamon in a bowl and mix thoroughly.

In a separate bowl, combine the eggs and lemon zest and beat until frothy. Add the warm oil a little at a time, stirring constantly with a wooden spoon. Stir in the dry ingredients, mixing until a smooth batter forms.

Pour the batter evenly over a well-greased jelly-roll cake pan or other shallow baking pan or pans. Place in a preheated 350° F (175° C) oven and bake for 30 minutes.

Remove from the oven and turn out onto a wire rack to cool. When cooled, cut into triangular shapes. Before serving, sprinkle with the powdered sugar.

EXTREMADURA-STYLE COOKIES
PIÑONATE
Extremadura

Preparation time: 1 hour 30 minutes
Cooking time: 40 minutes
Refrigeration: 1 hour
For 8 servings:
6 eggs
3 1/3 cups (27 fl oz/83 cl) olive oil
6 tablespoons (3 fl oz/9 cl) anise-flavored liqueur
3 cups (14 oz/400 g) flour
4 cups (32 oz/1 kg) honey
1 1/3 cups (8 oz/250 g) granulated sugar
6 tablespoons (3 fl oz/9 cl) water
1 egg white

Method:
Combine the eggs, 6 tablespoons of the oil, and anise liqueur in a bowl and mix together. Add the flour, knead into a smooth dough and let rest for 1 hour.

Roll the dough out on a lightly floured surface. Cut into matchstick pieces and twist them into a corkscrew.

Heat the remaining oil in a deep, heavy skillet. When the oil is hot but not smoking, add the dough pieces a few at a time and fry until lightly browned (about 30 minutes for all). Drain on paper towels and place in a large bowl.

Heat the honey, sugar and water in a pan for about 10 minutes, or until the mixture turns a caramel color.

Meanwhile, beat the egg white until it forms stiff peaks. Gently fold in the caramel. Pour this mixture over the fried dough pieces and turn them into a crown-shaped mold. Let cool for 1 hour and unmold.

EGG YOLK AND ALMOND CANDIES
YEMAS GLASEADAS
Castile-León

Preparation time: 30 minutes
Cooking time: 30 minutes
For 8 servings:
2 cups (14 oz/400 g) granulated sugar
1 2/3 cup (14 fl oz/40 cl) water
10 egg yolks
1 tablespoon almond oil

Method:
Heat 1 cup of the sugar and 2/3 cup of water in a saucepan over medium heat for 10 minutes. Remove from the heat and let cool.

Beat the egg yolks in a large mixing bowl. Add the sugar syrup a little at a time, stirring constantly. Turn this mixture back into the saucepan and cook over low heat for about 5 minutes, stirring constantly, until the mixture forms a ball and pulls away from the sides of the pan. Remove from the heat and let cool. Form into small balls.

Prepare another sugar syrup with the remaining sugar and water. Cook over low heat for 13 to 15 minutes until it boils and forms a white caramel. Roll the egg yolk balls in this mixture.

Coat a marble surface with the almond oil. Add the syrup-coated balls and let cool.

Córdoba fritters are powdered with sugar, attached to a ring and sold in packs of six (left).

ANDALUSIAN CARAMEL CUSTARD
TOCINO DE CIELO
Andalusia

Preparation time: 20 minutes
Cooking time: 48 minutes
For 8 servings:
Caramel:
4 tablespoons granulated sugar
1 tablespoon water

Custard:
1 1/3 cups (9 oz/250 g) granulated sugar
1 cup (8 fl oz/20 cl) water
12 egg yolks

Decoration:
12 small meringues

Food-lovers are enchanted by the lightness of the fritters and pine nut biscuits, specialties of Aranda de Duero in Castile.

Method:
To make the caramel: Place 4 tablespoons sugar and 1 tablespoon water in the bottom of a 9 by 7-inch (23 by 18 cm) baking dish. Cook over high heat, stirring constantly, until the sugar dissolves and the mixture turns a light caramel color. Remove from the heat immediately and tilt the pan to distribute the caramel mixture evenly over the bottom.

To make the custard: Mix 1 1/3 cups of sugar with 1 cup of water in a small saucepan and bring just to the boiling point over medium heat. Remove from the heat.

Place the egg yolks in a bowl and beat thoroughly. Beat in the sugar syrup a little at a time. When thoroughly incorporated, pour the custard mixture over the caramel in the baking pan. Place it in a larger baking pan full of enough hot water to reach about halfway up the outside of the custard pan. Place it on the stove and cook over medium heat until the water surrounding the custard mold comes to a gentle boil. Continue to cook until the custard is set, about 30 minutes.

Remove from the heat and let the custard cool in the water bath. Run a knife around the edges of the custard and invert it onto a serving plate. Serve decorated with the meringues.

CHOCOLATE TURNOVERS
EMPANADILLAS DE CHOCOLATE
Valencia

Preparation time: 30 minutes
Cooking time: 40 minutes
For 6 servings:
Pastry:
6 tablespoons (3 fl oz/9 cl) olive oil
6 tablespoons (3 fl oz/9 cl) white wine
Pinch salt
Pinch baking soda
2 3/4 cups (12 oz/350 g) flour

Filling:
2 cups (16 fl oz/50 cl) milk
4 tablespoons unsweetened cocoa powder
4 tablespoons granulated sugar
2 tablespoons cornstarch

To Finish:
Oil for frying
Sugar for dusting

Method:
Combine the oil, wine, salt, and soda in a small bowl. Place the flour in a large mixing bowl and form a well in the center of it. Add the oil mixture and gradually incorporate the flour into the center. Knead the dough lightly into a ball.

In a small saucepan, combine 1 3/4 cups of the milk with the cocoa powder and stir until well mixed. Add the sugar and bring to a boil. Combine the remaining 1/4 cup milk with the cornstarch, stirring until well blended, and stir this mixture into the saucepan. Cook, stirring, until the cream thickens. Remove from the heat and let cool.

On a lightly floured work surface, roll the dough out thinly. Cut into 6-inch (15 cm) rounds. Brush a little of the chocolate cream over the surface of each dough round. Fold each round in half and crimp the edges together by pressing down firmly with the tines of a fork.

Add enough oil to a deep, heavy skillet to measure at least 1 inch deep. Heat over medium heat and fry the turnovers three at a time until lightly browned on both sides, about 5 minutes. Remove from the oil, drain on paper towels, and roll the turnovers in sugar.

CATALAN CUSTARD
CREMA CATALANA
Catalonia

Preparation time: 10 minutes
Cooking time: 10 minutes
For 6 servings:
4 cups (32 fl oz/1 l) milk
1 stick cinnamon
Zest of 1/2 lemon
6 egg yolks
1 1/3 cup (9 oz/250 g) granulated sugar
3 tablespoons (1 1/2 oz/50 g) cornstarch

Method:

Place 3 1/2 cups of the milk in a saucepan with the cinnamon stick and lemon zest. Bring to a boil over medium-high heat, then remove from the heat.

Combine the egg yolks and 1 cup of the sugar in a mixing bowl and beat together thoroughly with a whisk.

Remove the cinnamon stick and lemon peel from the milk, and pour the hot milk into the egg yolk mixture a little at a time, stirring constantly. Turn the mixture back into the saucepan.

Combine the remaining 1/2 cup milk with the cornstarch and stir to blend thoroughly. Add the cornstarch mixture to the custard and warm over very low heat, stirring constantly, until the cream thickens, being careful not to allow it to boil.

Remove from the heat and pour the mixture into 6 individual earthenware or glass ramekins and let cool.

Shortly before serving, sprinkle about 1 tablespoon of the remaining sugar evenly over the top of each custard. To caramelize the sugar, run the custards quickly under a hot broiler until lightly browned and crunchy, being careful that the sugar does not burn.

LA MANCHA CAKE SOAKED IN MALAGA WINE
BIZCOCHOS BORRACHOS
Castile-La Mancha

Preparation time: 20 minutes
Cooking time: 45 minutes
For 8 servings:
Cake:
8 eggs
1 1/2 cups (11 oz/300 g) granulated sugar
2 1/2 cups (11 oz/300 g) flour,
 plus 1 tablespoon
1/2 tablespoon butter

Syrup:
1 1/4 cups (11 fl oz/30 cl) water
1 1/2 cups (11 oz/300 g) brown sugar
1 1/2 cups (11 oz/300 g) granulated sugar
1 2/3 cups (14 fl oz/40 cl) Málaga or other
 sweet fortified wine

To serve:
2 tablespoons ground cinnamon

Method:

To make the cake: Heat an earthenware bowl in the oven for several minutes until hot. Add the eggs and 1 1/2 cups of granulated sugar and beat together until a thick syrup forms. Add 2 1/2 cups of the flour a little at a time, whisking constantly, until it is thoroughly incorporated.

Grease the bottom and sides of a large shallow metal baking pan with the butter and sprinkle with the remaining tablespoon flour. Pour the batter into the pan. Place it in a preheated 375° F (190° C) oven and bake for 45 minutes.

Meanwhile, prepare the syrup: Heat the water in a saucepan. Add the brown and granulated sugars and cook over medium heat for about 25 minutes until a clear, thick syrup forms. Remove from the heat and let cool. Add the wine and mix thoroughly.

Remove the cake from the oven and let cool slightly before turning it out of the pan.

Cut the cake into slices and arrange them on a platter. Pour the syrup evenly over the cake slices and sprinkle with the cinnamon.

ASTURIAN SPONGE CAKE
BIZCOCHOS DE ESPUMA
Asturias

Preparation time: 20 minutes
Cooking time: 6 minutes
For 6 servings:
4 eggs, separated
2/3 cup (4 oz /125 g) granulated sugar
Grated zest of 1/2 lemon
1/4 cup (1 oz/25 g) corn meal
1/4 cup (1 oz/25 g) wheat flour
1 tablespoon butter
2 tablespoons powdered sugar

Method:

In a large mixing bowl, beat the egg yolks, granulated sugar, and lemon zest with a whisk until foamy. Mix the corn meal and wheat flour together and add them a little at a time to the egg mixture, whisking constantly.

In a separate bowl beat the egg whites until stiff peaks form, and delicately fold them into the batter.

Grease the bottom and sides of a rectangular cake pan with the butter. Turn the batter into the pan and place in a preheated 425° F (220° C) oven to bake for 6 minutes.

Remove from the oven and unmold immediately. Let cool. Sprinkle with the powdered sugar before serving.

THE BLOOD
OF THE
EARTH

Spain produces world-famous wines such as Riojas, Catalan Cavas, and Jerez. Quality wines that are less well known outside the country include Albariño from Galicia and Txakoli from the Basque region (above). This 1875 bottle of Rioja wine, the oldest in La Merced restaurant cellars in Logroño, capital of Rioja, would make more than one collector ecstatic (facing).

Spain, steeped in the Mediterranean wine-making culture, is a great producer and exporter of wines. It is impossible to imagine Spain without wine — the taste of Spain is inextricably linked to the taste of its wines, which are as marvelously varied as its topography and its cuisines.

In terms of acreage, Spanish vineyards are the most extensive in the world. In terms of production, however, Spain lags behind Italy and France, and its per capita consumption figures put the country only in eighth or ninth place, after Chile and Argentina.

The history of Spanish wine is not as well documented as that of France or Italy. Certainly the Roman colonizers planted vines for their own use, but with the growth of the major urban areas and city clienteles, Rome decided to apply protectionist measures to encourage export of its own wines. The development of vineyards in Tarragona and Lusitania was prohibited, and only those of Baetica were allowed to expand.

These protectionist rules date from the rule of Caesar Augustus, when Rome was a great wine producer. Prior to the Augustan decrees, however, vineyards had been planted extensively by Roman legionaries, and there were vineyards planted by Jewish communities that had existed since ancient times on the Iberian Peninsula.

Only a few years ago in Navarre, in 1990, *vitis vinifera* was discovered growing wild whose origins could well date back 5,000 years.

The oldest of the Spanish wines is probably Pedro Ximénes, which is produced in the Andalusian region of Moriles-Montilla (Córdoba) and, to a lesser extent, in Jerez. This wine is still made exactly the same way as it was in Carthage and the Phoenician world before the Punic Wars and the destruction of Carthage by the Romans.

This method consists of spreading the grapes on mats and leaving them to dry in the sun until they shrivel and are gorged with highly concentrated sugar. They are then pressed to extract a dense juice that is very difficult to ferment. The Romans were extremely fond of this wine, which may explain why they exempted Baetica from their protectionist laws — the region's limestone hills were ideal for the production of full-bodied wines.

The expansion of Spanish vineyards occurred mainly during the Middle Ages and during the wars of the Reconquest. The driving force behind this expansion was the monks from the great French abbeys established in Spain, especially those of Burgundian origin and, to a lesser extent, the Jewish community, who purchased land left behind by owners who went to fight the Moors.

The Benedictines and especially the Cistercians were experts on wine production in France, and wine was among the principal sources of wealth for the monasteries and great abbeys of Burgundy. Thus, vineyards surrounded monasteries and abbeys wherever they were founded by these monks from the North.

The Templar knights also planted vineyards and produced wine in their Catalan and Castilian fiefdoms. An *appellation contrôlée* was recently awarded to the Catalan region of Conca de Barberá, whose

VICTORIA
HEREDEROS DEL
MARQUÉS DE RISCAL
ELCIEGO (ALAVA)
1875
CONCEDIDA. MARQUE DEPOSÉE. TRADE MARK. SCHÜTZ MARKE
PHILOMATHIQUE
BEAUX-ARTS
INDUSTRIE
COMMERCE
XIIIe EXPOSITION
BORDEAUX
DIPLÔME D'HONNEUR
1895

All the wild beauty of Andalusia is concentrated in Jerez, the unique and generous wine from the vineyards of Jerez de la Frontera and Sanlúcar de Barrameda.
Both the classic Málaga dessert wine and Montilla, which strongly resembles the Jerez, are also from this region.

vineyards began under the tutelage of the Bernardine Cistercians and the Templars. The wines produced there are mainly white and rosé, the latter made with the *trepat* grapes (of French origin), which are ideal for this rose-colored wine.

One of the most complex and delightful wines in existence is Jerez (also called sherry or Xérès), which is the Spanish wine par excellence, and whose versatility and production methods make it unique in the world.

Its *appellation d'origine* is in the province of Cádiz, around the town of Jerez, with a maritime sub-region in Sanlúcar de Barrameda that produces a Fino, the Manzanilla.

Further north, in the province of Córdoba, is the Moriles-Montilla area which makes a family of wines closely related to the Jerez, but with less sophisticated production methods and in much smaller *bodegas.*

These nevertheless enjoy great prestige among enthusiasts of full-bodied wines.

The major difference between the wines is that the Jerez is made from the *palomino* grape, while the Moriles-Montilla comes from the *pedro ximenes* variety. Both types grow in soil known as *albariza*, which is extremely chalky earth of a strange white or gray color. This soil was once the bed of an ancient sea, and was formed by millions of mollusk shells crushed and worn into a kind of sand. This curious feature is one that the Andalusian and the French Champagne vineyards have in common.

Another feature of both Jerez and Champagne wines is that the base liquid is neutral and uninteresting until it undergoes the process that will transform it into some of the world's most brilliant and distinctive wines.

These are wines that fully justify the

saying, "God sends the harvest, man makes the wine."

However, there is another element that influences Jerez wine: climatic conditions, particularly the wind. Two winds, in fact: the *levante*, a warm, dry east wind that "cooks" the grapes on the vine, producing metabolic changes, and, even more important, the *poniente*, a humid Atlantic wind without which there would be no appearance or spread of the microscopic fungus *saccharomyces beticus* (the *flor*), a dense, odorous film of mildew-like growth that covers the surface of the Finos, sometimes very thickly.

The appearance, or not, of this magical *flor* determines which kind of Jerez wine will be produced.

If the *flor* appears, the wine will be a Fino. In other words, a dry, ivory-pale wine of 15 -16 percent alcohol, with the aroma of the *flor* predominant — this imparts a distinctive nutty flavor to the sherry, or a fruity olive or apple aftertaste in the case of the Manzanilla.

With little or no *flor*, the wine will be Oloroso, which sometimes turns into the finest of the Jerez wines. This is a fragrant, dense dry wine of a rich amber color, with an admirable bouquet, dry fruity aftertaste and enduring aroma.

From Fino is derived another product: the very dry Amontillado. When particular Finos are aged in wood they undergo a process of oxidation, and after eight or ten years of this they become Amontillados. The best of these are unforgettable. Fresh hazelnut and ginger are the preferred aftertastes, with a faint scent of cinnamon or plum.

The incredible Palo Cortado is nothing short of miraculous, for it is not created by human hands at all, and occurs in only one cask among one or two thousand. It can be classified somewhere between an Amontillado and an Oloroso, and is divided into three categories according to its quality: *dos cortados, tres cortados* or *cuatro cortados*.

None of these wines would exist, however, without the unique process used for Jerez wines: the *solera* blending system.

A *solera* is a long row of casks at floor level, on top of which are placed seven or eight additional tiers of barrels, called *criaderas* — sometimes as many as fourteen of them for the best Sanlúcar Fino Manzanillas.

The *solera*, the row on the bottom, contains the oldest wine, from which a third is drawn off each year for bottling. The casks from which wine has been drawn are topped up with younger wine from the tier above, and so on up to the highest row, where wine from the present year's harvest is added to the last. This system is the secret of the balance and consistency of Jerez wines. *Soleras* can still be found that contain tiny amounts of wine from the last century.

Naturally, the process is closely followed and controlled by expert blenders. Their

In Jerez de la Frontera, the storeroom of the González Byass residence, built by Gustave Eiffel, is an architectural masterpiece (left).
The silence and meditative atmosphere in the soleras is essential to the quality of Jerez wines (below).

The Jerez region not only produces exceptional wines like Fino, Amontillado, and the rich Oloroso, but is the capital of brandy, a superior eau-de-vie very different from cognac (above and at right).

The venenciador, the emblematic supervisor of the Jerez cellars, uses a silver siphon, the venencia, with elegance and dexterity to draw wine from the vats and thus monitor the vinification process (facing).

work requires the use of a *venencia*, a metal recipient — often of silver — attached to a long, flexible handle, which is lowered into the casks to draw up the wine and pour it, without spilling a drop, into the traditional Jerez wine-tasting cup. Served straight from the barrel, as it is done in the *bodegas*, by the deft hand of a professional *venenciador*, Fino or Oloroso wine is one of the great joys in this world.

Jerez are usually considered aperitif wines because of their high alcohol content. For a long time this wine was "taken over" by the British, who imposed their curious etiquette and habits on its use, as they did with port. Those days are over, however, and even though respect and even admiration is due to the quality and style of Victorian life, it is nonetheless a fact that the best way to drink Jerez is at a carousing Andalusian revelry, or by downing a half-bottle or two, particularly of lovely cool Fino, to accompany lashings of giant prawns or *pescaito frito*.

Jerez wine is inseparable from the Andalusian concept of quality of life. Light, color, horses and bulls, dancing and singing, the magnificent grace of Andalusian women, the architecture and cuisine of the region, all are in perfect harmony with Jerez wine and ev-

erything connected with it. The casks and barrels, the *venencias*, which transform the act of serving wine into a kind of ritualized bullfight maneuver or dance step, the wine-tasters and glasses, the enormous range of flavors and tastes, all create a web of pleasure and what I would call a philosophy of life that is distinct from anything found elsewhere in Spain.

Jerez are today the only white wines that are aged for a long time in wood. The practice of maturing white wines in oak, which was once fairly common in Spain, has now almost disappeared, and in the rare instances in which barrel-aging is done at all, it is never for longer than a few months.

But wine is made throughout Spain, including its rainiest, coldest regions with the least sun, such as Galicia and the Basque Country, whose white Albariños and "green" Txakoli are splendid adjuncts to their very individual cuisines. Catalonia is another great producer of white wines, both still and sparkling; its champagne-method wines known as *cavas* are gaining international renown. The base wine is a blend of three varieties of sugar-rich grapes whose characteristics remain constant from one harvest to another, and this ensures a reliable product whose quality improves steadily

from year to year. Differences in grapes, climate and soil create the distinction between *cava* and champagne. Any value judgement as to quality would be very subjective indeed.

Some 250 firms vie for the national and international *cava* market, in addition to the sector's two giants, Freixenet and Codorniu, who have *bodegas* not only in Catalonia but in California and elsewhere abroad.

Although the Catalan firm Miguel Torres, in Villafranca del Penedès, dominates the export market in fine red wines, the major producing area in this field is La Rioja.

Quality control is extremely strict nowadays in Rioja, whose best wines come from *tempranillo* grapes, to a lesser extent from the *garnacha* (whose wines resemble those of the French Côtes du Rhône), and from the *mazuelo* and *graciano* variety.

The Riojas' labeling indicates the length of time they have been aged in wood. There are three categories: *crianza* (a minimum of three years), *reserva* (four years), and *gran reserva* (six years). A Rioja can age long and well, but as a rule they reach their peak ten years after harvest.

Riojas are sometimes compared with wines from Bordeaux. This is a mistake. The character of the vineyard, production methods, vinification (in redwood instead of Limousin oak), and the different varieties of grapes, give the Riojas a distinctive personality of their own. If they are to be compared with another type of wine, it would have to be, as I have mentioned, the best Côtes du Rhône.

The bouquet of the Riojas is redolent of red fruit and plums. These wines are suitable for drinking young (the year they are made), and are a pleasant accompaniment to all kinds of meat and cheese. Their aftertaste is rich, with a touch of vanilla, and the overall impression is noble and straightforward.

Now that the fabulous 1970 vintage is no longer available, enthusiasts will get great satisfaction from the 1980, 1981, 1982, 1985 and 1986 wines.

These years also yielded extraordinary wine from Ribera del Duero, an *appellation contrôlée* that was little known until recently, despite the fact that it produces the famous Vega de Sicilia, which is considered by many the best of all Spanish red table wines. It is the only one, at any rate, whose composition includes several varieties of Bordeaux grapes, in addition to *cabernet sauvignon, malbec* and *merlot*. Vega Sicilia is a French-style "chateau" wine, whose best-known (and most expensive) label, the Vega Sicilia Unico Reserva, is aged in wood for a minimum of ten years — although in fact it is not bottled for sale until the firm's specialists feel that it has reached the height of its maturity.

Two other labels, Tercer Año and Valbuena, are excellent, fruity wines. Exploring the Ribera del Duero area can turn up some surprising discoveries, including local wines stored in cellars deep in the earth (some of them over 260 feet down), with extraordinary ventilation "chimneys" that give the landscape a beautifully exotic appearance. It is delightful to drink these clarets in the cool depths of the earth, accompanied by lamb chops, chorizo or fried blood sausages..

Vega Sicilia was the first Spanish *bodega* to introduce French stock into its vineyards. Its founder, a millionaire from Bilbao, was a

Ribera del Duero produces excellent wines of international renown, such as the Vega Sicilia, but also simple, traditionally made wines that age well. These deep cellars are characterized by strange ventilation chimneys, which add an exotic touch to the landscape (above).
The subsoil of the Aranda de Duero is a maze of tunnels, once used as refuge in the wars of Reconquest. As their temperature is ideal for storing wine, the tunnels have been transformed into cellars (facing).

The Condado de Huelva family in Andalusia produces full-bodied white wines that combine well with local dishes (above). Strangers rarely use the bota or porrón to drink wine, as this demands exceptional skill (right). Ribeiro wine from Galicia, a red wine with a strong tannin content, is drunk in tazas, special cups in which the wine leaves a deep purple mark (facing).

lover of Bordeaux wines, and wanted to produce a similar variety in Spain. Nowadays, making wines with grapes of French origin, even in *appellation contrôlee* areas, has become common practice. For some time *cabernet sauvignon* was the fashionable grape for red wines, and *chardonnay* was popular for whites. Now there are Merlots, Muscats, Rieslings and Gewürztraminers made by major Spanish firms and small-scale artisans alike.

Commercial incentives were undoubtedly the determining factor in this gallicization of Spanish wine, with an eye to the large North American market, whose tastes have been shaped by Californian products. Also, Spain needs wines whose price and taste will enable them to stand up to the flood of French, Italian and Portuguese wines that EEC freedom of trade will unleash upon the country.

To demonstrate the versatility and scope of Spanish wines, I would place side by side a wineglass full of Valdepeñas and a cup containing Ribeiro.

I doubt that anywhere else in the world can one find two wines from the same country that are so different, not only in taste and aroma, but also in custom and usage, and in the reflection they give of attitudes to wine. There is a world of difference between a wine that is drunk from a wineglass, or preferably a tiny *chato* glass, and one drunk from a china cup. The first dissimilarity is obvious to the eye.

The wines from Valdepeñas in La Mancha are a clear, fine ruby color; they are best served at cool temperatures and do indeed need to be drunk in a glass. The Galician

Ribeiro wines, on the other hand, which have a low alcohol content, are rather opaque, with a dark blackberry color and a pleasantly acidic taste. Its rich color can be better appreciated when a drop rolls down from the rim and is set off against the white china.

The Ribeiro cup is an original, typically Spanish recipient for wine, but Spanish drinkers also possess two other objects characterized by region and the kind of wine: the *porrón* and the *bota*.

Porrónes are Mediterranean, and made of glass. *Botas* are leather, typical of Castile and the North. Both provide one of the most delightful ways possible for drinking wine, which is pouring it from the height of the extended arm in a thin stream straight into one's mouth, splashing onto the upper lip and the teeth. This is quite a skill, and one that requires practice and a sense of style, for not a drop must be lost in its elegant execution.

The *porrón* is a common feature on the Mediterranean table, whereas the *bota* is essentially nomadic, a practical invention that enabled shepherds to carry wine from one pasture to another.

In addition to the style of drinking they impose, they share another point in common: they are utensils for collective use. Both *porrónes* and *botas*, at table for the first, outdoors or at the bullfight for the latter, are passed from hand to hand to be shared in a totally hygienic way, for the drinker's mouth never comes into direct contact with the vessel.

The interiors of the leather *botas* are lined with a coating of pitch, which gives the wine an unmistakable taste of broom that the Spanish find very agreeable. When the *bota* is new, it is "primed" with distilled liquor or brandy before being filled with wine, to tone down the tar-like flavor. A good-quality, well-treated *bota* improves with age, although a point is reached when it finally gives up the ghost. To prolong its life, it should be kept filled with wine at all times — never water, which is fatal.

The bota is a leather gourd of Castilian origin that should be seasoned with eau-de-vie before being filled with wine. It is passed around at parties, corridas and other popular events (above). Contino, one of the most prestigious Rioja wines, ages in oak casks (right).

In the same vein as the *chateo* that winds from bar to bar, *botas* are meant for use away from the table. In Spain, much of life is carried on outside the home, and many Spanish wines are produced specifically for extra-domestic consumption rather than as table wines.

Beer and spirits have dealt a serious blow to the tradition of wine as an aperitif in pubs and bars, although wine is certainly a far healthier drink. Nevertheless, this has not eliminated the average Spaniard's fondness for wine, nor the peculiar Spanish ways of drinking it.

The Spanish in general are fairly indifferent to the niceties of coordinating food and wine, and they generally drink the local wines with whatever there is to eat. However, many continue to respect the principle that the *chatos* should be white wine in the morning, and red wine in the evening.

Among the hidden treasures of Spanish wine cellars are sweet wines. Unfortunately, these are currently out of fashion, despite the sublime quality of the Spanish Málagas, Pedro Ximenes, Moscateles and Malvasías.

Particularly worthy of mention among the latter are the Canary Island Malvasías, especially those from Lanzarote, whose vineyards grow on volcanic soil with a mineral composition unique in the world. Many British, from William Shakespeare to Virginia Woolf, have adored them.

One could also lament the virtual passing of Spanish mellow (*rancîo*) wines, which held pride of place on the great European tables in the nineteenth century. One survivor is the Fondillón from Alicante, which is now made in only one *bodega*, the Casa Poveda, using methods described by Cervantes himself.

Clearly, Spain produces excellent wines. However, they do not enjoy the world recognition they deserve, and the Spaniards are mostly to blame for it.

The relationship between people and wine, which is a revealing indicator of the psychology, sociology, and even the economic and political patterns of wine-producing countries, was for centuries rather uncertain in Spain.

For hundreds of years foreign travelers gave accounts of a society that disapproved of drinking, and that deemed it a practice worthy only of the dregs of society.

Bottling, labeling, and the use of *appellations contrôlées* are relatively recent phenomena. Wine used to be sold in barrels or wineskins, and its alcohol content and taste varied wildly. It was fit for drinking

only in cheap taverns or in the streets.

Fortunately, things have changed, and the consumption of bad wines has decreased considerably in favor of beer and spirits. Owners of vineyards have made spectacular increases in the installation of bottling plants.

The shift from wine to beer, especially among young people and a violent fringe of soccer fanatics, has helped give respectability to wine in Spain. It has also given credence to the idea expounded by Maurice Barrès, who saw beer as a symbol of barbarity, but wine as a mirror of the aesthetic refinement of Latin civilization.

WINE AND POPULAR WISDOM

Many Spanish popular sayings extol wine's benefits to health. *"Quien bebe, vive"* ("He who drinks, lives"), and *"La verdad y el vino, son buenos amigos"* ("In vino veritas"), are two common phrases.

The virtues of wine are often emphasized by comparing it with water, which is considered rather unpleasant:
"El agua cria ranas y el vino no tiene esas mañas" (Water breeds frogs, but wine, never).
"El agua hace mal y el vino, cantar" (Water makes you sick, but wine makes you sing).

Other sayings attribute virtues to specific wines: *"Vino de Jerez, bueno para la vejez"* (Jerez wine is good for the old), and *"Vino de Illana, todo mal sana"* (Illana wine cures all ills).

How should wine be drunk? *"Por la mañana puro y por la tarde sin agua"* (Pure in the morning and without water in the afternoon); and:
"Antes de comer, unos vasitos has de beber. En comiendo, otros vasitos seguiás bebiendo. Mas después de haber comido, tampoco te sentarán mal más vasitos" (Two glasses before eating. Another two while you eat. But after you've eaten, another few won't hurt you).

There is no shortage of advice on combining food and wine, such as:
"Comer sin vino, comer mezquino" (Food without wine makes a stingy meal);
"Pan de antedía, vino de año y medio y carne de ese día" (Yesterday's bread, wine a year and a half old, and meat fresh today).

Wine can be a proof of friendship, as in the saying *"Al buen amigo, tu pan y tu vino. Al malo, tu perro y tu palo"* (For a good friend, your bread and wine. For a bad one, your dog and a stick); *"El vino, para que sepa a vino, bébelo con un amigo"* (For wine to taste like wine, drink it with a friend);
"Vino y amigo que se torvieron, nunca a ser bueno volvieron" (No wine or friendship gone sour ever was made good again).

Finally, when old age creeps up, one should remember that *"Viejo que vino no bebe, cerca está de la muerte"* (An old man who drinks no wine has one foot in the grave).

COFFEE
LIQUEURS
AND
CIGARS

Tradition dies hard. Spaniards love coffee, a digestive liqueur after a meal, and a good cigar, either Havana or domestic. Spaniards smoke more cigars than anyone else in the world. And the Spanish (who, don't forget, brought tobacco to Europe in the first place) are certainly the smokers most impervious to anti-tobacco campaigns.

Coffee, liqueurs and cigars are intimately linked with Spanish social life: conversation, family or friendly gatherings, soccer and bulls. And, of, course politics — or political gossip, anyway. But the distinguishing feature of these three phenomena, and one that does not meet with total approval in the modern world, is that the world of coffee, liqueurs and cigars excludes women. It is misogynous.

For the male contingent at the repast or party, coffee, liqueurs and cigars are a way to prolong the evening and the conversation. They may be indulged in at home, after a family meal when the women have gone off to talk about their own interests, in a restaurant, or at the corner café where the men meet specially for this purpose.

In Spain a meal is never complete without a liqueur. The most frequently served are aniseed liqueurs and brandies from Catalonia and Andalusia. The sloe-based pacharán is a recent addition.
Aniseed liqueur, however, remains the time-honored classic, and bottles with extraordinarily beautiful labels grace the paintings of Picasso and Juan Gris (right).
A good cigar is an essential complement to a Spanish dinner. Although Spaniards are fond of Havana cigars, they also appreciate the national production from the Canary Islands as well as the popular Farias, a cigar manufactured by the national tobacco company (facing).

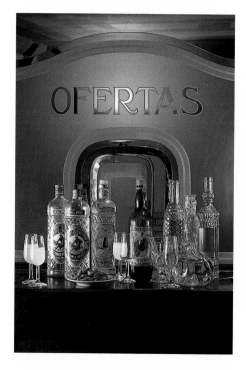

Being admitted to adult company for coffee, liqueurs and cigars is a rite of passage for young men.

What liqueurs are drunk with the coffee? The traditional Spanish drink is Jerez or Catalan brandy, but there is also aniseed liqueur, Cazalla, a popular brandy, derivatives such as *pacharán*, which is based on sweet or dry anis and sloes, and in Galicia in particular, Orujo, a brandy made from the skins and pips of grapes.

Because of international laws protecting French cognac *appellations d'origine*, cognac-style alcohols are known by the British name of brandies, although everyone calls them *coñacs*.

The great brandy producers are the Andalusians, especially in Jerez, and the Catalans, but there are some excellent alcohols made in La Mancha as well.

There is a wide difference, however, between Jerez and Catalan vinification methods. The distinctive, deliciously aromatic Jerez brandies are made by the same *solera* technique as the Jerez wines, while the Catalans use the method employed for French cognacs. Among the former, the Sanchez Romate and Domecq brandies are especially good, and among the latter, those produced by the firm of Torres are the best.

Anis has its own aesthetic characteristics, brought to the attention of the world by the great Spanish masters of Cubism, Pablo Picasso and Juan Gris.

Anis is made all over Spain, but Ojén and Cazalla in Andalusia, and Chinchón near Madrid, have their own special versions. It can be sweet or dry in varying degrees, and its ingredients include other seeds and herbs besides the aniseed itself.

Many anis liqueurs are worth buying for the bottle alone, such as the excellent Machaquito; in fact, anis bottles are often collectors' items. Machaquito belongs to a large family of liqueurs that go by the name of *torero*.

Many Spaniards prefer the Galician Orujo, with or without herbs, to accompany coffee. This is a very strong, dry distilled

liquor, or marc, whose quality depends on the honesty of the distiller and the quality of the Orujo, or grape skins used. It is better to be wary of Orujo produced by local artisans, which sometimes has a higher methyl content that it should.

The Spanish like to put a dash of a favorite alcohol into coffee after a meal. This mixture is called a *carajillo*, and can also be drunk first thing in the morning, with breakfast.

The Catalan *cremat* is also a combination of coffee and alcohol, but the alcohol is flambéed in the coffee cup — the ideal drink for raw winter mornings in the Mediterranean.

According to some writers, including Alvaro Cunqueiro, *cremat* was the source of a ritual Galician ceremony, the *queimada* (burning), to which some overactive imaginations attribute ancient and mystical origins.

Cunqueiro claims, reasonably enough, that the *queimada* originated during the Spanish Civil War, when it was prepared by Galician soldiers fighting on the Catalan front. It was gradually refined into its present complicated form, and has even turned into something of a symbol for supporters of the Galician autonomy movement.

Briefly, a large quantity of first-class Orujo dotted with grains of coffee, orange or lemon peel and spices is flambéed in a recipient. The alcohol must burn for quite some time to reduce considerably, while being stirred with a large spoon to agitate the blue flames. A lively Galician get-together rarely finishes without a *queimada*.

Despite the excellent cigars produced in the Canary Islands, the Spaniards prefer Havanas. The most popular Spanish cigar, however, is the humble, unsophisticated Farias, which has thousands of fans and even fan clubs. Connoisseurs of this cigar can tell from the very first puff in which of Tabacalera's factories the cigar was made.

"La" Farias, as it is popularly called — almost as though it were a famous singer or flamenco *cantaora*! — is a short, tough cigar that fits well into the corner of the mouth and can be held easily in the teeth. A good one produces a compact gray ash. Its intense, strong flavor is a perfect complement to brandy or rum *carajillos*. The Farias-lover begins the smoking ritual early in the morning with a coffee and a glass of brandy or anis, and the cigar will not leave his mouth for the rest of the morning, even if it goes out momentarily.

Farias are cigars for the common man, for smoking at the bullring or the soccer field. They got their name from a Galician, Hector Farias, a member of a Spanish family who emigrated to Mexico, and who invented a machine for making the cigars. However, they were eventually produced in Spain by Don Amós Salvador Rodrigáñez, director of the Compañia Arrendataria de Tabacos in 1890.

Evoking the name of this popular cigar brings this book on the taste of Spain to a close. In fact, without a whiff of Farias in the air, the taste of Spain would somehow be altered. Something would be missing — something so omnipresent that it is rarely noticed, but when it is, it can only be acknowledged with tenderness and appreciation.

Xavier Domingo (above).
The Escarchado can still be tasted in the older bistros. It was once known as the preferred drink of prostitutes (facing).

Oceano Atlántico

Betanzos
Gijón
Santander
San Sebastián
Guetaria
Anglet

Oviedo
Asturias
Cabrales
Cantabria
Bilbao
País Vasco
Tolosa
St-Jean-Pied-de-Port

Santiago de Compostela
Galicia
Matalavilla
León
Vitoria
Beasain
Perpignan

Cangas de Morrazo
Minho
Villalón de Campos
Burgos
Navarra
Pamplona
Barbastro
Cataluña
Figueres

Vigo
1
Castilla y León
Valladolid
Aranda de Duero
Rioja
Logroño
Zaragoza
Lérida
Arbeca
Arenys de Mar

Zamora
El Burgo de Osma
Aragón
Fraga
Villafranca del Penedés
Barcelona

Fuentesaúco
Sepúlveda
Garraf

Salamanca
Cantimpalos
Segovia
Vilanova i la Geltrú

Guadalajara
Tarragona

Madrid
Madrid
Teruel

Plasencia
Jaraíz de la Vega
Chinchón
Menor

Alcántara
Tajo
Toledo
Aranjuez
Castellón de la Plana
Palma

Cáceres
Las Pedroñeras
Benisano
Mallorca

Extremadura
Mérida
Guadiana
Castilla la Mancha
Valencia
Islas Baleares

Peloche
Valencia
Ibiza

Campanario

Jabugo
Córdoba
Alicante
Mar

Carmona
Jaén
Murcia
La Mata
Mediterraneo

Ecija
Montilla
Andalucía
Murcia

Sevilla
Moriles

Osuna
Estepa
Granada

Grazalema
Trevélez

Sanlúcar de Barrameda
Málaga
Almería

Jerez de la Frontera

Cadis
Medina Sidonia

VVVVVV Winegrowing Regions

Islas Canarias

Santa Cruz de Tenerife

Las Palmas

Map of the regions of Spain highlighting places discussed in the text and the principal vintages:
1. Ribeiro (Galicia)   2. Valdeorras (Galicia)   3. Rioja (Rioja)   4. Navarra (Navarra)   5. Campo de Borja (Aragón)   6. Ampurdán Costa Brava (Cataluña)   7. Rueda (Castilla y León)   8. Ribera del Duero (Castilla y León)   9. Cariñera (Aragón)   10. Priorato (Cataluña)   11. Tarragona (Cataluña)   12. Penedés (Cataluña)   13. Alella (Cataluña)   14. Méntrida (Castilla la Mancha)   15. La Mancha (Castilla la Mancha)   16. Valdepeñas (Castilla la Mancha)   17. Utiel-Requena (Valencia)   18. Valencia (Valencia)   19. Almansa (Castilla la Mancha)   20. Yecla (Murcia)   21. Jumilla (Castilla la Mancha)   22. Alicante (Valencia)   23. Condado de Huelva (Andalucía)   24. Xérès (Andalucía)   25. Montilla-Moriles (Andalucía)   26. Málaga (Andalucía)

A
GOURMET'S
GUIDE

A GOURMET'S GUIDE

The author has personally selected the restaurants mentioned in this guide. The reader may be surprised not to find certain prestigious addresses, but the point of this list and the book itself is to avoid the beaten track.

Arzac
Alto de Miracruz 21, San Sebastián (Guipúzcoa).
Tel: 27 84 65.
The specialties of this great restaurant include cornmeal puff pastry with cod accompanied by basil-flavored tomato sauce, baked turbot with fried vegetables, steamed lobster in asparagus stock, truffles stuffed with potatoes, fried pistachio cream and homemade sherbets.

Peixerot
Passeig Maritim 56, Vilanova i la Geltrú.
Tel: 815 06 25.
In a popular maritime setting, local specialties, fish and seafood including the catch of the day, and a wide variety of rice recipes.

El Caballo Rojo
Cardenal Herrero 28, Córdoba.
Tel: 47 53 75.
Wide variety of Andalusian dishes: oxtail, lamb with honey, mid-Eastern desserts. Luxurious and characteristic atmosphere.

Las Camachas
Cádiz-Málaga road, km. 445, Montilla.
Tel: 65 00 04.
Andalusian cuisine. Excellent *pata negra* ham and other pork specialties.

Hispania
Real 54, Arenys de Mar.
Tel: 791 04 57.

One of the best restaurants in Spain. Catalan cuisine: lobster with potatoes, cod casserole, old-style rabbit, pork specialties, Catalan cream.

Patxiku Kintana
San Jerónimo 22, San Sebastián.
Tel: 42 63 99.
Traditional Basque cuisine. *Zurrukutuna* (bread and cod soup), turbot and whiting, stuffed lamb, Basque plum pie.

Pepe Simón
Balea 3, Cangas del Morrazo.
Tel: 30 00 16.
Seafood, oysters, scallops with candied onions, fish soup, baked bass, *empanadas* stuffed with lamprey, squid, cockles, etc.

Jockey
Amador de los Rios 6, Madrid.
Tel: 319 10 03.
A classic and luxurious restaurant that, paradoxically, serves some of the best Madrid-style tripe.

Edreira
Linares Rivas 8, Betanzos.
Tel: 77 08 03.
Bistro. Exceptional Spanish omelette with potatoes.

Bolaviga
Enrique Eguren 4, Bilbao.
Tel: 443 50 26.
Tiny bistro with just two dishes on order: *bacalao al pil-pil* and *bacalao a la vizcaína* — cod with peppers and Biscay-style cod. Heavenly.

Guria
Gran Via 66, Bilbao.
Tel: 441 05 43.

Innovative cod dishes in a contemporary setting. Lamb fillet, rice with milk and *tocinillos de cielo*.

Bermeo
Ercilla 37-39, Bilbao.
Tel: 443 88 00.
One of Spain's best hotel-restaurants. Lobster with sweet pepper cream, *kokotxas* with *salsa verde*, "Ranero Club" cod.

Els Tinars
San Feliu-Girona road, km. 25, Llagostera.
Tel: 83 06 26.
Catalan cuisine: chicken with cod tripe, monkfish with garlic and parsley, tiny cuttlefish Ampurdán-style, skate with vinaigrette sauce.

Casa Botin
Cuchilleros 17, Madrid.
Tel: 266 42 17
The suckling and roast lamb are delicious in this characteristic and time-honored restaurant.

Levante
Virgen del Fundamento 15, Benissanó.
Tel: 278 07 21.
Only the orthodox, traditional version of *paella de la huerta* (from Spain's heartland), is served in this popular restaurant.

Galvis
Marva 28-30, Valencia.
Tel: 380 94 73.
Unrivalled in rice dishes, especially paella with duck, Ribera Alta rice, and *all i pebre*, baby goat with young garlic. Well-known restaurant with an elegant atmosphere.

Elcano
Herrerieta 2, Guetaria.
Tel: 83 16 14.

Baked turbot, lobster salad and Basque-style anchovies are the main specialties.

Currito
Pabellón de Vizcaya, Casa de Campo, Madrid.
Tel: 464 57 04.
Madrid's major Basque restaurant. Serves tuna *escabeche*, *kokotxas* with peppers, baked scorpion fish, charcoal-grilled sardines, and *marmitako* (a tuna and potato dish).

Hartza
Juan de Labrit 19, Pamplona.
Tel: 22 45 68.
Mixed vegetables, bass cooked in foil, whiting with cider, pigeons with *foie gras*, eel salad.

Rincón de Pepe
Apóstoles 34, Murcia.
Tel: 21 22 49.
Excellent salt fish and vegetables, salmon with lemon leaves and Murcia-style suckling lamb.

Virrey Palafox
Universidad 7, El Burgo de Osma.
Tel: 34 02 22.
This Castilian restaurant serves excellent pork dishes, including their own specialty, the meat of an animal that is a cross between a pork and a boar. Also *migas canas* (garlic-flavored fried bread).

Mesón de la Villa
Plaza Mayor 1, Aranda de Duero.
Tel: 50 10 25.

This restaurant features the fabulous but little-known Castilian cuisine. Partridge *escabeche*, duck and chicken, charcoal-grilled calf sweetbreads, rice blood sausages, rice with squirrel, grilled vegetables, and *flor de sarten*, a house specialty, for dessert.

Nicolasa
Aldama 4, San Sebastián.
Tel: 42 17 62.
Contemporary Basque cuisine in a refined atmosphere. *Kokotxas* with peas, eggs with kidneys and mushrooms, bass with *salsa verde*.

Ampurdán
Spain-France highway, km. 763, Figueras.
Tel: 50 05 62.
The major restaurant in a region famed for its gastronomy. Cod with *aioli* mousse, veal head and veal feet, tiny broad beans in salad with mint, cannelloni with chicken and truffles. Wild game in season.

Coto de Antonio
General Godet 13, Santa Cruz de Tenerife.
Tel: 27 21 01.
Cuisine from the Canary Islands. *Sancocho*, rabbit *salmorejo* (a cold soup), scallops with coriander, baby goat *escabeche*, potatoes with garlic and fresh coriander.

Florian
Bertrand i Serra 20, Barcelona.
Tel: 212 46 27.

Angler fish in puff pastry, *butifarra de perol* (Catalan sausage) with beans, oxtail, and in season, an excellent choice of mushrooms.

Roig Robi
Séneca 20, Barcelona.
Tel: 218 92 22.
Home-style Barcelona cooking in a modern and pleasant setting. Swiss chard on toast with Vendrell blood sausage, fish soup, loin of lamb with lamb brains, and a wide variety of rice dishes.

Can Leopoldo
San Rafael 24, Barcelona.
Tel: 241 30 14.
In the heart of the Barrio Chino, this may be Barcelona's best fish restaurant. Excellent turbot, bass, mullet, but also Catalan-style tripe and extraordinary *coca* (bread stuffed with tomato).

Principe de Viana
Doctor Fleming 7, Madrid.
Tel: 259 14 48.
The emphasis here is on vegetables, particularly cardoon and borage. Angler fish with peppers, delicious pork and veal meatballs. Sumptuous atmosphere.

Casa Maera
José Leon 17, Seville.
Tel: 434 36 05.
Family bistro in the Triana *barrio* serving freshly caught fish and seafood from Isla Cristina, ideally accompanied by a Fino wine from Jerez.

COOKING GLOSSARY

Achiote: Vegetable coloring from the red annatto seed, a seasoning and colorant basic to Mexican cuisine.

Aïoli: To make an aïoli sauce, place 2 peeled cloves garlic and a little salt in a mortar and grind to a paste with a pestle. Add 1 cup (8 fl oz/25 cl) olive oil in a very slow, steady stream, whisking constantly to form an emulsion.

Amanite Imperial: An edible member of the Amanitas family of wild mushrooms, which also includes some of the most poisonous mushrooms known.

Black truffles: One of the rarest and most costly of all the wild mushrooms, the black truffle (*Tuber melanosporum*) grows underground near the roots of certain oak trees in Spain (as well as in France and several other countries). Fresh black truffles, which have an intense, earthy flavor, are difficult to find. Canned black truffles can be found in many specialty food shops.

Bodega: Cellar for storing or selling wine.

Brandy: Spanish cognac.

Butifarra: Pork and tripe sausage from Catalonia and the Balearic islands. *Butifarra blanca* is a white Catalan sausage spiced with cinnamon, cloves and nutmeg. If unavailable, substitute a sweet Italian sausage, braised or poached slowly until thoroughly cooked. *Butifarra negra* is a flavorful blood and rice sausage. If unavailable, substitute a fresh blood sausage, or simply omit from the recipe.

Cachelos: Galician potatoes that grow along the coast.

Calçot: A variety of elongated onion that resembles a leek.

Carajillo: A coffee and alcohol mixture served in a coffee cup.

Caramel, liquid: To make liquid caramel, combine 3/4 cup of sugar and 1/3 cup water in a small heavy saucepan. Cook, stirring, until the mixture turns a light caramel color. Add 1/3 cup water and stir to cool slightly.

Cava: Spanish bubbly wine made according to the champagne method.

Cebiche: Raw fish marinated in vinegar or lemon juice.

Chato: Small glass of red, white or rosé wine.

Chorizo: The most typical and available of all Spanish sausages, chorizo is a dried pork sausage flavored with paprika and garlic. In Spain it is produced in strong and mild versions, and may be lightly cured or air dried. It is used in a wide range of Spanish dishes and can be found in Spanish specialty markets and gourmet shops. If not available, a good-quality mild pepperoni may be substituted, although it will not give the same results as an authentic chorizo.

Churrasco: Term used in Argentina to describe grilled meats.

Churro: Elongated sweet fritter usually served with a cup of chocolate.

Cocido: Spanish stew.

Earthenware pans: The earthenware *cazuela* is a traditional multi-purpose Spanish pan that diffuses heat evenly and also retains the heat once the dish is removed from the stove. The most common variety is round, wide and shallow, rough on the outside and glazed on the inside. They come in a multitude of sizes and are attractive enough to use for serving. A new earthenware *cazuela* should be treated before being placed over an open flame to prevent it from cracking. The traditional method is to rub the unglazed exterior with the cut side of a garlic clove, then with oil. Place about 1/4 inch of oil in the casserole, and heat in a 300° F (150° C) oven for 20 minutes. Discard the oil and the casserole is ready to use.

Escudella: Catalan stew.

Fish broth: To make your own fish broth, boil the heads and backbones of several non-oily white-fleshed fish such as whiting or sole in a saucepan filled with water, 1/4 cup dry white wine, a bay leaf, and a few peppercorns, for 30 minutes. Strain through a sieve.

Gazpacho: Chilled Andalusian soup.

Gazpacho manchego (or **alicantino**): Castilian-La Mancha pancake prepared with small game, mutton or baby goat.

Guacamole: Chopped or pureed avocado salad (Latin America).

Huerta: Irrigated and cultivated plain (Valencia, Murcia), or a large vegetable garden.

Ikurrina: Basque national flag.

Jerez: Spanish wine from the region of Cádiz and Sanlúcar de Barrameda.

Kokotxas: Basque term for the muscle in cod and hake next to the lower jaw. Hake *kokotxas* is particularly appreciated in Spain.

Laburu: A sun symbol in the shape of a rounded cross, seen on tombs in the Basque region.

Lactarius: One of the finest of the Spanish wild mushrooms, it is a shiny light reddish-orange and exudes a milky substance when its flesh is broken.

Mojama: Dried, salted fish, often tuna.

Mole: Mexican national dish; it contains chocolate.

Morcilla: a blood and rice sausage, frequently flavored with onions. Although chorizo is generally available in specialty markets, *morcilla* is often difficult to find outside of Spain. Any kind of blood sausage may be substituted, or *morcilla* can simply be omitted from the recipe.

Olla podrida: A rich stew from an ancient Spanish recipe.

Pacharán: An aniseed-flavored liqueur popular in Spain.

Paella: Name of the two-handled pan in which this dish is prepared; paella is made with rice, vegetables, poultry, seafood or meats, and saffron.

Parrillada: Grilled meat, fish or seafood.

Picadas: Sauce made with almonds and hazelnuts.

Picatoste: Thin slices of bread fried in butter or grilled.

Porrusalda: Basque soup made with puréed leeks and potatoes.

Porrón: Long-beaked wine carafe.

Puchero: A type of stew.

Quesada pasiega: A cheesecake made from an old Spanish recipe.

Romescu: Spicy Catalan sauce served with grilled fish and meat.

Saffron: Red-gold saffron strands (actually the dried stigma of a special variety of crocus) add an intense and distinctive flavor to many Spanish dishes. Although this ingredient is very expensive, a little bit goes a long way — only a pinch is needed. It can be purchased in two forms: saffron threads, which are the strands of the dried stigma, or in powdered form. The powder, though widely available, is a poor substitute for the highly flavored threads.

Salmorejo: A variety of Andalusian gazpacho.

Serrano: Serrano ham is a highly prized cured ham used in a wide range of Spanish recipes. The best comes from Jabugo, a small Sierra Morena village. It can be found in many specialty shops and Spanish markets. If it is not available, Italian prosciutto can be substituted.

Sevillana: Large, medium-green or dark green olive.

Sobresada is a large soft Spanish sausage made with ground pork, seasoned with salt, paprika and other spices. It is available in mild and strong versions, the latter seasoned with hot peppers. It can sometimes be found in Spanish specialty markets in the United States. If not available, a mild, not too dry chorizo sausage or a mild, good-quality pepperoni sausage can be substituted.

Solera: Characteristic vinification of Jerez wines.

Squid: To clean squid, pull out the tentacles and peel off the silvery ink sac located underneath the tentacles, being careful not to break it. Reserve the tentacles, discarding the slimy white portion below the eyes. Remove the quill and rinse the squid body thoroughly inside and out.

Tapas: Tiny appetizers served with aperitifs.

Tiznao: A variety of *bacalao al ajo del arrier* (cod with garlic).

Verdeo: Preserved or semi-preserved olives.

Zarzuela: A Catalan specialty: fish and seafood casserole.

GLOSSARY

Agulló, Ferrán: Early 20th-century Catalan politician, journalist and writer. Author of *Llibre de la cucina catalana*.

Alarcón, Pedro Antonio de: Late 19th-century Spanish writer. His novels describe the power of the clergy, the separatist movements in the provinces, and his own struggle for freedom.

Arrieros, maragatos: Muleteers from the province of Leon who transported goods, including cod, from the north to the Andalusian plains.

Audot, Louis Eustache: 19th-century French writer, author of *La Cuisinière de la Campagne et de la Ville.*

Berlanga, José Luiz: Major contemporary Spanish film director. Directed *El Verdugo, Carretera nacional, Bienvenudo Mr. Marshal.* His neo-realistic films are noted for their black humor. Xavier Domingo acted in several of his movies, including *Carretera nacional* and *Moros y cristianos.*

Botero, Jean: Contemporary French scholar who decoded the Babylonian tablets containing the oldest recipe in existence: quail *empanada.*

Botin, Jean: French cook and adventurer who took refuge in Madrid in the early 17th century and founded the famous Hosteria de Botin restaurant. This restaurant still serves wonderful suckling pig and lamb.

Brillat-Savarin, Jean Anthelme: 18th-century French magistrate and writer. Became famous with *Physiologie du goût* in which he presents culinary art as a total science.

Carême, Antonin: 19th-century French cook and confectioner. Headed Talleyrand's kitchens for twelve years and demonstrated his talents throughout the courts of Europe. Carême wrote *L'art de la Cuisine au XIXe siècle* and is considered the founder of modern French cuisine.

Cortés, Hernán: 16th-century Spanish conquistador. Defeated the Aztecs in 1521.

Dubois, Urbain: 19th-century French cook. Worked mostly outside France, particularly in Russia and Germany. Author of *La Cuisine classique* in collaboration with Emile Bernard.

Escoffier, Auguste: Early 20th-century French chef. Worked mostly in Britain and wrote *Ma Cuisine, Le Guide culinaire* and *Le Livre des menus.* The pêche melba is his most famous culinary creation.

La Chapelle, Vincent: 18th-century French cook and author of simple, easy-to-duplicate recipes. His book *Le Cuisinier moderne* was still very popular in the early 20th century.

Linnaeus, Carolus: 18th-century Swedish naturalist, author of *Systema Naturae.*

Lopez, Cándido: Famed contemporary Spanish cook, specialist of grilled suckling pig according to Jean Botin's recipe.

Mata, Juan de la: Renowned 18th-century chocolate and pastry cook in Madrid, and author of a major work on pastry making.

Moctezuma: 15th-century Aztec emperor.

Paz, Octavio: Nobel prize-winning (1990) Mexican poet. Author of a biography of Sister Juana Inés de la Cruz.

Redondo, José: Famed 19th-century matador, gourmet and excellent cook.

RECIPE INDEX

ACKNOWLEDGEMENTS

The author is grateful to all those who participated in the preparation of this book, and particularly: Rosa Grau and Xavier Garcia of the Florian de Barcelona restaurant, who developed and perfected the mushroom recipes; publisher Angel de Miguel, for his valuable cooperation; those who assisted photographer Pierre Hussenot and Marianne Paquin, especially the Hispania restaurant in Arenys de Mar and the Mesón de la Villa in Aranda de Duero; thanks are also due to Leopoldo Pomès; the Moriles-Montilla, Jerez, Rioja and Ribera del Duero wine cellars; the pastry-making nuns at the Seville convent, who graciously allowed us to tour their kitchens; the administration of the Boquería market in Barcelona; and lastly, Florence Picard and Claude Montgaillard, for their efficiency. Marianne Paquin and Pierre Hussenot are grateful to the following for their hospitality and cooperation:
The Horta Callejo cheese dairy in Burgos; Mr. José Irizar Ansa of the Barkaiztegi cider factory in San Sebastián; Juan Luis Bega of the Gonzalez Biaz cellars in Jerez; Juan Rei Andrada, farmer and viticulturist; the Manuel Vidal bakery in Chinchón; Manolo Lopez Alexandro, who welcomed us at his antique oil mill in Almazara; the renowned baker, Josep More Rabassa in Argentona; Barcelona's distinguished chocolate-maker, Escribá; Jose Ignacio Inaz, who invited us to discover his wonderful cheeses; and the members of the San Sebastián gastronomic society, the Sociedad Gaztelubide de Donostia. Our thanks also go to those who offered us their specialties: Mr. Mariano Navas of the Navas restaurant in Huesca; Mr. Oppawsky of the Oromana hotel-restaurant in Alcala de Guadaira, Seville; Casa Bigote in Sanlúcar de Barrameda; Lolita, Paquita and Ramon of the Hispania restaurant in Arenys de Mar; the Casa Vallès *tapas* bar in San Sebastián; Arzak in San Sebastián; Guanito and Maria of the Pinocho bar in the Boquería, Barcelona; La Merced restaurant in Logroño; Jose Juan Castillo of the Casa Nicolasa restaurant in San Sebastián; Mr. Soriano Albandos of the Casa Miguel bar; Manuel Jimenez of the Taberna Salina in Córdoba; and Hijos de Alejandro Perez, the traditional confectionery in Casar de Cáceres.
Grateful thanks to the Rozimar, San Valero and O'Gallego Fatigué restaurants, and the Galerie Farnèse and the Tuile à Loup for their assistance in Paris.

The publisher thanks Jean-François Revel, who inspired this project and helped to make it possible.

INDEX